SENATOR
JOHN JAMES
INGALLS

SENATOR
JOHN JAMES
INGALLS

Kansas' Iridescent Republican

by

BURTON J. WILLIAMS

142828

THE UNIVERSITY PRESS OF KANSAS
LAWRENCE / MANHATTAN / WICHITA

© Copyright 1972 by the University Press of Kansas
Standard Book Number 7006-0086-8
Library of Congress Catalog Card Number 72-177898
Printed in the United States of America
Designed by Fritz Reiber

To

the late Professor George L. Anderson

Gentleman,

Teacher,

Scholar,

&

Friend

PREFACE

All too often the personages of history have been reduced to little more than statistical or political abstractions. This book is an attempt to "personalize" a sensitive, highly emotional, and intelligent man. It is also an attempt to present the historical record of that man, using the perspective of his own time and spatial limitations. As the title suggests, this is a biography of a man who, as a public figure, had achieved considerable but who somehow never seemed to be able to measure up to his potential.

Historically, he has been stereotyped as an insensitive, vindictive, partisan politician. However true this may be, he was also much more than this. He dabbled in and often succeeded in many things: territorial and state politics, the military, law, literature, banking, real estate, the newspaper business, prospecting, public speaking, speculating, townsite "booming," and finally as a U.S. Senator. Throughout all this he was a man with an unfathomable mental and spiritual burden. His specific political stance could be as mercurial as the weather in Kansas. Certainly it is not easy to characterize or stereotype such a complicated figure. And since this has been the tendency, there exists the need for a more balanced historical account.

In his lifetime (1833–1900) Ingalls witnessed the technological revolution which was reshaping not only America but the world as well. His recent critics have accused him of failing to comprehend the resulting changes and the subsequent impact upon American society. Perhaps their criticisms are justified. Nevertheless, there is a tendency to recite the failures of the personages of the past through the "gift" of hindsight. If Ingalls failed, there was no one more critical of his failing than he himself. His was the "Gilded Age," an age that people today are supposed to regard as especially corrupt and short-sighted, according to popular historical tradition. It seems ahistorical to accuse Ingalls of being no better than his age, no matter how "gilded" or "tarnished" that age might be.

It is sincerely hoped that the stereotyped characterization of Ingalls will be revised to encompass the broader spectrum of his life, including the successes that accompanied his failures.

ACKNOWLEDGMENTS

For assistance received in the course of this effort, the author gives special thanks to Mrs. Constance Ingalls Barnes, General Ellsworth Ingalls Davis, Mrs. Sally Ingalls Keith, and Mrs. Frances Davis Price, all of whom are surviving grandchildren of John James Ingalls. To them the author is deeply indebted, not only for the fact that they preserved the manuscripts of their grandfather and made them available to the author, but also for the fact that since this work was undertaken they have graciously donated their respective collections of Ingalls manuscripts to the Kansas State Historical Society in Topeka, Kansas.

Grateful appreciation also goes to Nyle H. Miller, Secretary, Robert W. Richmond, State Archivist, Joseph W. Snell, Assistant Archivist, and Elsie Beine, Archives Clerk, all of the Kansas State Historical Society, for their generous help in making the research facilities of the Historical Society available to the author. In addition sincere appreciation is expressed to James C. Malin, professor emeritus of the Department of History at the University of Kansas, for suggesting Ingalls as a topic of historical research and for his patient and helpful suggestions along the way.

Special acknowledgment goes to the late Professor George L. Anderson, who, at an earlier stage, directed this study as a doctoral dissertation at the University of Kansas. I thank him for the generous contribution of his time, for his constructive criticisms, and especially for his encouragement.

In addition, I would like to express my thanks to the University of Kansas for a research grant which was essential in the preparation of this manuscript and to the Office of Research and Development of Central Washington State College for a grant which enabled me to complete it. Finally, my sincerest thanks to Millie, who not only typed the manuscript, but who also patiently labored to decipher my "scrawl."

Burton J. Williams
Central Washington State College
Ellensburg, Washington

CONTENTS

1

A NICHE
NO ONE ELSE COULD
OCCUPY

On a cold winter day John J. Ingalls was born in the crossroads village of Middleton, Massachusetts. The date was December 29, 1833. In genealogical order John J. was the eighth generation of Ingallses descended from Edmund Ingalls, a Puritan immigrant. He, with his brother Francis, founded the town of Lynn in Essex County, Massachusetts, in 1628.[1] Now, some two hundred years later, the nation was peopled by those who had survived two wars for independence. Memories of the "Second War for Independence" were still vivid in the minds of the adult population, while the very old survived as witnesses to or participants in the American Revolutionary War itself.

In spite of the emerging nationalism, America's colonial heritage was still deeply impressed upon the nation at large and New England in particular. This in spite of the fact that "Jacksonian Democracy" was approaching flood tide. Historians have categorized the 1830s as marking the close of America's early national period; however, the generation of that day was not aware of it. For them it was a time of beginnings. America was emerging from infant and adolescent nationalism, and destiny beckoned ominously for her to fulfill her "manifest destiny." Fate and destiny were to become significant words in John J. Ingalls' vocabulary. In later years he pondered the reasons for his existence and concluded that his birth was "a link in the chain of fate."[2] Fate, so he reasoned, decreed him indispensable in nature's mysterious and inexorable process. A Washington or a Napoleon was no more nor less significant in this "chain of fate" than he was. Ingalls believed that his presence on earth "filled a niche that no one else could occupy."[3] This statement was not prompted by egotism. It was prompted by a morose sense of fatalism, a fatalism that was frequently characteristic of his contemporaries. Ingalls was the product of a century which has been described as a century suffering from an acute consciousness of "the agony of being." Whether there is substance to such claims or not, Ingalls proved to be the personification of the diagnosis.

John J. was the child of parents who took pride in their ancestry. His father, Elias Theodore, was proud of his colonial heritage. His mother, Eliza Chase Ingalls, boasted the same legacy. She was a descendant of Aquila Chase, who settled in New Hampshire in 1630. Throughout their married lives Ingalls' parents facetiously bickered back and forth as to which family possessed the proudest heritage. As a result John J. acquired an absorbing interest in the "dynastic" traditions of his parents, and determined to preserve and enlarge the family heritage.

John J. was the first of nine children born to his parents. His father, Elias T., had been reared in reduced circumstances owing to the death of his father when Elias was only seven. In spite of meager means, Elias's mother, Ruth Flint Ingalls, managed to enroll Elias in preparatory school. It was her wish that he enter the ministry. Her wish was never fulfilled, for in the course of his preparatory studies Elias fell in love. The object of his amorous attentions was the woman who was to become his wife, Eliza Chase. She was the daughter of a well-to-do shoe merchant of Haverhill, Massachusetts. Elias was only nineteen at the time, and his love for Eliza took precedence over everything else. With the conclusion of his preparatory studies, Elias abandoned all plans of continuing his education. He became an apprentice to Eliza's father in order to be near her. Apparently Eliza's parents were unaware of Elias's romantic interest in their daughter. When this became obvious, however, they were deeply troubled and did their best to discourage the impending match. Nevertheless, when threatened with elopement, Eliza's parents reluctantly consented to the marriage of their daughter to Elias. The wedding took place on December 27, 1832.[4]

After their marriage Elias found his relationship with the entire Chase family to be tenuous, even strained. Because of this unpleasant relationship, he severed connections with his wife's father in the first year of their marriage. He took his bride to Middleton, Massachusetts, and there set up a meager shoe factory himself. Middleton could hardly be styled even a village. It was a crossroads.

The young newlyweds moved into a large, barnlike two-story frame house far removed from any neighbors. It was in an upstairs room of this house that Ingalls first confronted the world. Middleton proved to be a remote and lonely place for a child to begin life in. In later years John J. recorded his impressions of these first years in Middleton in a morbid fashion. While still a youth, he composed an autobiographical essay entitled "The Sun Lover, or The Autobiography of a Monomaniac."[5] In this essay he described his innermost thoughts. He claimed that he could read at the age of two and that at the age of four he "was a wonder."[6] Nevertheless, childhood for him was generally a melancholy, if not morose, experience. He complained that his parents were poor, that he had no companions, and that he was desperately lonely.

One of Ingalls' childhood pastimes was the solitary contemplation of the "moors and the lowlands," as he described them. His nights were frequently filled with frightful nightmares or were spent in sleepless horror. Before his eyes danced visions which proved indescribable but which he diagnosed as his mind's efforts to grapple with the awesome questions of infinity and fate. On one occasion he dreamed that an invisible army of the dead passed in endless procession past his window. On still another occasion he dreamed that he was chained to a mountain, holding a tiny spade and compelled to move the mountain a spadeful at a time. These incidents exemplify the mind of Ingalls as a youth. His morose moodiness caused him to state on more than one occasion that he wished he had died the day he was born. His parents were aware of these "eccentricities," as they described them, while they fretfully contemplated what the future held for their gifted but tormented son.[7]

Perhaps the frailty of John J. contributed to his emotional problems. His health was always rather delicate. To compound the problem, Elias proved to be a severe disciplinarian in the rearing of his first-born. He demanded more from his young son than the son was able to deliver. The severity of his discipline caused Elias in later life to ask John J.'s forgiveness, while at the same time explaining that he had acted out of a desire to serve his son's best interests.[8] In spite of the harsh discipline, John J. always felt closer to his father than to his mother. He did hold his mother in great esteem, but somehow he could never communicate with her as he could with his father. He spoke affectionately of her, claiming that she was "kind and faithful," though never "affectionate nor demonstrative."[9] He described her as a person possessing a philosophic spirit. She belonged to the church, but still Ingalls could not describe his mother as being religious. She was patient, did not grumble, and accepted conditions pretty much as she found them. She lived her life with others but still remained somewhat alone, a quality characteristic of John J. Although Ingalls had complained of being lonely, his mother pointed out that he had never been inclined to seek the company of others.[10]

The question of religion is important in any discussion of Ingalls, for this question plagued him throughout his life. Although his mother was a member of the Congregational church, she did not attempt to force religion upon her young son. Elias had been skeptical of Christianity throughout his early life and did not "confess religion," as that term was commonly used, until after the birth of his first son, John J. As a young man, Elias claimed that he had read "infidel" books, claiming further that he came away from them convinced that he could destroy the whole fabric of the Christian faith.[11] However, John J. never knew this side of his father's disposition. His first memories of his father's religious interest were at age three "in the old Baptist Church" and not in "the church of his fathers."[12] With marriage and parenthood, plus the imminent prospect of death and utter annihilation, Elias began to look into the "evidences of Christianity." Out of all this came a calm religious assurance, not by reason or knowledge, as he put it, but by faith. He described his transformation as a gift from God and expressed hope that his son's religious experiences would ultimately parallel his own.[13] However, this never came to pass.

Questions of religion were raised from time to time in later years as father and son corresponded. Upon reading Charles Darwin's epic work on evolution, Elias was not shaken in his religious faith or in the Genesis account of creation. What is more important, he was not even angered by it all. He enjoyed the book, was even fascinated by it, but felt that Darwin was some distance from arriving at any definitive conclusions.[14] One can only assume that such a frank religious exchange took place between father and son during John J.'s youthful years. In any event, Elias was concerned about his son's religious welfare from an early age; however, for some inexplicable reason John J. was not baptized into the Congregational church until he reached the age of six.[15]

Although the young John J. thought he had a "hard lot" in life, by all outward appearances he enjoyed a normal and relatively comfortable home life. Nevertheless, the fabric of young John J.'s mentality was anything but ordinary. He prematurely struggled with the awesome questions of life and death, lamenting his own existence while dreading its termination. Still, seemingly small things burdened Ingalls as a child. Once he complained that one of "the great griefs" of his youth had been the want of nice clothes. But in spite of the overall melancholy picture thus far posed, Ingalls' childhood and youth had its bright side. In quick succession eight brothers and sisters were added to the family, and this dispelled the solitary loneliness that he had so bitterly complained of. Treasured among his memories were happy frolics, scratched faces, and morning piecrust eatings. And indeed his memory was uncanny. As a young man of twenty-five he recorded his childhood memories under the title "Pictures from Memory." In all, twenty-five "pictures" are described and numbered. They appear to be in chronological order, and if they are, they include a major memory for each of the first twenty-five years of his life. It is also reported that at age thirteen he kept a meticulous journal. Also at that age he had some of his compositions published in the Boston *Transcript*. It is claimed, however, that he used a fictitious name, therefore the compositions cannot be identified.[16]

In 1838 Elias took his family back to Haverhill, a move that was at least partially predicated on economic necessity arising out of the Panic of 1837. Here he resumed his trade as a cobbler. The returns were meager. For several years it was a struggle simply to provide the basic necessities of life, but in time fortitude was rewarded by fortune. Elias was a man with an inventive mind, and by the time John J. had reached his early teens, his father had perfected and patented a device for cutting leather into shoe soles.[17] Fortune continued to smile, and the fruits of modest prosperity altered the family's style of living. Young Master Ingalls now had the clothes that relieved one of his "great griefs."

There is little on record as to the details of the early education of John J. other than the fact that he graduated from "old Haverhill High." After this he was placed under the guidance of tutors, preparatory to entering college. Upon completion of these studies, the next question was not whether, but rather where, he should go to college. For some time it appeared that he would enter Harvard; however, when the decision was finally made, the choice fell on Williams College in Williamstown, Massachusetts. Williams was a small Congregational school; and since the Ingalls family was Congregationalist, this may well explain why it was chosen. The celebrated Mark Hopkins was serving as its president when Ingalls enrolled as a freshman in the fall of 1851. The college faculty consisted of a total of eight persons, including the president. The student body numbered 208.[18] The student-faculty ratio, though not unusually small, provided for a camaraderie not easily duplicated today. On the other hand, if there is any truth in the adage that familiarity breeds contempt, then this, too, could occur at Williams. In Ingalls' case the college bred contempt. He resented the *in loco parentis* role of the faculty and administration and seldom denied himself the pleasure of disparaging his alma mater while a student there. As in other church colleges of its day, chapel attendance and religious observances were stringently required at Williams. Absences from such services were punishable by fines. In addition a record was kept of delinquencies in these requirements, with a report of the deportment of each student being sent to his parents or guardian at the close of each term.[19] Surprisingly, Ingalls was not unduly remiss in complying with these requirements and rarely found himself confronted by disciplinary action.[20]

Though often contemptuous and hypercritical of college life, Ingalls was an energetic participant in school activities. He was president of the Adelphic (debate) Union, a member of the Philotechnian Society, editor of the *Williams Quarterly* and a member of the Sigma Phi social fraternity.[21] In overall scholarship he was outstanding.[22] In spite of all these commitments Ingalls found time for the "extracurricular" activities of the day. In short, Ingalls would be classified as something of a campus activist by today's standards. One example of his "activism" occurred during his freshman year. In a letter to a friend Ingalls explained that President Hopkins, for reasons of inclement weather, had denied the class a traditional holiday. In consequence the class voted to take it anyway. Ingalls described this as rather a bold move and boasted that indeed they did take it. The class journeyed to nearby Stockbridge to while away their mutinous time. While there, Ingalls visited the English novelist G. P. R. James, whom he described as a slovenly John Bull.[23] He also visited the houses of Hawthorne and Heady and other prominent homes in the town.

In this same letter he discussed current social and political topics. He spoke of Harriet Beecher Stowe's *Uncle Tom's Cabin*, exclaiming that it was the topic of nearly every conversation, so much so that he was sick of the very name of it. He did regard it as an extraordinary book, however, in spite of his complaint. Politically he referred to the nomination of Franklin Pierce by the Democratic party by humorously, almost prophetically, asking, "Why did they not nominate me?!!"[24] In summarizing his freshman thoughts on mutiny, literature, and politics, he concluded that the Stockbridge incident, though sufficient grounds for expulsion from college, would result in nothing more than fines, which proved to be the case.[25]

Ingalls' literary and oratorical talents became increasingly recognized during his junior year. A number of his rather pensive poetic compositions were published in the *Williams Quarterly*.[26] By the time he reached his senior year, his campus fame had spread still more, and his pensive prose was displaced by his peevish prose. He became openly critical of the faculty and administration. He continued to claim that the environment at Williams was far too paternalistic. One specific example was described in a letter he wrote to his brother Morris. The sophomore class stole some beer which the freshman class had cached for a future celebration. However, the freshman class had learned of the impending theft well in advance and had "treated" a half-dozen bottles with a strong dose of tartar emetic. According to Ingalls' account, "About ten sophomores employed the night and part of the next day in vomiting."[27] The trick was not inconsequential. A small but ominous civil war seemed eminent. Knives and pistols were carried openly; but President Hopkins apprehended the ringleaders, and according to Ingalls, he "put an end to the fun."[28]

Though college had its fun side, for Ingalls it served primarily to intensify his habit of engaging in morose introspection. This is evidenced in a number of his poems and essays that were never published. In a poem entitled "Give Me Neither Poverty or Riches," he described a seemingly meaningless existence by stating that neither pleasure nor woe was the reward of "having what I want by wanting what I have."[29] Another of his compositions was first titled "Essay on Faith," but later changed to read "Knowledge and Self Knowledge." A line from this composition succinctly expressed his persistent and perplexing dilemma: "Man is but knows not whence or whither going. . . . He is a cry between two silences."[30] Very early in life he reasoned that human existence was not compatible with, perhaps not even related to, ideas of reason, justice, or mercy. He saw all of creation as a combination of opposites, of "infinite adversities."[31] His inability to find satisfactory answers to questions concerning life, death, infinity, eternity, and God was a mental burden he was never able to lay down, at least for any great length of time. He was so tormented by such questions that at times he bordered on being mentally unbalanced. He once described his state of mind as a "madness which I felt crowding and gnawing at my soul."[32] He claimed his only relief came from intense physical and mental excitement, exclaiming further that his "godless debaucheries and scholastic attainments became proverbial."[33] For a time he could not cope with the world of reality and conceded that for fully five years he lived in a dream world.[34]

Ingalls' inexorable pessimism was also in constant conflict with his vague and more often frustrated sense of idealism. Though reared and educated in the Christian climate of eternal hope, he found little help or hope as proffered by the Christian creeds. He often doubted, even disbelieved, the basic tenets of the Christian faith. However, he did accept the churchly premise that mankind was in a fallen condition. Nevertheless, in an essay entitled "The Admirable Crichton" Ingalls found an occasional exception to the rule, though he lamented the fact that the exceptions were too far between and too few. He declared that the vast majority of men were counterfeits. But on occasion an exceptional person appeared upon the scene, a Crichton. Such exceptions, reasoned Ingalls, kept nature from going bankrupt. Upon the credit of Crichtons the enormous and "spurious issues of the Bank of Humanity," as Ingalls described the masses of humanity, would be "dropped without an epitaph into the agricultural aberrations of death to fertilize the earth which they cumbered while upon its surface."[35] In other words most men are born losers. Concerning the fate of Crichton, a winner, Ingalls was silent.

If Crichton is an accurate reflection of Ingalls' reasoning, then it is obvious that he believed fate consigned the vast majority of men to failure. Ultimately this "senseless" existence would be destroyed "without a dirge or epitaph," and nature would become a "blanched and bleaching skeleton."[36] Even God, if there was a God, was subject to the immutable verdict of fate. And years ahead of his time Ingalls forecast the "death of God." Though he himself had been baptized, he never claimed church membership in any strict sense of that term. Later in life he did attend church with a degree of regularity, usually the Episcopal church. But church to Ingalls as a college student was insufferable. He described Sunday religious services as "emblems of the weekly lie." He argued that pagan rituals were more acceptable in "angels' eyes."[37] Christians were hypocrites, and church was their promotional agency. In all, much of Ingalls' cynicism was not uncommon for college students of his day or ours. Nevertheless, he was something of an enigma. Even his appearance was at times beyond explanation. While in college, for example, he let his hair grow so long that it hung to his shoulders "in curls like a sissy boy."[38] In spite of his crossed-purpose reasoning and perplexing personality, he did receive an excellent education in the classical tradition. But like students of every age, he complained of a lack of relevance.

Though Ingalls had been something of an "activist" in college, which was not unusual in the nineteenth century, he was nevertheless chosen to deliver the commencement address at his own graduation exercises. The administration and faculty later conceded that this was a mistake. Ingalls had avoided any serious infractions of the college regulations and their subsequent penalties, but he had chafed under the constant threat of disciplinary action. As was customary, he was required to submit a draft of his address for faculty approval, which he did. The faculty directed that major alterations be made before they would consent to its presentation. Ingalls complied with their request. However, when the time actually came for him to deliver the address, he substituted a sarcastic and highly critical speech in place of the approved draft. He entitled his address "Mummy Life." He used this title to convey the contempt he had for the maternal environment of the college.[39] The address was brutally contemptuous. Although there is no extant copy of the address, the substance of his feelings is contained in a line from a later comment of his on Williams College. Ingalls stated that it was no more than "a four years course of attention to whiskers, driveling flirtations, kid gloves and Lubin's extracts, with non attendance on vulgar prayers, and a hideous array of flunks."[40] President Hopkins and several faculty members tried to intervene, but Ingalls would not be denied, in spite of the fact that his own mother was among those seated in the audience. In retaliation President Hopkins refused to present Ingalls with his degree.

Some four months later Ingalls referred to this incident in a letter addressed to a friend named John Graham. He claimed he had not been "abused" for what he had done, other than the fact that he had met "prex . . . and the old wretch wouldn't look at me!"[41] Ingalls' friend had obviously communicated earlier that he wanted to get revenge on the Williams College faculty for the ill treatment he believed they had accorded Ingalls. He planned to handle them "without gloves." Ingalls feigned shock and horror by claiming that the faculty was such a loathsome lot that touching them bare-handed would be unthinkable. "Get buckskins of thickness immense," he wrote, "get a brace of boat hooks—Gods! get one of Prof. Al's morning prayers, (that would be long enough) or Miss Carrie Hopkins nose (longer still) or her father's genitals rather than touch one of those peripatetic dung hills."[42]

It would be a gross understatement to say that there was no love lost when Ingalls departed Williams College. And this remained the case for many years. In the *Williams College Class Report,* published in January of 1857, a brief progress report is carried for each member of the class of 1855. Ingalls' report reads in part as follows: "For an exhibition of dignity, distance and ice, in a letter writer, commend me to my learned . . . friend in Haverhill." Following this, a portion of Ingalls' letter to Williams College is quoted:

"Let us not be too much acquainted. In all things I would have the island of a man inviolate. Let us sit apart, as the gods, talking from peak to peak all round Olympus."[43] In summary, the editor of the class report wrote, "The distressing cold of last week wouldn't bear comparison a moment." In spite of all this, Ingalls later came to admire Mark Hopkins and eventually claimed that "the ideal college is Mark Hopkins on one end of a log and a student on the other." Although President James Garfield has been credited with coining the phrase, it was Ingalls who popularized it.[44]

After graduation, or alienation, from Williams, whichever may be more accurate, Ingalls returned to Haverhill and "read law" in the office of John J. Marsh. In the year of the Panic of 1857, Ingalls was admitted to the Essex County Bar at Newburyport, Massachusetts. Educationally, he was now ready to "wrestle with fate."

During these preparatory years, events in the life of the nation had transpired in epic fashion. The years since Ingalls' birth had witnessed the rise and fall of the Whig party. Abolitionist propaganda had increased in intensity. The Panic of 1837 wrecked havoc with the nation's economy. There was the Oregon question and its peaceful resolution after considerable bluster and bragging in this nation. Then there was the Texas question and war with Mexico, and manifest destiny was consummated as fact. There was the discovery of gold in California, and one of the epic migrations in history took place as 49ers streamed across the continent in serpentine fashion. The sectional crisis loomed large, but for a time was quelled by the Compromise of 1850, only to be resurrected with renewed vigor with the passage of the Kansas-Nebraska Act in 1854. As a junior in college, Ingalls described this act as an epic event. "Destiny closed one volume of our annals," he stated, "and opening another, traced with shadowy finger upon its pages a million epitaphs ending with 'Appomattox.' "[45]

Subsequent to admission to the bar Ingalls was lured by the romance of the West. Kansas beckoned or fate decreed, as Ingalls would have put it. The temptation was too great; he could not deny himself the fascination of the frontier.

2

WESTWARD TO THE UNPROMISING LAND: SUMNER, KANSAS TERRITORY

"J ust landed myself in that Promised Land, supposed to be flowing with milk and honey" was John J. Ingalls' way of announcing to his father that he had newly arrived in Sumner, Kansas Territory, on the great bend of the Missouri which separated Missouri and Kansas.[1] The "promised land" that Ingalls beheld that day rudely shattered any illusions he may have held that Sumner was the rising emporium of the West. His eyes scoured the steep riverbank with its squalid clutter of irregular cabins and shacks and its single gullied "street," searching in vain for the spires of churches, the chimneys of factories, the smoothly graded streets bounded by tidy bungalows, and all such signs of thrift, industry, and cultural refinement. "I am quite unable to convey to you any definite idea of disappointment, not unmixed with anger and mortification with which I contemplated the state of affairs here. I wish I could give a photograph of the place, but a new western village is truly indescribable in language. It can only be compared to itself."[2] Ingalls' bitter disappointment at what he found in Sumner poses a problem with regard to his motive for migrating to Kansas.

The actual circumstances surrounding his decision to go to Kansas are not as clear as the more romantic accounts of his migration seem to indicate. Many years later Ingalls' eldest daughter, Ethel, wrote the following: "Over in Haverhill, Massachusetts, young John James Ingalls was indulging in dreams of empire. He had been in Boston to hear Charles Sumner, Senator from Massachusetts, make one of his brilliant courageous speeches, in which he denounced slavery and the Kansas and Nebraska bill."[3] Ethel believed that Senator Sumner had fired the imagination of the New England youth and that in Kansas he saw a dynamic future.[4] Near the close of his life Ingalls himself cited the moral argument employed by his daughter Ethel as the reason for his migration to Kansas; however, his letters written en route to Kansas and after his arrival at Sumner give no indication of any moral commitment as a reason for his migration.[5] On the contrary, the letters are replete with accounts of the disappointing routine required merely to keep "body and soul together." Free Statism, as a moral cause to which Ingalls was allegedly committed, is not even seriously referred to. A thorough study of Ingalls' letters and his activities in Sumner make it clear that he did not journey to the West in order to apply a "Free State tourniquet" to "bleeding Kansas."[6] As a matter of fact, Kansas had, in a sense, come to Ingalls.

Town-site "booming" was in the American tradition. In the course of booming Sumner, Kansas Territory, an enterprising, or more accurately a dishonest, agent of the Sumner Company approached Ingalls with numerous reasons why anyone going west should choose the site of Sumner as his western terminus. In addition to verbal persuasion, the agent unrolled a beautifully colored lithograph which he claimed was a picture of Sumner. The lithograph was a display of church spires, lovely graded streets lined with tidy white bungalows, factories with all their productive potential, and steamboats literally waiting in line to discharge their cargoes upon the teeming levee. There were schools, hotels, shops, and all that was needed to depict a bustling, prosperous emporium. Ingalls later described this picture as "lithographic" and pointed out that it was an "alluring picture, in which all the attractions of art, nature, science, commerce and religion were blended."[7] Apart from the personal persuasion of an agent of the Sumner Company, there appear to have been other factors that also contributed to Ingalls' decision to migrate to Kansas. From October through December of 1857, four letters of William Gilpin were published in the *National Intelligencer,* in which the Great Plains were described in a most praiseworthy fashion. Gilpin had journeyed with John C. Fremont's exploratory expedition of 1843, and had served with the United States forces in the Southwest during the war with Mexico. He was, therefore, in an excellent position to comment on those regions. One of his letters referred to the Great Plains as "the pastoral region of the world" and stated specifically that "these plains are not deserts, but the opposite, and are the cardinal basis of the future empire of commerce and industry now erecting itself upon the North American Continent."[8]

Whether Ingalls read Gilpin's views as published in the *National Intelligencer* is not known. It is recognized, however, that the promoters of the Sumner Company did read them and exploited them to the limit of credibility. In the course of booming their town, the Sumner promoters published a weekly newspaper which they entitled the Sumner *Kanzas Gazette*. In its first edition the *Gazette* quoted a portion of one of Gilpin's letters under the heading "The Pastoral Region of the World." The letter was prefaced with remarks by the editor of the *Gazette*, who cited three reasons why Sumner would become the leading emporium of the West, that is, "the pastoral development; the gold, silver and salt production of the Sierra San Juan; the continental railroad from the Pacific." It is more than likely that the Sumner Company agent, who urged Ingalls to migrate to this "promised land," was amply armed with copies of or clippings from the *Gazette*. Also, in this same edition, was an article entitled "Sumner, Its Rise and Progress." The description of Sumner that ensued was more the product of fancy than fact; nevertheless, to one uninitiated to the ways of the West, Sumner would appear to fall into a category somewhere between the New Jerusalem and Shangri-la.[9] Later press reports contained in the Sumner *Gazette* only buttressed its claims of being a "delectable city."

On August 21, 1858, the *Gazette* carried a feature story entitled "Sumner An Important Kansas Town." The article played up all the natural and fancied advantages of the town, calling attention to the fact that it was situated "on the Great Western Bend of the Missouri." In addition the *Gazette* claimed that as of July, 1858, Sumner had one thousand inhabitants, "with two hundred and eighteen houses, among which are large blocks of brick stores and hotels, two three and four stories high." As a final salute to its prowess, the newspaper declared that "in position and commercial advantages Sumner stands first in Kansas, so also is it becoming the Manufacturing town of the Territory." In the light of such fabulous claims it is not difficult to imagine the shock, followed by despair and depression, which swept over Ingalls as he gazed upon this disorderly and destitute settlement on that October morn. In a moment of forlorn reflection he asked himself "whether or not in my hunger after the Western horizon I have eaten my own happiness."[10]

In searching for the motives behind Ingalls' migration, perhaps his wife came as close to the answer as anyone, for in a simple statement recorded sometime after her husband's death, she claimed that "he realized that better opportunities awaited a young man in the West and decided on Kansas."[11] But there is still more than this to explain Ingalls' decision to go west. He had an adventurous spirit, and the challenges and vague promises held forth by a new territory would of themselves be alluring to his pioneering aspirations. Once he gave poignant expression to the love he held for the dramatic West with the words, "He is unfortunate who has never felt the fascination of the frontier; the temptation of unknown and mysterious solitudes; the exultation of helping to build a State; of forming its institutions, and giving direction to its career."[12] Ingalls revealed that his westward migration was just the kind of "medicine" he needed. "I am quite sure," he wrote, ". . . that the discipline is what I need to develop that part of my character which has not hitherto been called into exercise, and it remains to be proved whether there is any heoric stuff in my mould."[13] Perhaps Ingalls was of the same opinion as Edmund Burke, whom he later read and admired, for in Ingalls' personal copy of one of the volumes of Burke he noted a line which reads as follows: "Great men are never sufficiently shown but in struggles."[14] In substance all one can say is that a combination of circumstances conspired to bring Ingalls to Kansas, or as he would have put it, "Fate decreed it."

The trip to Kansas began when Ingalls left Haverhill, Massachusetts, on September 23, 1858. His journey west was via Boston, Elmira, Buffalo, Cleveland, Cincinnati, St. Louis, and Kansas City. He reported from Boston that he had purchased railway tickets to St. Louis, rather than Sumner, "after inquiring about the best method of getting West."[15] What Ingalls obviously learned here was the fact that the western terminus of the railroad was at Jefferson City, Missouri. From this point he would be required to travel by steamer, and the combined costs of the railway and steamer passage he reported to be $29.75. Ingalls carried a letter of introduction to Albert Dean Richardson, a New York City newspaperman who was living in Sumner, Kansas Territory, at the time, gathering material for his book *Beyond the Mississippi*. With this introduction he boarded the New York and Erie Railroad for "the West," assuring his father that he was "in good health and spirits but somewhat sleepy."[16]

Ingalls' next communication was dated at Cleveland. He reported that en route to that place his train had reached Buffalo just moments too late to catch the Cleveland train. He was not sorry, as this gave him the long-coveted opportunity to visit Niagara Falls. Finally he boarded the "Lightning Express" for Cleveland at 10 P.M., and arrived there at 6:30 the next morning. His impressions of the Great Lakes were such that he claimed "it was a scene of enchantment and gave me a new idea of those great inland seas which are the glory and pride of our country." On September 26 he left Cleveland by rail, headed for Cincinnati. He expected to reach St. Louis on Tuesday, September 28, and his final destination, Sumner, on Thursday, September 30.[17] As it turned out, he did not reach Sumner until October 4.

Ingalls' next correspondence was a letter to his father dated at St. Louis which was replete with his experiences and impressions gained while traveling from Cincinnati to St. Louis. He had not left Cincinnati on schedule, as a heavy cold had forced him to lay over there until Tuesday the twenty-eighth. On this date he boarded a train of the Ohio and Mississippi Railroad and traversed the 340-mile distance between these two river cities in eighteen hours. He recorded his impressions of Indiana in melancholy terms, describing that state as seemingly absent "of those qualities which I have been accustomed to consider of value and significance in life. The effect on me was distressing in the extreme." If Indiana was so depressing to Ingalls, then doubtless he would have to undergo a major metamorphosis to find any satisfaction in Sumner. He described a scene near the present site of Vincennes, Indiana, as the place where he had his first sight of a prairie, "a vast open expanse, reaching in silent desolation to the horizon." He continued his description by pointing out that as "seen by the twilight through which we were traveling, it looked more like the saltmarshes of Salisbury or Ipswich [Massachusetts] than anything else to which I can liken it."[18]

Upon reaching the bank of the Mississippi River opposite St. Louis, Ingalls reported that the travelers were ferried across its waters sometime during the night. He described this city as a "very dirty, ill built place—air full of pulverized lime stone and all manner of stenches, water like a thin decoction of soap suds and food swimming in grease. Armies of pigs and Irish swarm the streets," he continued, "the signs on the shops are nearly half in dutch and all together, the aspect is quite strange and foreign."[19] He reported that he would start for Jefferson City, Missouri, by rail on the same day, September 29, and continue from that point by boat, expecting to arrive at Sumner in the slow time of approximately two and one-half days, as the water was low and navigation difficult.[20] He explained that since boats left St. Louis heading up the Missouri River nearly every day, there was a time advantage of some thirty-six hours by taking the train and catching up with the boat that had left St. Louis the preceding day. Ingalls' westward-bound train overtook the steamer he was scheduled to board late that night near the town of Herman, Missouri. The conductor informed the rail passengers that they could board the steamer then and there if they liked, or they could continue by rail to Jefferson City and board the boat at that point. By boarding at Herman they would be assured of better accommodations. Ingalls humorously described the stumbling, cursing passengers as they scrambled down the steep riverbank, in the black of night, in order to avail themselves of the "sumptuous offerings" of their steamer, the *Duncan S. Carter*.[21]

The first few hours of the river journey were exciting for Ingalls, but they soon turned to monotony, which was made even more disagreeable by poor meals, a rowdy group of cursing, gambling passengers, and miserable accommodations. These features, however, were not enough to squelch a spark of romanticism which he associated with the whole migratory adventure. In the darkness of the night he stood at the rails of his puffing packet and reflected on "the mighty stream [Missouri River] whose very name is a drama: that stream of which I had so often dreamed."

Upon reaching Kansas City, Ingalls wrote that he improved an hour of transfer at this point on Sunday morning by walking about the town. He was impressed with its "New England look of thrift and business" but quickly perceived that the language of the place was not consistent with its appearance. He described the Western manner of speech as "strong and peculiar." He illustrated this point by repeating a conversation he had overheard where a "very respectable man in appearance, speaking to another on the boat, expressed his belief that he could thrash him in this way: 'I allow that I could clean you out quicker than greased lightning would pass a funeral.'"

Departing from Kansas City on October 3, the captain informed the passengers that the boat would reach Sumner at about one the following morning. A weary and travel-worn Ingalls remarked, "Knowing that everybody this way was a liar, I went to bed in perfect peace and arose to breakfast at the usual hour, still 10 miles below Sumner." At about 8:30 A.M. the "walls of that delectable city came in sight, and precisely at 9 A.M. (10½ by Haverhill time) I landed on the levee at 'Sumner.'"[22] Ingalls then understated his despair by saying that he "was not surprised at not finding a Boston or New York."[23]

Ingalls proceeded to the "hotel," which he described as being "as destitute of carpets as its walls are of paper or its table of decency." It was a large building and resembled its representation "in the lithographic fiction more nearly than any other feature of the 'city.' " An upper room, with unlathed walls, rented for four dollars per week, while a lower room, with lathing, brought five dollars. The only "graded street" in Sumner was Washington Avenue, which Ingalls described as "immensely steep; more like the roof of a house than anything else . . . so gullied with the rains, so interspersed with rocks and stumps of trees, in many cases several feet high, that a New Hampshire teamster of ordinary temerity would shun the task of traversing it."[24] The engineering and grading of this street had been done the previous year by J. B. Gridley of Nebraska City, Nebraska Territory, in contract with the Sumner Company.[25] Needless to say, the town did not fit the visual or verbal impressions that had been conveyed. The Sumner Company agent and the Sumner *Kanzas Gazette* had either erred or lied, and Ingalls believed the latter. Ingalls' dismay and mortification have already been alluded to, but it is imperative to read his vivid descriptions of Sumner if a real appreciation of his situation is to be conveyed. He reported that the town itself consisted of some two hundred houses, "twenty or thirty of which are visible from any one point . . . without windows and doors, some without chimneys, some without shingles or clapboards, nearly all without cellars and situated on heaps of stones or the stumps of old trees and distributed without any regard to order or regularity."[26] Apart from the number of houses, practically everything else Ingalls had been led to believe about Sumner proved to be fictional.

Ingalls arrived in Sumner on Monday morning, October 4, 1858, which happened to be election day. This gave him an excellent chance to see what kind of persons made up the citizenry. He described the local inhabitants as appearing to be "without any exception . . . a shabby, ill-dressed, unthrifty people, most like the inhabitants of the Irish quarter of a large city, wearing upon their countenances a look of ill-concealed discontent akin to despair—as if written over their hearts was the legend fabled by the Italian poet to be inscribed above the gates of hell: 'All hope abandon ye who enter here.' " He continued by pointing out that there were "no churches in the place, instead of four, as was represented to me. No respectable residences; no society; no women except a few woebegone, desolate-looking old creatures; no mechanical activity; nothing which would seem to indicate a large and intelligent energy; no schools, no children; nothing but the total reverse of the picture which was presented to me. On the engraved romance a 'college' was imagined, of which no person here of whom I have inquired has even so much as heard the idea advanced. . . . There is apparently no trade, no commercial exchange with other states or other parts of the territory, no commission business; no reshipment or forwarding, and the few small grocery shops seem to contain only those articles demanded by a wretched and destitute population." Ingalls seriously deliberated the propriety of leaving Sumner at once. "What is best for me to do under the circumstances I do not know—," he remarked, "whether to stay here and get posted in the laws, earning nothing meantime, or return East for a few months." He concluded, however, that if he could find some means of support, he preferred to remain, and commented on the fact that he felt better than he had felt for some months, but conceded that this was probably the result of the stimulation produced by his travels.[27]

The question of remaining permanently in Sumner was frequently discussed in his letters to his father. He thought of the possibility of moving to good points up the Missouri River, without committing himself to a river-site location, for he was aware of the potential of the railroad which he believed would have an important effect upon the relative importance of towns.[28] Perhaps the whole prospect of his position can be summed up in his own words: "Being once fairly embarked, I am ready for any movement which gives promise of success."[29] He alluded to the Pike's Peak gold diggings and envisioned the prospect of Kansas becoming another California. The overall prospects appeared promising; for the immediate present, however, the pickings were extremely lean. On October 23, 1858, Ingalls argued his first legal case in Sumner and represented a "Dutchman" who was being sued by a doctor for an exorbitant bill. Ingalls reported that he got the greater part of the bill disallowed and that the "Dutchman's gratitude was profuse in words, but he had no dimes, and I am consequently as poor as ever."

If Sumner was destitute of opportunity, as Ingalls inferred, he nevertheless conceded that the weather in the late October days of a Kansas Indian summer was "inexpressibly fine." But as roses have thorns, so Kansas had mud. Ingalls referred to it as "incomparable," and stated that in the mud line, Kansas was a "perfect triumph." He described it as "slippery as lard, adhesive as tar, cumulative as a miser's gold, and treacherous as hope, it forms a compound unique and peculiar that defies description. There are three colors—black, red and clay, differing in no respect except chromatically. It sticketh closer than a brother, entering every crevice, and then accumulating in varied laminae and strata, many shaped and many colored, that can neither be kicked off nor scraped off, nor in any way avoided. It dries as hard as a mortar wall. A brush glides over it as it would a lapstone or the Farnese Hercules, leaving a hammer and an old case knife the only resource." Ingalls went on to describe another method employed to clean boots, which consisted of taking them by the straps and banging them against a brick wall. "It is quite efficacious, the only objection being that the process would soon bury the house as effectually as Vesuvius did the city of Pompeii." In conclusion, Ingalls suggested still another method, which consisted of boiling the boots in a great vat. The idea was suggested, he claimed, by the fact that the drinking water looked and tasted as if the operation had been performed in it.[30]

In spite of the fact that Ingalls found much to complain about, he conceded that he had been treated kindly. He believed that this was a result of the fact that he was, as he put it, "the only freestate lawyer in the county—a county which was, and still is, the focus of border ruffianism and proslavery propagandism."[31] This statement puts both Ingalls and Sumner in a somewhat better political perspective. It remains true, however, according to Ingalls' own testimony, that he was concerned primarily "with any movement [that is, locating at any place or site] which gives promise of success."[32] As for the town of Sumner, it too was more interested in success than it was in becoming sacrificed in the cause of Free Statism. Sumner was named after Charles Sumner, the well-known champion of Negro civil rights and United States Senator for the state of Massachusetts. This indicates that the town was at least sentimentally associated with the anti-slave or Free State forces of Kansas. Apart from its place name, however, there is little substance to the argument that it was a Free State stronghold. The Sumner town-site project was a commercial affair whose purpose, like that of so many other Free State towns, was to make a profit. The town was conceived in the mind of John P. Wheeler, who, as a young man in his early twenties, migrated to Kansas in 1855. After initiating the organization of a company, a constitution was drawn up and adopted on April 3, 1857. The constitution contained seventeen articles. Article Two stated the specific object of the company, which was "to build upon and improve a town site, situated upon the Missouri River on section No. Twenty (20) in township No. Six (6) South in Range No. Twenty one (21) east of the 6th P.M." The only intimation that the promoters were at all concerned with the moral questions of the territory was made by the fact that Article Three stated that the town should be named "in honor of the Hon. Charles Sumner Senitor [sic] of the American Congress from Massachusetts." Those who signed this constitution were John Wheeler, John A. Fitch, Perry Domuls or Daniels, William Wheelock, Albert Adams, and Tom Wheelock.[33]

Although the town's constitution did not state anything specific about the Free State cause, the Sumner *Kanzas Gazette* of April 23, 1859, made specific references to this issue. In fact, some of these *Gazette* statements were so specific as to be highly questionable. In this issue of the *Gazette* just cited, an article appeared under the title "Facts For Emigrants to Kanzas." Thirty-one reasons were given to encourage emigrants to Kansas to settle in Sumner. Several of these "facts" are quoted here so as to give some indication of the optimism of those who were promoting this particular town site: "Kanzas is the garden of the United States. . . . All the Indian tribes are friendly to the Free State men, so far as they know. . . . While Kanzas is the country for the poor man, it holds out advantages equally encouraging for the man of limited fortune. . . . Sumner is nearer the interior of the Territory than any other River town as it [is] situated at the western extremity of the great bend of the Missouri River. . . . There are most excellent roads leading from Sumner to all parts of Kanzas. . . . Sumner is situated on very high ground and entirely free from miasmatic influences of the fever and ague districts." Item thirty-one of the list was the strongest statement with regard to Sumner's Free State status and reads as follows: "Sumner is an original Free State town, settled by free state men, for the sole purpose of developing the industrial resources of Kanzas, originating free state enterprise, establishing free institutions, and having at least one port on the river, where free state men can make a landing, do their shipping and other business on free state principles, without trouble or being subject to imposition." This article extolled all the supposed and fancied "natural" advantages of the town site, while simultaneously associating the whole project with a moral and/or political cause. This kind of appeal was very common and highly attractive. Such exaggerations, however, required a most intensive application of the old adage that "beauty is in the eye of the beholder."

In spite of the shortcomings of Sumner, Ingalls humorously noted that his own prospects were promising, because "offices are filled by dolts, and posts of honor and profit by irresponsible persons, because there are more positions than there are worthy candidates."[34] He had indicated earlier that even though his first impressions of the place were disappointing, he had become inclined to think of it more favorably. A partial reason for his changing views resulted from his conversations with Albert D. Richardson, whom he described as "the Kansas correspondent of the Boston Journal." From these talks he gained a more favorable insight into the "machinery."[35] This insight enabled Ingalls to at least partially comprehend the bizarre manner in which Western towns were built. He regarded this as having arisen from the "audacious enterprise of the age" and wondered "if the Plymouth Company and the Massachusetts Bay Company of two or three centuries ago were organized like these western corporations." In a prophetic mood, he closed his commentary on the topic of the town-site development by stating, "We may become historical yet."[36]

The whole question of deciding upon a permanent location in the West, however, troubled Ingalls for several months; and a good potential town site was his preference rather than settling down in an established town or city.[37] But what makes a good potential town site? Ingalls concluded that it was not geographically determined. He rejected the thesis that great rivers gave rise to great cities and pointed out that if this were so, then Alton, Illinois, and Cairo, Illinois, would theoretically have unequaled advantages. In summarizing his views on this topic, he pointed out that both Alton and Cairo had been "exceeded by points which have no geographical position whatever," and therefore, "the soil is essentially democratic and has a noble scorn of all factitious distinctions."[38]

The most urgent business at hand, however, was not so much where he should finally locate but, rather, how was he to earn his living? His first impulse had been to build up a legal practice, and in consequence of this prospect, he wrote to his father, stating that some twenty or thirty volumes of law books were indispensable if he were to begin to practice. Within a few weeks he sent his father a list of supplies plus titles of books that he considered essential. In all, some eighteen books were requested, plus some warranty, quit-claim, and trust deeds, mortgages with power of sale, a few bonds, leases, and some half-dozen sticks of bright-red sealing wax.[39] These supplies were received in due time, but the major problems to beginning a legal practice in Sumner arose from two factors: the "bogus problem" and a want of customers or clients. Ingalls pointed out that there was a conflict over two codes of law, adopted by two hostile legislatures (Pro-Slave vs. Free-State), and that each called the other "bogus." He indicated that the two codes were taken largely from the Missouri and Ohio constitutions respectively, with the former being adopted by the higher courts and the latter by the lower courts. He optimistically believed that in time the two codes would be simplified and consolidated. The problem of acquiring clients was another matter which is best described in Ingalls' own words: "If you happen to know any dissatisfied swain who aspires to the milk and honey of Kansas, who would exchange the granite quarries of Middleton for the black, inexhaustible mines of prairie fertility, who would dispense with the plough and the hoe and gain of fabulous crops without labor, who would have winter mitigated by the skies of Italy and summers tempered by perpetual breezes whose fragrance exhilarates without satiety, who would grow rich while he slept and bequeath to his children a certainty of wealth instead of their few cold, barren ancestral acres, if you know any such, I would be obliged if you would put me in correspondence with him, for the per cent on all sales here is extremely satisfactory."[40]

Ingalls' first legal case had ended with his receiving no remuneration for his services, as his client had no money. A subsequent case saw him a wiser man, and consequently he wrested an agreement from his client whereby he was to receive fifteen dollars for his services if he won the case. When Ingalls won, his client rose and proceeded to leave the room, whereupon Ingalls reminded him of their agreement. The conversation proceeded as follows: "How about that order [money]?" "Oh I aint going to pay you anything!" "Why?" "Oh, you did it so easy it aint worth anything." Ingalls concluded by stating that the rest of his own remarks "were more forcible than polite."[41]

These first months in Kansas were generally unremunerative and depressing for Ingalls. His father encouraged him by telling him he had an extraordinary talent for letter-writing and suggested that he might secure employment as a correspondent for an Eastern journal. He cautioned, however, that he might get into trouble with his neighbors by being a "little bit too racy." He pointed out that Judge Lecompte would hardly like the verbal picture Ingalls had painted of him and that "your picture of Sumner would be anything but inviting to western emigrants."[42] In time, the advice of his father proved to be prophetic.

3

POLITICAL PRETENSIONS AND LEGITIMATE ASPIRATIONS

Ingalls had been in Kansas slightly more than a month before he made mention of his political activities. He reported, almost curtly, that he had been chosen president of a political meeting one evening, November 5, and that he was to attend the Territorial Convention which was to meet at Lawrence the following week.[1] For some unexplained reason, however, he missed this political gathering. Nevertheless, he managed to keep informed of its proceedings, and he commented on some of the leading political sentiments. He pointed out that there were two major proposals under consideration: "whether the Free State party should go into a distinctive Republican organization at once, and whether immediate steps should be taken to gain admission into the Union as a State." Ingalls concluded that public sentiment was negative on both points. He also indicated that there was a movement under way to secure the division of the Territory of Kansas into two parts, forming an eastern and a western territory. If such a measure came about, he concluded further that the struggle between freedom and slavery might be renewed. He agreed with the idea that the Territory should be divided into two parts, however, stating that it was 700-miles across, which he considered to be "an impractical distance through which to transmit the feeble vitality of a state government."[2]

If the Territory of Kansas was having difficulties with regard to administration and finance, then Sumner was having the same problem in microcosm, but with even less chance for favorable solutions. As early as November, 1858, Ingalls had alluded to the difficulties the town was having. He indicated that a city government was to be organized in the coming winter months and that taxes were to be more equally distributed. In summarizing his comments on the existing conditions, he added the simple fact that "the Sumner Co. is financially embarrassed."[3] The organizational meeting was held in December, and Ingalls was chosen chairman of a committee to prepare a charter for the reorganization of the City of Sumner. This, in turn, was to be presented to the Territorial legislature, which would open its session on the first Tuesday in January, 1859. But first the charter had to be approved by the citizens of Sumner in a special election. Whether special or otherwise, Sumner was accustomed to elections; and if numerous elections are to be equated with democracy, then Sumner was democratic by the widest of possible margins. A few days later Ingalls reported that changes had been made in the organization of the Sumner Company that would effect material changes in the board of control and that a new promotional policy was being developed. John P. Wheeler was elected president, replacing C. F. Currier, and a Mr. Lewis from Pennsylvania, "a young man of wealth and business capacity," was elected secretary, taking Wheeler's old position. Samuel Harsh, whom Ingalls described as a Leavenworth banker originally from Ohio, "of large means and extended experience, and one of the best financiers in the Territory," remained treasurer. Plans were made to distribute a large number of lots with general improvements effected, and the whole project was to be energetically promoted. Ingalls stated that the charter he was drafting would help to create a sense of local pride, which he believed was presently lacking. The big news, however, was word that negotiations were under way with the Governor, as Ingalls put it, to have "Hockaday, Burr and Co., by which the Salt Lake mails and Govt. trains for Utah are [operated], . . . start from Sumner subject to the approval of the Secretary of the Interior." He conceded that the prospect was not certain, but nevertheless there appeared to be an excellent chance of securing this all-important communication and transportation facility.[4]

On the evening of December 21, 1858, Ingalls related, he had the honor of presenting to the citizens of Sumner a draft of the new city charter, which was "to be engineered through the next legislature." He explained that the charter met with the approbation of the Sumnerites, "as it could not well otherwise do, insomuch as none of them knew anything about such things, and I read it with such immense rapidity that one section must have been erased from their memory by the incursion of the next." He pointed out that it was short and simple, that it called for no salaried officers at the present time, and that it contained nothing that was ornamental, but was strictly designed for utility. He also noted that it was not by any means original, but that after examination of several other city charters and after consultation it was decided that Sumnerites would do best by adopting the latest charter of Lawrence, Kansas, as the basis of their own. In summary, Ingalls related how he had protected himself from having to serve in any administrative capacity by inserting a clause in the charter requiring prospective officers to have at least a six-month residence in the Territory to become eligible.[5] Nevertheless, Ingalls had permitted himself to be elected to another post, that of a Director of Common Schools. In addition a tax of $600 was voted, and the Reverend Daniel Foster was employed to teach about one hundred pupils.[6]

Sometime late in November or early December, Ingalls paid a visit to Atchison, the rival river town just two miles upstream from Sumner. He had visited there before; but on this occasion his impressions were unusually vivid, and he recorded them in a long letter to his father. He described Atchison as one of the oldest, if not the oldest, place in the Territory, stating that it was started more than four years earlier. It was named "in honor of old Dave R. Atchison," and according to Ingalls it was "until last year . . . the headquarters of border ruffianism in the Territory." He referred to the bad odor of the town and pointed out that it was situated in an unhealthy bottom and that altogether it contained about three hundred houses and twelve hundred people. "It presents a very fine appearance viewed from the river, having a thrifty flourishing look, rising gradually from the levee to the grassy horizon. Nearness dissipates the illusion, and entry destroys it." He extolled the commercial progress of Sumner as compared to that of Atchison and claimed that Sumner had increased its business activities ten times over the past year, while Atchison's had remained the same. He believed that Sumner was destined to outstrip its upstream rival within four years. He also called attention to geographical location and the manner in which both towns talked about their superior location upon the "Great Western Bend" of the Missouri River. Ingalls concluded that the western extremity was, in fact, situated between the two towns, but that in any event the supposed advantage was so insignificant that any dispute about the matter seemed ridiculous. He conceded that an important town would develop in the immediate vicinity, "not a St. Louis or a Cincinnati perhaps, but a large, wealthy and enterprising city. It depends upon individual energy and intelligence, whether Sumner or Atchison shall exceed, or perhaps future growth may consolidate the two into a great Western Metropolis." He closed prophetically with the statement that "the location of Railroads is exercising the public mind just now, and their route will decide forever a great many of these vast pretensions based upon supposed natural advantages."[7]

Within a few weeks Ingalls' political interests required him to journey to Lawrence via Leavenworth. He commented upon the rapid growth of Leavenworth, claiming that its population was approximately ten thousand persons. He expressed the belief that this city would become the great point in Kansas. He also commented upon a question of "coincidence or law" whereby it appeared to him that forts gave birth to great cities, and named as illustrations Pittsburgh, Chicago, Cleveland, Cincinnati, and St. Louis. Upon his arrival in Lawrence, he wrote his father that he was there as "lobby member" of the legislature. He described the several members of the legislature who were already there "rolling logs and pulling wires," and explained that the session would be required to meet at Lecompton, twelve miles west, but that once there, they would immediately adjourn to Lawrence.[8]

Ingalls' purpose as a lobbyist was to obtain legislative approval of the new Sumner city charter and also a charter for a newly formed "Pike's Peak Express Company." He pointed out that the Pike's Peak fever was expected to bring thousands of emigrants through eastern Kansas en route to the gold fields farther west. The object of the company was to transport and feed persons going to Pike's Peak for fifty dollars each. Ingalls regarded the express-company franchise, which he said would cost nothing, as a very valuable thing; and as he was to be one of the corporate members, he lacked no enthusiasm in seeking to secure passage of the measure.[9]

Ingalls' efforts proved successful, and he reported that the charter measures had been passed by the Territorial legislature and that the Sumner city charter was creating considerable excitement among the office-seekers. The charter provided for twenty-two offices, including twelve aldermen, and Ingalls boasted that he had been offered any position he might choose to accept. However, he declined the small political honors that were offered to him and once more expressed an interest in the possibilities of going west in the spring.[10] Although he had made some progress in gaining political notice in Kansas, he was still hard pressed to make even a subsistence living. At Lawrence he had secured election to the position of clerk of the Territorial senate. Initially this was to have paid him three dollars a day, but later this figure was upped to five dollars.

When payment for these services was finally received, the figure was again raised so that Ingalls received six dollars per day for his services. Unfortunately payment was made in scrip. Since the Territory had no cash, this was the usual manner of "robbing Peter to pay Paul." In consequence of these financial difficulties the Territorial legislature passed a bill whereby the Territorial debt was to be funded. Bonds were to be issued, payable in New York in 1865, which would pay 10 percent interest. To secure cash, Ingalls bought some of these bonds with his scrip, hoping to be able to sell the bonds for cash at par. In the meantime he was forced to rely upon his father for the money necessary to meet his day-to-day expenses.[11]

The problems that beset the struggling Territory of Kansas are suggested in the descriptions that Ingalls wrote of the legislative proceedings. He pointed out that most of the business conducted was of a local and uninteresting nature. Something that proved to be interesting, however, was "the economy of Mr. Secretary Walsh." Ingalls reported that this gentleman had used the contingent fund in private speculation and now was "disinclined to disgorge." In addition, bulletins were received daily from the "rebellious counties" in the south. In summary, Ingalls reported that the town was full of "lobby members engineering through schemes of plunder in the way of charters, town grants, franchises and perpetual privileges."[12] Such critical descriptions once more led Ingalls' father to write him some words of caution. In a most discreet manner he suggested that he had no intention of dictating what his son should say; however, he advised him to "be more judicious if you would ever have any valuable or permanent popularity—If you do not like vice, you are in the same predicament in regard to it as Henry Ward Beecher toward the potato—But he genially and devoutly thanks a Kind Providence that there was a race of Irish created especially as it would seem to him, to eat them up, and considers them the Irish very useful for that purpose if for nothing else. Sarcasm is good, but should be used sparingly and in order not to recoil upon us, should always have *proper* and definite objects to be exercised upon." In summarizing his advice, he concluded with the optimistic hope that his son would "remember and adhere to strict rectitude—let no bribe tempt you to vary one iota from the strictest integrity—You will find that honesty will be the most valuable characteristic that you can possess."[13]

Such advice was timely, since Ingalls had begun a journalistic career by writing a few articles for his hometown newspaper, the *Gazette* of Haverhill, Massachusetts, but more importantly because he had also contracted to write for the New York *Evening Post* for a salary of four dollars per day. Ingalls was expected to write accounts of the proceedings of the Territorial legislature, which he did in the "racy" manner his father had cautioned against. One of the Territorial issues of national interest, which the legislature considered, involved the status of slavery in Kansas. In a letter to his father Ingalls reported that bills to abolish slavery had been introduced in both houses of the Territorial legislature, which gave "a fine opportunity to the members to ventilate their vocabularies." He believed that some act would be passed that would make Kansas at least a nominally free Territory, while at the same time he recognized this would have serious repercussions, as there were a number of slaves owned in Kansas. He pointed out that most of the slaves were owned by persons living in the southern part of the Territory and that a project was under way that, it was hoped, would alter the Territorial boundaries so as to cut off the lower portion of the Territory. This portion of Kansas was then to be joined with a northern portion of the Indian Territory (present-day Oklahoma), a combination that would ultimately lead to the formation of another slave state.[14] Ingalls did not indicate just who proposed such a measure, nor did he state his position on such a proposal. Although the bill to abolish slavery passed both houses, it did not become law. It was vetoed by Governor Samuel Medary.[15]

Ingalls' stay in Lawrence, though in connection with the Territorial legislature, was not devoted solely to political interests. He commented upon the location of the town and its history. He described the Kaw (Kansas) River as being about half as wide as the Merrimac of Massachusetts and pointed out that originally Lawrence had been called Wakarusa, but that "someone who had a genius for investigation discovered that in the original the apparently romantic name had a significance which I can only properly paraphrase by the term 'hip deep,' in consequence of which the appellation was abandoned for the present term." While in Lawrence, Ingalls attended church for the first time since coming to the Territory and noticed that "there was as much style and fashion in the audience as would be seen in an eastern city."[16] Obviously the appearances of Lawrence's citizens contrasted sharply with those of Sumner's, whom Ingalls had earlier described in unflattering terms.

With the close of the Territorial legislature's sessions in Lawrence, Ingalls returned to Sumner to continue the pursuit of his fortunes. Success was not, however, to come to him via the rise and progress of the city of Sumner. In a communication to his father he unconsciously prophesied the town's ultimate doom with the announcement that the Hannibal and St. Joseph Railroad would be open to travel throughout its entire length on February 28, 1859.[17] Any connection with that line would, of geographic necessity, be required to pass through Atchison if it were ever to extend to Sumner. At best this would put Sumner in the position of acting as a tail to the Atchison kite, and whatever progress Sumner might hope for would inevitably be dependent upon the fortunes of Atchison. Nevertheless, Ingalls' optimism for his city was, for the time being, sustained by the reports of gold discoveries in the Pike's Peak area. In a reference to the now-celebrated ignorance of Easterners with regard to Western geography, he spoke of a party from Massachusetts who proposed going to the Pike's Peak gold fields by constructing a small steamboat in which they planned to sail up the Kaw to its junction with the Smoky Hill Fork and thence on to Cherry Creek. "It looks prettily on the map," Ingalls reported, "as you will see by referring to the atlas hanging in the front hall at home, but unfortunately that stream is only navigable by catfish, and by them only at certain seasons of the year." Ingalls facetiously claimed that this pioneer party purchased a steamboat of about "one mule power" and six-inch draught and set sail one summer morning. By evening they ran aground on a sandbar, disembarked, and as a result of their mishap became the unwitting founders of the city of Topeka. Ingalls satirically claimed that a similar comedy of errors was the cause of the founding of Manhattan also.[18]

By March of 1859 Ingalls achieved two additional minor milestones in his Kansas career. He was elected city attorney for Sumner and received a commission from Governor Medary as a notary public. Ingalls commented that the former office was composed of "more honor than profit" and, of the latter, that had Governor Medary known of his recent characterization of him in the New York *Evening Post*, "it is highly probable he would not have favored me with a commission."[19] Medary's hostility to the Republican party was cited by Ingalls as one of the major motivating factors behind the growing discussion concerning statehood for Kansas. He described the course of action proposed by those advocating statehood, which called for a vote to be taken in the very near future for the purpose of framing a new constitution. If that was successful, then delegates to a constitutional convention were to be elected in June and the convention would then convene in Wyandotte in July. The constitution emerging from the convention would be submitted to a popular vote in October, and if approved by the voters, the next step would be the election of officers in December. Although Ingalls favored the statehood movement, he realistically concluded that the Territory was unable to bear the expense of becoming a state.[20]

By May of 1859, Ingalls' political star had begun slowly to climb. He was elected a member of the Republican Central Executive Committee,[21] and in June was elected a delegate to the Wyandotte Constitutional Convention. He boasted that he received the largest plurality in the county nominating convention and that his election on June 7, 1859, as a delegate on the Republican ticket, found him running far ahead of the ticket in the county. He closed on a melancholy note, however, pointing out that "the democrats carried every other county on the [Missouri] river."[22] In the same communication he once more referred to the number of slaves in the Territory, estimating the number to be some five hundred. He also pointed out that the number was increasing "by virtue of the Dred Scott decision," and that a family had only recently moved from Kentucky to Sumner bringing five slaves with them. As for the affairs of Sumner, Ingalls noted "the only excitement aside from politics being thunderstorms and taxes."

As the date of the constitutional convention neared, Ingalls made his preparations to journey to Wyandotte. He went from Sumner to the convention site via the steamer known as the *Southwester*. Upon his arrival in Wyandotte he noted that the Republicans had a majority of eighteen, which gave them "entire control." He described the convention's organizational activities, commenting that they were effected without much difficulty, although the "democrats made all the opposition they were able." Ingalls described the fifty-two assembled delegates as a body that was definitely not superior. He anticipated that the session would last three weeks and noted that the per diem was three dollars, payable in scrip. As for his part in the proceedings, Ingalls claimed that he was on some of the most important committees and would be obliged to do some hard work. His work load was multiplied because he was simultaneously writing for the press, which, as he put it, was necessary "to eke out my means of existence."[23]

Ingalls detailed certain events which took place during the course of the convention in a manuscript entitled "The Row in the Wyandot Convention."[24] The proceedings were frequently characterized by disorderliness and shouts of "liar," "coward," and other vigorous phrases. Not infrequently threats of physical violence lent an ominous note to the proceedings. He described William C. McDowell, who on one such occasion was seated with a "rather inflamed face, veins knotted in his forehead, and looking generally hot and uncomfortable, and as the Sergeant at arms approached him he took the loaded cane which he had carried for some purpose during the entire session and shook it at the officer saying 'Let him try if he dares.' There was a tremulous motion about it, I think, which some attributed to fear and others to rage. I have no opinion in the matter," concluded Ingalls. All of this chaos was urged on by chants from the background, and McDowell was encouraged by a zealous admirer who shouted, "Go on, Mac, go on." In such an atmosphere of sweetness and light the convention lurched on. Ingalls surmised that "this rolling up of sleeves, brandishing loaded canes and disorderly yelling, appeared like an attempt to bully and intimidate, but as it had not that effect," he facetiously concluded, "it is fair to presume that there was no such intention."

Order was finally restored by William McCullough, whom Ingalls described as a gentleman of Scotch descent. McCullough "stepped into the aisle with considerable alacrity . . . commenced turning up the sleeves of his coat disclosing a hairy bulge of muscle and a most ominous length of limb. Mr. McCullough is not a pigmy and his frame seemed to expand and dilate into unwonted proportions. A facetious gentleman remarked that he would rather have an elephant tread on him or a jackass kick him that [sic] have Mac strike him, though I am quite sure no such considerations occurred to the unterrified democracy. He said something about having order preserved, accompanying his remark by an excusable use of the name of one of the Holy Trinity, at the same time smiting his hands together with a sound like the concussion of two anvils. Several other gentlemen also came from the Republican side of the house and I noticed some glaring eyes, some suppressed breathing, some distended nostrils and clenched hands." The apparent object of McCullough's request for order was "Colonel" John P. Slough, a Democrat from Ohio, whom Ingalls described as a gentleman who had "been expelled from the Ohio Legislature for indulging in the gentlemanly amusement of striking or kicking somebody." McCullough prevailed, and Ingalls reported that "all of a sudden gentlemen took their seats. A malicious person remarked that the Colonel [Slough] looked as if 'something had crawled into him and died,' a statement which I believe," claimed Ingalls, "to be a wilful perversion of the truth and base fabrication. There was evidently something unfinished about the programme," he continued, "which perhaps arose from the fact that the Republicans did not send cowards to represent them at the Convention." In summary, he stated that the official debates would contain an account of the affair, "to which I defer entirely."[25]

The Republicans' triumph in the convention was never in doubt, and their version of what the constitution should be was signed on July 29, 1859. As chairman of the committee to draft the final version of the constitution, Ingalls reported that "the language, expression and arrangement are mine." He pointed out that the amount of superfluous matter rejected, of verbiage pruned and solecism corrected, could not be fully appreciated unless the original drafts of the constitution, as submitted by the various committees, were compared with the finished document which he had edited. He boasted that even the opponents of the constitution confessed that "for accuracy of definition, conciseness of expression and terseness of language it is 'a model instrument.'" Those who did oppose the constitution, however, did so, in the words of Ingalls, "because it does not include Southern Nebraska and Pike's Peak, because it does not exclude free Negroes and on account of an apportionment which cannot fail to secure a large Republican majority in the state organization." Ingalls explained that this was done by grouping counties together to the advantage of the Republicans. Counties that were largely Republican were grouped with doubtful or Democratic counties, "in such a manner that success is a certainty." He described the anger of the Democrats as a result of this "Gerrymandering" tactic and remarked that some "temporizing" Republicans had attempted to smooth the matter over with explanations and "euphimisms." "I adopt a different ground," he continued, "and in a speech which I made at Atchison at a mass ratification meeting last evening, I told them distinctly that I assisted in making the apportionment and voted for it, because I thought it was one that *would win*, that I was not aware of any extreme favors or kindness extended to the people of Kansas in the last four years by the democratic party which warranted any very delicate consideration from the party in power to-day." In summary, Ingalls conceded that the "ruffians" hooted some, but that the majority expressed their approbation. Interestingly enough, years later Ingalls claimed that he submitted the original design and the motto for the Kansas State Seal.[26]

There is some doubt as to whether Ingalls was actually so blunt in his Atchison speech in behalf of the Wyandotte Constitution. A portion of his speech, written in his own hand and entitled "Wyandot [sic] Constitution," indicates, if he followed the text, that he adopted a more conciliatory posture. The text of the address called for nonpartisan cooperation in the attempt to achieve statehood under the proposed constitution. After this general appeal Ingalls went on to define a constitution as "merely a written compact between society and each of the persons of which it is composed, comprising a common fund of rights conceded by individuals to secure the greatest good for the whole." He cautioned, however, that "the problem to be solved is the least possible limitations of individual rights consonant with the permanent organization of society." The important question Ingalls posed for his audience was whether or not the proposed constitution called for too great a concession of individual rights. Obviously Ingalls felt it did not, and by using a simple but effective piece of psychology, he won their confidence by stating that this was a matter for the people to decide for themselves. He continued his address with an attack on the Democrats, claiming that they had harassed the proceedings of the constitutional convention "from the noon of the 5th day of July to the night of the 29th." The Democrats opposed the constitution, declared Ingalls, because of the boundary, the black law, and the apportionment.[27]

With the advent of September, Ingalls became increasingly confident that the Wyandotte Constitution would be adopted. On the other hand he was "by no means sanguine of our admission under it into the Union." He conceded that the Democrats were opposing it along Party lines. However, he estimated the Republican majority in the Territory, which he apparently assumed would support it along Party lines, to be some five thousand, "which would assure a Republican victory." In this same communication he commented upon the "stagnation" of Kansas commerce and trade with "nothing to sell and no money for speculation." He stated his belief that all depended upon the prospective railroads, some of which were partially surveyed westward "towards the Rocky Mountains and the Pacific." In closing, he mentioned that the telegraph was in working order as far west as Atchison, which he claimed put its terminus there some fourteen miles farther west than any other station on the continent.[28]

In October, Ingalls reported to his father that the constitution had been adopted by the five-thousand-vote margin he had predicted. He also noted the slate of candidates that had been nominated for constitutional offices, remarking that they "would hardly rank third class in New England, but the poorest state government would be preferable to this condition of none at all." Nevertheless, Ingalls saw a paradox in statehood, that is, a more efficient government at greater expense, as opposed to the existing cheaper but inefficient Territorial government. In the meantime his own political fortunes had taken another mild turn for the better with the announcement that he had been offered the position of probate judge of Atchison County. These aspirations were quickly dashed, however, for he explained that while he was absent from the nominating convention, another person was given the nomination and, as some kind of solace, he had been offered the nomination for district attor-

ney by acclamation. Ingalls declined this "inferior" honor and
indicated that he held hopes of being nominated for the state senate
"if there is no other slip between the cup and the lips." He pointed
out that even this position was not very important, but that it put
the word "Honorable" before a man's name and that it would also be
a long stride towards Congress.[29] However, he did not get the nomination and thus was thwarted in taking this "long stride."

Ingalls speculated that if Kansas were to be admitted to the
Union, this would bring about the distribution of school and railroad
lands which would give impetus to business and generally serve as
a revitalizing force upon the affairs of Kansas. His optimism caused
him to state that "climate, soil and position all combine in prophe-
sying a grand future for Kansas." Ingalls understood, however, that
a "grand future" depended upon the victory of the Republican slate
of officers in the impending December election. The Democrats, on
the other hand, had some grand designs of their own, which consisted primarily of defeating the Republicans. Ingalls had no serious
qualms about an inevitable Republican victory and in fact stated his
belief that the Democratic participation in the upcoming election
would enhance the chance of Kansas' early admission into the
Union.[30]

As Ingalls had predicted, the Republican slate of constitutional
candidates was elected in December, 1859. The headlines of the
Atchison *Freedom's Champion* heralded the Republican victory in
terms so zealous that they might easily have been employed to
announce that the "elect" had suddenly been caught up in the air to
meet the returning Messiah.[31] Ingalls himself expressed no elation
over the Republican triumph. This is easier to understand when it
is recalled that thus far he himself had been frustrated in most of his
county and Territorial political aspirations. He had failed to secure
the nomination for the office of probate judge and consequently had
declined the dubious distinction of becoming the Atchison County
district attorney. He had not secured the nomination for the Territorial senate, and his political hopes were seemingly at a stalemate.
In letters written to his father in late 1859, he portrayed his personal
plight. He complained of being unable to negotiate his scrip, that
bills were hard to collect, debts were repudiated, and that he was
considering doing the same thing with regard to his own bills. He
pointed out that he had assets of several hundred dollars, but was
unable to raise enough cash to pay even his room and board.[32]

Although Ingalls' letters often seemed to border on despair,
there was, occasionally, encouraging news of a general nature to
cheer his prospects. The long-dreamed-of railroad connection be-

tween Atchison, Kansas, and St. Joseph, Missouri, was about to be realized; and continuing reports of a sizable gold strike in the Rockies were hopeful indications of potential prosperity for Kansas.[33] Personal prosperity always seemed just out of reach for Ingalls, however; and in January, 1860, he wrote that he was still undecided on what course he would adopt in the coming spring, "whether to remain on the frontier or get on the foremost wave and rush for Denver City."[34] His interest in the Pike's Peak area was such that while he was lobbying at the sessions of the 1860 Kansas legislature, he became an incorporator in some half-dozen unsurveyed towns, "an insurance and telegraph company, and sundry other schemes of visionary and speculative wealth." He was aware, however, that in the Far West "the social condition is rather uninviting to one who doesn't like the idea of being perforated or lynched." But he concluded that "all accounts unite in declaring the country extremely healthy and picturesque and undeniably fertile in minerals."[35] His chances of going there were, nevertheless, somewhat dependent on whether Kansas was admitted to the Union, which he regarded as the only possible stimulus for business for the remainder of 1860. The economy of the Territory was in such bad shape, according to Ingalls, that exports of corn, pork, and hides did not produce enough income to pay for the whiskey that was drunk each month. He claimed that the populace was living on assets that they brought into the Territory when they migrated, or else they were living on the charity of friends. He cited as an example the fact that the best quality of corn, delivered in sacks on the levee, brought only thirty cents a bushel. Hides brought from four to six cents a pound, and the wheat crop was suffering badly from being winterkilled, which he claimed resulted from the lack of snow.

In spite of Ingalls' gloomy appraisal there were small signs of success of a political nature to which he could point. In January, 1860, he had been appointed chairman of a board of five commissioners who were to serve as Territorial bank inspectors. He reported that he was "to examine into the condition of Kansas Banks this year and report to the legislature at its next session; a position which does not pay much but is very respectable. I don't know much about banks," he continued, "but suppose I can tell by looking round in the vaults, about how the machine works."[36] His next small success occurred when the Republican Territorial convention convened at Lawrence in April, 1860. The temporary organization of that body resulted in the election of Ingalls as secretary. His hopes for the permanent secretaryship were soon dashed, however, for when the election for the permanent organization was held, he was replaced as secretary by the joint election of J. Stotler and J. E. Hayes. Ingalls was not elected to any other position at the convention and was not nominated to go to Chicago as a Kansas delegate to the Republican National Convention.[37]

Shortly after this latest political setback the city of Sumner suffered a final misfortune which sealed its fate. It was struck by a tornado on June 2, 1860. The severity of the damage is not clear. Later reports claim that the town was literally devastated, but contemporary accounts do not bear this out.[38] The Atchison *Freedom's Champion* described the tornado as "one of the most terrible," but in describing its path of destruction, Nemaha was the only town named as suffering any appreciable damage.[39] This is important in light of the claims that the tornado was the reason for Ingalls' moving from Sumner to Atchison.

It is true that he had already begun a law practice in Atchison in partnership with F. G. Adams and C. M. Leland; however, he remained a citizen of Sumner for some time and commuted between the two towns. He once commented on this in a letter to his father, remarking that it was not inconvenient to commute from Sumner to Atchison, as it was merely a pleasant ride of some two miles' distance.[40] Ingalls described Adams as "the senior partner, a grave elderly gentleman, of New York birth, quiet deportment, bald and bearded, and was the first judge of Atchison county." He also mentioned that he was "an old Kansas soldier." Leland was described as "a Southerner and a very studious, learned and excellent counselor."

Ingalls' role in the partnership was to argue the cases before the jury. He claimed to be very successful in this, characterizing his opponents as an "ignorant, detestable set of saddleheaded numb skulls and blackguards." He claimed that he preferred the role of advocate to counseling, as it paid better, brought earlier success, and afforded "a surer avenue to the higher walks of political preferment." He also claimed that he knew and was known by every prominent man in Kansas and that he had their undivided good will. In addition he stated that he had assurance of any position he wanted under the prospective state administration. In summary, Ingalls referred to the prospective establishment of a "central newspaper as the organ of the party [Republican]" if Lincoln was elected in the impending national elections. He claimed that he had been offered the position as editor-in-chief, if the paper materialized, but that even though the position would be influential, it would also be "delicate and harassing" and therefore he was not overly interested. With regard to his long-range political ambitions, he stated, "I do not regard the Governorship or a seat in Congress beyond the range of my legitimate aspirations in the next ten years."[41]

The next step toward achieving his "legitimate aspiration" was taken at the Republican county convention, which met at Atchison on October 13, 1860. John A. Martin, who was chairman of the county executive committee, called the meeting together and after stating its objectives, nominated Ingalls of "Sumner" for president. Ingalls was duly elected, and in addition to this honor was selected to be a delegate to the Republican Territorial convention. He was also named as a member of the Republican county executive committee and later became secretary of this group. Such pretentious positions called for a speech, and Ingalls complied by addressing a "Republican Meeting" in Sumner on November 1, 1860.[42]

To all outward appearances Ingalls now seemed well on the way to achieving his political ambitions, but these early, small successes were unable to carry him to those "legitimate aspirations." Nearly thirteen years would pass before he would be sent to the Congress of the United States as a Senator for the state of Kansas.

Shortly after these local political successes of late 1860, Ingalls finally moved from Sumner to Atchison. The exact date is not known. For approximately two years Ingalls and Sumner had struggled to achieve their respective ambitions. Neither had succeeded. Sumner's schemes and dreams all proved iridescent. Atchison had secured the stage lines, the railroad, the telegraph, and in addition became the county seat. These were the factors that caused the decline and eventual demise of Sumner. And these were the reasons that prompted Ingalls to move from Sumner to Atchison. Nevertheless, whatever initial success and notoriety Ingalls had achieved had been accomplished as a resident of Sumner. This Free State town had put Ingalls into the arena of local and Territorial political activity.

4
CIVIL WAR
AND
SPECIAL SEDUCTIONS

The two years of 1859 and 1860 made it increasingly apparent that the nation was facing an impending crisis. In October of 1859 John Brown attacked and seized the Federal arsenal at Harper's Ferry. He was tried for treason that same month, found guilty, and hanged the first week in December. And thus a national martyr and/or monster, as you please, was simultaneously and instantaneously thrust upon the American public. He became symbolic of the forces that were busy marshaling the nation into opposing camps. Although Ingalls was seriously concerned with respect to national issues, his correspondence conveyed a deeper concern for the affairs of Kansas Territory. Very likely it was a combination of local and national political interests that found Ingalls among the welcoming party for Abraham Lincoln's visit to Atchison on December 2, 1859, the very day that John Brown was hanged. However, in Ingalls' extant correspondence from this period there is no reference to this occasion nor any comment about Lincoln. Ingalls was not overly impressed by Lincoln's charisma.

Events of the spring and summer of 1860 made the growing political tensions still more taut. The Republican party of 1860 was more than just a political fact, its platform, with respect to slavery, made it anathema to the South. The Democratic party had split into two factions, while remnants of the old Whig and American parties combined to create the Constitutional Union party. As November drew near, there was a confusing array of Presidential candidates and issues. Out of this confusion Lincoln emerged the Presidential victor, and the wheels of secession were set in motion. South Carolina led off by unanimously passing an ordinance dissolving its union with that of the United States. Intelligence of such momentous matters was slow in reaching Kansas. The winter of 1860–1861 was a hard one in Kansas, and blizzard conditions interfered with communications. This proved to be extremely aggravating to Ingalls, who was eager to learn the status of the Kansas admission bill, the Pacific railroad bill, and conditions in the South, in that priority. In Kansas, the Territorial legislature, where Ingalls was serving as secretary to the Council, was busy "endorsing Major Anderson [of Fort Sumter], and divorcing everybody who applies for rupture of the bonds of matrimony [secession]."[1] As always, there were intensely mixed political emotions in Kansas, and the concept of secession seemed a salutary solution to some, while being repugnant to others.

Ingalls viewed secession as a catastrophic specter. He hotly disputed the right of peaceable secession, and if it were allowed, he saw it as making the Federal government a "stupendous practical joke." He viewed those who favored secession as "traitors and paupers" who must be stopped "once for all." And this, he concluded, would involve the "iron logic of the cannon of the volunteers of the north."[2] Kansas was preparing for this imminent contest by organizing a militia for "self defense." In the process of this effort Ingalls was appointed aid-de-camp to the Major General, with the rank of Colonel. In response to his appointment Ingalls' only comment was that "titles are cheap just now."[3]

When the legislative sessions closed, Ingalls returned to Atchison and made arrangements to have the journal of the Council published.[4] The *Champion* claimed that "Mr. Ingalls has been Secretary of the Territorial Council during the last two sessions, and discharged the duties of his office with eminent ability. He is one of the very few men in Kansas who has received office on account of his fitness for it."[5] The article continued by pointing out that Ingalls would be a candidate for the position of Secretary of the State Senate and speculated that he would, "no doubt, be elected. Certainly, if that body wishes the most capable, obliging, attentive and courteous officer that can be found in Kansas, he will have no opposition for the post."[6]

Kansas was admitted to the Union on January 29, 1861. Secession was approaching flood tide. Six states had seceded prior to the admission of Kansas, and three days after Kansas was admitted, Texas seceded. Texas' action completed the secession of the Lower South. But for the *Champion* the big news was the admission of

Kansas to the Union. It was a "glorious" event that was likened to the arrival of the millennium, at least on the local level.[7] Ingalls immediately planned a trip to Topeka, the new state capital, and mentioned that President Lincoln had declared that no state appointments would be made until United States Senators were elected.[8] Consequently, he surmised that the real question was not who would be preferred, but rather who was going to win?[9] Of the several candidates in the field only four were of any prominence. The four Ingalls named were Marcus J. Parrott, Samuel C. Pomeroy, General James H. Lane, and Frederick P. Stanton. He pointed out that the first two named lived north of the Kansas River and the other two lived south of it.[10] Ingalls believed that Parrott, who was his own personal choice, would win. As for Pomeroy, he concluded that "if abdomen was a test he would be sure to triumph, but as brains enter into the contest somewhat, his chances are small."[11] Ingalls looked upon Lane as another of Kansas' notorious characters; nevertheless, he admitted that Lane was one of the most remarkable characters he had ever known.[12] He described him as "a perfect demagogue, charlatan, knave, everything that is infamous and detestable in private life, and yet possessed of a certain indefatigable energy, magnetism and nerve which conquers adversity and achieves success." As for Lane's election to the United States Senate, Ingalls concluded that "the chances are immensely in his favor." Stanton was mentioned as a "pro-slave 11th hour Republican who had served ten years as a Congressman from Memphis, Tenn."[13]

A short time later an Ingalls letter criticizing Pomeroy must have fallen into the latter's hand. Pomeroy confronted Ingalls with excerpts taken from the letter, and a heated exchange between the two ensued. A sadder, but wiser, Ingalls regretted that he had carelessly circulated his criticisms.[14]

Contrary to Ingalls' wishes, Pomeroy and Lane were elected United States Senators for Kansas. And in spite of the recent confrontation with Pomeroy, Ingalls could not refrain from further elaboration on "Pompous Pom" Pomeroy. "Pomeroy is of Massachusetts birth," he wrote, "a blacksmith by trade, about fifty years old, and as fat, mean and hypocritical an old canter as can well be described. He has fattened upon the calamities of the public: and his election to the Senate is the greatest calamity of all."[15]

Ingalls' "eulogy" for Lane was no better than the one for Pomeroy. He described Lane as one of the "free state" leaders in Kansas of some three or four years earlier, "and subsequently as the murderer of Jenkins at Lawrence." His description of Lane grew more elaborate with the pronouncement that "he is an unmitigated scoundrel and a demagogue of the [first] water. His personal appearance is striking and peculiar: lean, sinewy, bronzed and savage, he resembles a fiend in bad condition: his eyes small, deepset and fiery, shine beneath a cavernous forehead and long shaggy brows: his dress is negligent and carelessly worn, exhibiting a cross between a backwoodsman and a prosperous barber. His ability is average and his attainments as a lawyer fair: upon the stump he is unequaled, though his oratory is of no sort described in the books: his deep gutterals are rasped from a raging throat and in his frenzy he nearly denudes himself before his audience. The magnetism of his manner is unbounded: he wins and persuades by a certain indefinable plausibility of tone and gesture which no enmity can withstand." Ingalls concluded his discourse on Lane by stating that "He is energetic and laborious to a miracle and unscrupulous as a devil. For six years he has bent his entire effort to the attainment of this result, without money or popularity and his triumph indicated his power."[16]

In the meantime the law firm of Adams, Leland, and Ingalls was dissolved. Ingalls pointed out that Leland had been appointed receiver in a land office, and Adams became a district attorney in Nebraska. As a result Ingalls' own fortunes took another turn for the worse. He complained that Kansas was hard put for currency, and having no banks of her own, the currency was altogether Illinoisan, Wisconsinan, and Missourian. He pointed out that the depreciation of the stocks upon which this currency was based had made it almost worthless."[17] Perhaps in an attempt to minimize his financial distress, Ingalls' father and his brother Robert Morris bought fifty shares of Sumner stock, which Ingalls owned, at three hundred dollars per share. There is good reason to believe that the cash to the amount of $15,000 never exchanged hands in this sale. Ingalls received some cash from his father and brother, who in turn probably tried to sell the shares back East. No doubt there was a mutual understanding concerning the finances of this transaction, with any balance owed being dependent upon turning the shares over at par or for a profit, and all of this being in the realm of "hopes and wishes."[18]

If doing a job well merits a reward, then Ingalls received appropriate accolades for his part in the proceedings of the first legislature of the new state of Kansas. This first session had the awesome task of electing Senators, creating courts, and defining the jurisdiction of both the new and the old courts. On top of all this was the burden of patronage. At the conclusion of the first momentous sessions at Topeka, the *Champion* claimed that "Hon. John J. Ingalls

Secretary of the State Senate reached home from Topeka on Sunday morning last. He has discharged the duties of his office to the satisfaction of everybody."[19] In less than a week after the completion of his service in the state Senate, Ingalls wrote his father that he was leaving Atchison at once, mounted on a bay mustang headed for the Rocky Mountains. He expected to return no later than the last of September and asked that his mail be directed to "Denver City, Colorado Ter.," until August 25.[20] Ingalls made no mention of his "military" obligations which committed him to "defend" Kansas. Kansas had achieved statehood; Lincoln was in office; the nation was in a state of civil war; but for Ingalls in particular and Americans in general it was "business as usual" insofar as conditions permitted. But for Ingalls conditions did not permit the usual. Consequently, with the dissolution of his law partnership and the downward trend of his political fortunes, the lure of the "elephant" became irresistibly attractive.

Ingalls' next extant communication was written from Colorado and dated August 23, 1861. He claimed that the mines there were abandoned, the mills closed, the cabins shut up, and the people so discouraged that they were leaving. His impression of the opportunities there was so poor that he concluded his letter with the remark that he would "start for America" by the twelfth of September or the fifteenth at the latest.[21] In a subsequent letter dated at Central City, Colorado Territory, he boasted, or complained, that he had ridden fifteen hundred miles since July twelfth and had changed clothes just twice in that time.[22]

Ingalls returned to Atchison in September, a wiser but poorer man. He wrote that he had kept notes of his journey and gave a detailed account of his trip home, which was by stagecoach.[23] Atchison was described as "quiet," with the comment that the opponents of the Governor had fled and their property had been "jayhawked."[24] By October, 1861, military preparations were on the increase in Kansas as the result of the growing Civil War. Ingalls referred to the organization of the home guard as the "Homely Blackguards as we are maliciously termed by the envious," and stated that they were drilling constantly in preparation for the exigencies of war. He boasted that he was a "high private" and could go through the motions or manual of arms, with tolerable facility, though he confessed that military glory at thirteen dollars per month held no "special seductions" for him.[25] In this same communication he told how he had been nominated for state senator at the "Union Convention," with fifty out of sixty votes on the first ballot.[26] Again his political prospects seemed about to blossom. His finances, however, were in the usual state of depletion. He related how he had been holding fast to his last five-dollar bill only to learn too late that the bank had "gone up." He lamented that he had passed up several good chances to pass the bill just the day before, but now regretted his folly. He pointed out that corn was only a dime a bushel, apples thirty cents, and beef was to be had for the asking, therefore he did not foresee immediate suffering.[27]

Ingalls' father had suggested that he write a book about his Rocky Mountain experience. Ingalls concurred with his father's suggestion and reported that he had kept "copious notes" of his proceedings and that he intended to write them out for the gratification of himself and his friends, and possibly for publication, if there was some chance for remuneration. He stated that he had never seen any work conveying a "graphic and definite objective idea of life on the Plains and at the mines," such as he thought he could give. "The region has a peculiar fascination to the mind," he exclaimed, "and I had already selected as a clap trap alliterative title, 'The Platte, the Plains and the Peak.'" He concluded that if nothing should ever come of his proposed book, at least he had acquired abundant health, an unshaven face, and the ability to sleep on a blanket in the dirt, all of which he regarded as being somewhat on the credit side of the whole episode. In fact he enjoyed this journey so much that he mentioned that he was already planning a trip to Santa Fe or to the headwaters of the Missouri River.[28]

Ingalls' political fortunes were once more nipped in the bud when in November of 1861 he was defeated in his bid for a seat in the state senate.[29] He ran a "good" last on a ticket comprised of three nominees. On top of this the campaign had cost him a thousand dollars.[30] Where he secured his campaign money is questionable, although it is possible that at least a part of the funds came from his father and brother, who had purchased his Sumner shares. Ingalls also mentioned that he was investing all surplus money in "wild lands" and other property, at such figures that the taxes would not be overburdensome. He concluded with the comment that he was planning a trip home next year.[31]

In the meantime, Kansas politics continued to be plagued by charges of corruption. Ingalls referred to a sale of bonds to the Indian Department in Washington, D.C., and claimed that Kansas, in a single transaction, had been swindled by her own state officers out of one hundred and fifty-eight thousand dollars. He pointed out that "Old Pomeroy rode into the Senate on the cry [a need to weed out swindlers] and made probably $50,000 from the contributions of generous simpletons, who indulged in the amiable luxury of feeding the hungry and clothing the poor."[32] Pomeroy's motives and general character were frequently questioned. One interesting query came from Ellsworth Chesebrough, who was running as a candidate for mayor of Atchison at the time.[33] Chesebrough wrote to Pomeroy and informed him that he had been unanimously nominated for mayor by the "Unconditional Union Citizens" of Atchison and that the secessionists had nominated a ticket headed by M. R. Benton and C. M. Leland.[34] He continued by stating that the Benton-Leland ticket was pledged to the "Pro-Slaveryites" who wanted to regain power in Kansas. The letter then focused sharply on a "summons" in circulation, which supposedly stated that Pomeroy was "pledged to Challis and others of this city to contribute $1,000.00 for the purpose of electing Benton—Glick [deleted]—, Hetherington—Challis—secesh piebald ticket." Chesebrough claimed that he denied the reports of such a deal; nevertheless, he declared, "Our unconditional friends . . . deemed it proper under the circumstances to drop you a line on the subject—so that if untrue, as I believe it to be, we can brande [sic] the whole story as a weak fabrication—for if not contradicted it will work serious injury to the cause we have so much at heart—and your own 'good name.'" Chesebrough added that the "Unconditional" party had passed resolutions against "secesh and Jayhawking." In an almost pleading fashion, he concluded by asking if he could make Pomeroy's reply public.[35] Although Pomeroy's reply is not available, a collateral reference to the incident is disclosed in a cryptic letter that Ingalls wrote to F. G. Adams. The letter referred to names identified only as "Bridgman" and the "Express" and stated that these parties had no information on the subject. Ingalls concluded, however, that the general conviction was that "the great & good man Pomeroy, has been guilty of intentional deception or is himself a dupe. Heaven save the man! If we lose faith in him," Ingalls facetiously continued, "what refuge is there for suffering humanity."[36] Whether Pomeroy was guilty of the charges raised by members of his own party remains a moot question. His later "performance," however, lends credence to these earlier suspicions.

In the meantime the Civil War waxed hot. Ingalls' father, however, told his son John J. that he would be more useful by not going into the fight "direct." He claimed to believe that Ingalls could "more effectively aid the Union cause with the head than the hand."[37] Perhaps in deference to his father's advice, or his own inclination, Ingalls resumed the pursuit of political office. Shortly thereafter he proudly announced that he had been unanimously nominated by acclamation as "Lieutenant Governor of the State of

Kansas" by the "Union Convention" at Lawrence.[38] He claimed that his prospects for success were good and that the movement was anti–Jim Lane. By October the political fortunes of the Union Party appeared brighter than ever.[39] Ingalls believed that this "Union, anti–Jim Lane" movement was gaining favor in the sentiments of the people, and he concluded that unless unforeseen circumstances occurred in the next two weeks, there was little doubt of success.[40]

Ingalls' next communication to his father told about the outcome of the election in a straightforward manner: "My defeat doesn't annoy me at all."[41] He claimed that his defeat was actually a triumph and would, somehow, be an advantage to him in the future. "My great gains on all the rest of the ticket," he wrote, "and my undeniable success as an orator during the campaign make me really the Representative man of the opposition. The swindlers and thieves are bound to be beaten some day, and then my turn will come." And then as if to dismiss the whole dismal business, he concluded by stating that "politics have been to me nothing but a recreation."[42]

Turning to ideas dealing with the future prospects of the Mississippi Valley, which Ingalls had suggested would someday be a "Western empire," it is interesting to note that such thoughts had also occurred to his father. Elias believed that it was "plain to any observer that the great Mississippi Valley is laid out for one people and interest, but it [is] only as the east and west unite that the Federal Government can be sustained even in the efforts against the South." The elder Ingalls also commented on the Emancipation Proclamation. He denounced the policy as an extremist measure that would only increase the anger and the resistance of the South.[43] John J. replied to his father's letter the same day he received it and commented that the border states had been worse than "the old man of the sea" upon the shoulders of the administration. He believed that the Emancipation Proclamation, which had not yet been formally promulgated, had partially shaken off the incubus, but feared that "Lincoln's constitutional timidity might drive him to the wall again after all."[44]

By the fall of 1862 John A. Martin, owner and editor of the Atchison *Freedom's Champion,* had joined the Union forces and with his unit had penetrated as far south as Nashville, Tennessee.[45] Martin had leased the *Champion* to G. I. Stebbins, whom he feared was managing it poorly as a result of "devoting his attention to Mrs. Crowell." He asked Ingalls to inquire into the matter quietly and report his findings "fully and freely." "I feel too great an interest in the old *Champion* to have it ruined for a termagant," he wrote. In this same letter, written the day after election day, Martin expressed his hope that Ingalls would be elected Lieutenant Governor and stated that he preferred the election of the "Union State Ticket to the Republican," with the exception of "Cart. Wilder." "The idea of Tom Osborn for Lt. Gov. is decidedly rich," he wrote, and continued by stating, "The fellow hasn't ability above managing poorly the commercial interests of a small peanut stand, and even as proprietor of such an institution he would involve it in ruin by getting drunk occasionally and kicking it over for sport." Martin's concluding judgment was that "Kansas can nominate some of the d--st smallest and most disgusting watery potatoes of any State in the Union."

Martin expressed his deep obligation to Ingalls and promised not to forget him when the opportunity came to repay. In summary, he referred to military operations and mentioned that General William S. Rosecrans had replaced General D. C. Buell and was now in charge in his area. He regarded this as a decided improvement as "Buel [sic] was the world's worst general." Rosecrans was not Martin's idea of a panacea, however, and he urged Ingalls to send a petition to Senators Pomeroy and Lane "to get us ordered back to join the remainder of the Regt." He held no great hopes for his unit's return, however. Martin's spirits rose at the end of his letter, as he reported that he had been commissioned a Colonel on November 8, 1862, and that the 8th Regiment was known as the "Kansas Greyhounds."[46]

On the "home front" in east Kansas, Ingalls commented on some of the social aspects during the Christmas season of 1862. He remarked that the people kept their houses open to receive their friends. Ingalls had suffered a bruised toe as the result of having dropped a chunk of stove wood on it early one morning; nevertheless, he wrote that he "hobbled around to one hospitable mansion where I found an excellent person engaged in the manufacture of a beverage composed of baked apples, hot water, loaf sugar, bourbon whiskey, Jamaica Rum and a Spoon. I do not know what it is called" he continued, "but as my host said, 'it neither cuts nor bites but acts like balm to the soul.'" Ingalls concluded that this concoction merited the encomium phrase "pronounced by the booth keeper at the county muster who averred that his lemonade was concocted seventeen thousand feet underground, by the light of a diamond, and stirred with the forefinger of Jenny Lind."[47] Returning to the subject of the Civil War, Ingalls claimed that Atchison's border position provided a practical illustration of the "beauties of emancipation." He stated that every nook and cranny of the town was rapidly filling with "our sable and fugitive brethren from Missouri and elsewhere. Male and female, the venerable Ned and the grinning picaninny, the bent and withered beldame and the ebony Juno with her stately gait and feing [sic] turban, the humble full blood Congo, and the pert smirking smart mulatto, of every shade from New Orleans molasses to that of a new pig-skin saddle, all have their representatives here, and form a new element of population."[48]

Ingalls thought of them as "Very decent, quiet, honest, and respectable. . . . Industrious and useful, and by no means obtrusive or annoying. Never noisy or drunk, and willing to do with their might what ever their hands find to do. The women wash, cook and work in families: the men saw wood, drive teams, tend horses and do the thousand odd jobs which need the strength of a man with the docility of a child." No one asked them where they came from, or if they had a master. Ingalls expressed amazement that such a vast social system could have been so entirely disrupted in two years' time in the border states. He pointed out that when he first arrived in Kansas, the fact of a fugitive slave being in town was not tolerated. But now no one would attempt to reclaim one, with law or without law.

Ingalls continued by boasting that he was a leading representative of the anti-slavery sentiment in the community and that, as such, "my colored brethren regard me as their ally and treat me with great deference." He concluded that this was a heavy penalty to pay, however, as the Negroes believed that if a man was an abolitionist, "he must be the personal friend of every Nigger in the country." He described a speech that he had made on the anniversary of West Indian Emancipation as being "an act of fatal condescension that I shall always regret." He concluded that "we are living in a great historical epoch, but the future delineator of the chief characters of the drama will find cause to deplore the absence of more heroic material than any harlequin President [Lincoln] and his Africa followers."[49]

A short time later Ingalls sent his father a copy of the Topeka *Record* containing the message of Governor Thomas Carney, whom he described as "the successful grocer of Leavenworth."[50] Ingalls was pleased, however, that Carney was favorably disposed to the local branch of the Union Pacific Railroad and remarked that all indications pointed to the future prosperity of Atchison. He was unhappy over the inflation arising from wartime spending, however, and warned that national prosperity could come only when "the national credit" was dead.[51]

Kansas suffered its worst Civil War catastrophe when William C. Quantrill raided Lawrence on August 21, 1863. Ingalls wrote that he had been appointed a delegate from Atchison to look into the relief needs of the stricken city.[52] His long, detailed description of the destruction contained a bitter denunciation of such guerilla warfare.[53] In the same communication he described his "experiment" in farming. He had a large crop of corn, oats, and potatoes and about three acres of tobacco. He expected to harvest about two thousand pounds of tobacco and hoped to receive no less than fifty cents a pound. In addition he and Judge Albert Horton had leased the Atchison *Freedom's Champion* from "Colonel Martin."[54] Ingalls claimed that this latest responsibility was "rather forced on us by the leading citizens here." Ingalls believed that the interests of the city and county demanded a more spirited and popular organ than the one they had been served by.[55] At the same time he hoped for "considerable additional emolument" for his efforts.

Under the Ingalls-Horton management, Martin learned that the *Champion* was now making expenses, and he expressed the hope that it would continue to do so.[56] In a letter to Ingalls, Martin criticized the war policy of occupying enemy territory and proposed instead that the rebel army be annihilated: "And the territory will need no army of occupation—it will come back of itself . . . destroy Lee's and Bragg's armies," he wrote, "and the war is practically ended—there will be nothing more than guerilla warfare which only cavalry can put down."[57]

Martin suggested that some newspaper accounts of military engagements were more accurate than others, and he seemed especially pleased with the articles appearing in the Cincinnati *Commercial*. He suggested that the account of the battle of Chickamauga contained in the *Commercial* be reprinted in the *Champion*. In addition he once more referred to his desire to return home and stated that his regiment had been reduced to one hundred and sixty-five able-bodied men as the result of battles and disease. Again he suggested that Ingalls appeal to Pomeroy and Lane, plus D. W. Wilder, and expressed the hope that together they might succeed in bringing the regiment home. Martin pointed out that his unit had served in the South for over two years and had only ten months remaining to complete its three-year enlistment. He speculated that by bringing it home, it could be recruited once more to the maximum number of men.[58] It was to be some time, however, before Martin could return home, in spite of the alleged influence of Pomeroy or Lane.

In the spring of 1864 Ingalls' business associate, Horton, went to Washington, D.C., to discuss the topic of Indian treaties and railroads with Senator Pomeroy of Kansas. In a letter to Ingalls, Horton revealed that considerable "log rolling" had already been done, which involved Pomeroy, George W. Glick, [J. H. or E. G.] Lawler and others.[59] However, he did not elaborate on any of the details of this apparently "lucrative cooperative effort." Horton related that Salmon P. Chase was a candidate for the Presidency, despite his denials, and that he was being aided in his bid for the candidacy by the fact that his followers were temporarily aiding John C. Fremont in his political aspirations. By this strategy, Chase's supporters hoped to weaken Lincoln's chances in the election scheduled for November, 1864. Horton believed that in spite of all contrary efforts, Lincoln would be reelected. Fremont's supporters, however, were of the conviction that "Lincoln *must* and *shall* be defeated." Horton also stated that Senator Lane was "very powerful" with Lincoln. As for Pomeroy, Horton claimed that he had "a good deal of influence with *Chase and the radicals,* but *none* with *Lincoln.*" Concerning the role of the House and the Senate, Horton claimed that he was "completely astonished at the weakness of the members." Horton concluded his letter by referring to an undescribed "good claim" that he was trying to push through Congress, but he admitted there was little chance for success.[60]

In the meantime Ingalls received a second commission as major on the staff of General George W. Deitzler of the Kansas State Militia. The letter of transmittal advised Ingalls to be "virtuous in which event you can scarcely fail to be happy."[61] Putting the question of virtue aside, Colonel John A. Martin remained unhappy as a "virtuous" officer still encamped in Tennessee. He once more wrote to Ingalls and lamented the candidacy of General George B. McClellan and the anti-Lincoln efforts of General John C. Fremont.[62] His letter referred to the Democratic candidates as being on the "Conservative—Peace—Copperhead—Sympathyzing Ticket." Martin claimed that he had always imagined that McClellan "would wind up in something of the kind." He concluded that McClellan and Fremont "ought to be yoked together" and that "it is proper and right that they should receive the support of traitors, cowards, shirks, and exposed corruptionists." As for the war itself, Martin claimed that if General William T. Sherman had fifty thousand more men, "he would humiliate the rebellion before the 1st of January. God speed the draft," he continued, "I hope old Abe will administer it in large doses. If he does he will get the unanimous support of the Army." In closing his letter, Martin became nostalgic and asked Ingalls, while "enjoying life and things" to occasionally remember him, especially "when drinking a sherry cobbler, or punch, or julep."[63]

Ingalls' "active" military service was confined to a "Camp near Big Blue Ridge, Missouri," in October of 1864, during the invasion of Missouri by General Sterling Price.[64] Ingalls reported that the Union forces at this time consisted of some fifteen thousand men and that they were concentrated at "Blue Ridge" in anticipation of engaging the enemy the "next day." He described the scene as "magnificent" in the "clear frosty light of the moon." He assured his father that he believed they would "come out all right" and that he had no personal fears.[65]

Ingalls did "come out all right" and resumed his political activities as a candidate for Lieutenant-Governor of Kansas on the "Union Ticket" once more.[66] Again he failed to receive the necessary support for his election, in spite of the fact that he had the dubious distinction of having the support of the Reverend Pardee Butler.[67] Before Ingalls' defeat in 1864, which was his last political candidacy prior to his election to the U.S. Senate in 1873, he wrote and asked his father and mother to come visit the shores of the "Beautiful River" at Atchison.[68] His father at this time was undergoing financial difficulties, and Ingalls assured him that "retrospection might not be more painful in one place than another."[69] Another phase of Ingalls' own career was coming to a close. Horton dissolved his relationship with the *Champion* on September 1, 1864.[70] Shortly after, Ingalls wrote to his father, explaining that Martin had returned from the army and that his own connection with the *Champion* would cease on January 1, 1865. He mentioned that a daily newspaper had been discussed and that it might possibly become a reality in the near future.[71]

Ingalls' closing editorial in the *Champion* was entitled "Valedictory." In this article he expressed gratitude to the readers, Colonel Martin, and others for their patronage, patience, and support during his tenure as editor.[72] In the same issue Martin published his first editorial since returning from the army, which was entitled "First Words." He extolled the competence of Stebbins, surprising as it may seem, also Frank A. Root, Ingalls, and Horton, and made himself ready to resume the reins as editor of the *Champion*.

As for Ingalls, the war years had enriched his experiences: From "high private" to Colonel. From a dusty Pikes Peak prospector to newspaper editor. From a land speculator to a town-site boomer. And throughout, a perennial political candidate. These were the "special seductions" Ingalls preferred. However, he would wait some years before the "seduction" of high political office would come his way.

5

THE INTERIM YEARS
AND
DREAMS OF DYNASTY

The close of the Civil War also marked the close of another chapter in the life of Ingalls. When Lee surrendered to Grant at Appomattox in April of 1865, Ingalls was thirty-one years of age. The exuberance of his youth was now mellowed by age. True, he still harbored political ambitions of the same magnitude, but these, too, were tempered with a greater sense of sobriety and patience. After Ingalls severed his connection with the Atchison *Champion* he devoted himself to the practice of law. As for his role in politics, he vigorously lent his support to the candidates and issues of his choice, and with equal vigor opposed everything and everyone he was not in sympathy with. Jim Lane was one of those whom Ingalls opposed; but in spite of Ingalls' opposition, Lane was reelected to the United States Senate.[1] With this mild disappointment clouding his thoughts, Ingalls busied himself with the routine of his law practice in Atchison. In the course of his business and social activities he met Anna Louisa Chesebrough. She was an intelligent, well-educated young lady of twenty-one when Ingalls first saw her. She and her father, Ellsworth Chesebrough, had migrated from New York City to Atchison in 1859. Her father had opened a general store in Atchison, and this brought him and his family into contact with a wide circle of acquaintances in and around Atchison.

Anna Louisa, or Lou as she was called by her family and friends, witnessed the changes in Atchison effected by the Civil War. "Social lines" were more distinct in Atchison in 1860 than they were after the war. So much so that she described the war as a "social melting pot." Prior to the conflict between the states, different classes and groups met at church or on public occasions, but never in each others' homes. There were no public schools in ante-bellum Atchison. There were, however, a few private schools. One was conducted by Miss Clara Kipp; another by a Baptist clergyman, who being a Southerner, according to Lou, was forced to close his school at the outbreak of the Civil War. This Baptist clergyman's school was a girl's academy, and Lou's sister, Frances Louisa, or Fanny, attended it for a time.

Another "young ladies school," which was also a Baptist school, was opened by a Mrs. Abbot. In addition a convent school was opened on North Second Street, near the old Catholic church and St. Benedict's Abbey, under the guidance of the Benedictine Sisters. This school was the foundation for the Mount Saint Scholastica Academy "where all my daughters received their first schooling," as Lou put it many years later.

Actual wartime conditions in Atchison brought about alterations in the routine of the community. There was a shortage of certain "table comforts," such as sugar, coffee, and flour. There was very little coal in Kansas, and wood was imported from Missouri for wartime fuel. Out "in the country" dried corn on the cob was frequently used for fuel, as it sold for only ten cents per bushel, if it sold at all. Generally speaking, there was no real food shortage, however, as grain of all kinds was abundant; and during the winter, especially at Christmas time, the shops were filled with dried buffalo meat, fresh antelope, turkeys, quail, and prairie chickens.

The latest war news was posted on the walls of the post office. Lou related that as telegraphic information was received, it would be posted there so that every one would have access to the "latest intelligence." Lou's sister, Fanny, commented that their step-mother, Mrs. Annie Euphemia (Pheme) Kearney Chesebrough, organized a women's society for the benefit of the wounded Kansas volunteers, "of which Momma is treasurer, Lou secretary, and myself on the committee on Resolutions."

Ellsworth Chesebrough and his daughter Lou had come to Kansas in advance of Fanny and Mrs. Chesebrough. They were seeking a healthy location in the West. Fanny was suffering from a lung ailment, or so it was believed, and Ellsworth and his older daughter had come to make advance preparations for the arrival of Fanny and her step-mother. Ellsworth was laboring under the delusion that the "desert air" of eastern Kansas would be beneficial to his ailing daughter's lung condition. In later years Lou described their migration to Kansas in the following words: "I little thought, when we left New York on the morning of July 5, 1858 [1859], that I was leaving my native city never to return as a resident. . . . First we journeyed to Buffalo, thence to Detroit.[2] We stopped at Ann Arbor and in Chicago. Our next stop was at Hannibal, Missouri. We crossed the Mississippi in a rowboat before sunrise, between Lyons and Clinton, proceeding to Cedar Rapids, where my father owned a farm which he had taken for a debt. Here we took a steamboat for Hannibal, then crossed the state of Missouri by rail, reaching St. Joseph, which even then was an old historic place." She continued by pointing out that their destination had originally been Leavenworth, but that "Samuel C. Pomeroy, afterward United States Senator, General Stringfellow and P. A. Abell had persuaded my father to go to Atchison." Their trip from St. Joseph to Atchison was by steamboat down the Missouri River, and when they landed in Atchison, they were escorted to the newly opened Massasoit Hotel, of which Thomas Murphy was the proprietor.

Ellsworth Chesebrough was no ordinary man. He was one of three sons of Enoch and Sally Sheffield Chesebrough of Stonington, Connecticut. His older brother, Amos, graduated from Yale in 1835 and became a Congregational clergyman. Nicholas, the younger brother, graduated from the New York City College of Physicians and entered the practice of medicine. Ellsworth's father had owned a general store in Stonington, and the experience that Ellsworth gained in his father's store charted his future course. He went to New York City and entered a firm of lace and silk importers against his father's wishes. Enoch wanted his son to emulate his older brother and enter one of the professions. While working and living in New York, Ellsworth met Anna Louisa Addison, whom he married on June 28, 1842. She was the daughter of Thomas Addison and Silence White Curtis. Ellsworth and Anna Louisa had only the two daughters, Lou and Fanny, when Mrs. Chesebrough became ill. She died on October 4, 1845.[3]

After the death of his wife, Ellsworth married Annie Euphemia Kearney of Newark, New Jersey. Although she was only twenty-two years of age at the time of their marriage, there were no children born of this union. Pheme, as the second Mrs. Chesebrough was called, conferred her maiden name of Kearney upon her two young step-daughters, Lou and Fanny.[4] This so angered the Chesebrough side of the family that the two girls did not receive their full share of their Grandfather Addison's estate when he died. As a child, Lou played with the children of "Professor" Samuel F. B. Morse at Gramercy Park Hotel in New York. She also liked to boast that she had heard Jenny Lind twice, "once in Triplus Hall at Eighth and Broadway." Her early education was at the hands of "visiting teachers and music masters." She studied French and German from a native of Germany, and English and Latin from a Presbyterian minister. After her arrival in Kansas, Lou was sent to the Convent of the Visitation in St. Louis, Missouri. She graduated from this school in June, 1861, receiving the "crown of Honor" as the outstanding scholar in the class.[5] Her study habits and wide range of interests persisted throughout her life, and even as a housewife and mother she reserved a part of each evening in order to read *Harper's Magazine, Littell's Living Age, Every Saturday,* the New York *Tribune,* and the Boston *Transcript.*

When Ellsworth Chesebrough came to Kansas, he carried letters of introduction to "prominent Westerners." Among this group was D. R. Anthony, editor of the Leavenworth *Times* and brother of the famous female-suffrage champion Susan B. Anthony. The Anthony and Chesebrough families became lifelong friends. Ellsworth was a man of considerable financial resources, and he became a strong Republican, though he had at one time supported Stephen A. Douglas. He was elected mayor of Atchison in 1862, and was a candidate as a Lincoln elector on the Republican ticket in 1864. Apparently he was on the way to even-larger political prospects, but he was taken ill quite suddenly and died on October 24, 1864.[6] W. F. Cloud replaced Chesebrough as a candidate for elector, and with the victory of the Republican ticket, he was so elected.[7]

Shortly after Ellsworth Chesebrough's death, the Leavenworth *Daily Conservative* listed his store for sale, under the heading "Rare Opportunity."[8] The ad claimed that sales for the store during the past year had exceeded two hundred thousand dollars, which indicates something about the magnitude of his business.

In February of 1865 Lou Chesebrough went to Washington, D.C., to attend the inaugural ceremonies for the incumbent President Abraham Lincoln. The fact that her father had been nominated as a candidate for a Lincoln elector and the knowledge that he would have been elected had he lived were instrumental in Lou's receiving an invitation to the inauguration and the subsequent ball. On the eve of her departure for Washington, her slight acquaintance with John J. Ingalls ripened into friendship. Ingalls and Lou had been invited to participate at the wedding of "a pair of madcap lovers." Their conversation en route was short of brilliant, as Ingalls remarked that he had never assisted "at an affair of this kind before." Lou simply replied, "Neither did I." The marriage ceremony was pronounced by an Episcopal clergyman, and after the vows the newlyweds left on their wedding trip. In was the custom in that day for the wedding party to travel some distance with the bride and groom, and to go as far as St. Joseph was not uncommon. Lou wrote about the trip and remarked that she was teased by her friends because "Mr. Ingalls, who merely came down to the boat to see the party off, decided to go on to the next landing place. Finally when he decided to remain on the boat until we reached St. Joseph, there was much whispered comment on the interest Mr. Ingalls was taking in the journey. When my friends discovered that he had brought along an air pillow for my comfort, they laughed a good deal."

After this romantic excursion, Lou went on to Washington, where she received a good deal of attention from "handsome" Senator James H. Lane, who was detested by Ingalls. Lane acted as her escort during the inaugural ceremonies. Lou described Vice-President Andrew Johnson, who was first to be sworn in, as looking "very ill for he was so white and he trembled so." She mentioned this to Lane, her escort, and remarked that he did not seem very sympathetic, for Lane replied that "Johnson needed an ice cap on his head." After Johnson was sworn in, the ceremony moved outside, where the oath of office was to be administered to Lincoln. Lou described her position as "just below the platform on which Lincoln stood," and commented that she "could look directly up into his face and hear all that he said in his inaugural address." At first she was astonished at the appearance of Lincoln and remarked that "it seemed strange to see in a man who was taking for the second time the oath of the highest office in the gift of the people, a certain uncouthness of bearing, a manner of standing that was almost slouchy, but as soon as he began to speak," she went on, "that impression gave place to wonder at the simple dignity in his bearing, the benign expression on his face and the sense of greatness he produced. In a few moments of time my impression changed completely." Later that evening she attended the inaugural ball, escorted by Kansas' Governor Samuel J. Crawford. She remarked that the cards of admission cost twenty-five dollars, "so it was more expensive than the inaugural balls of today [1913?]."[9]

By May of 1865, after her return from Washington, Ingalls began to see Lou regularly; and often in the late afternoons they would go horseback riding together.[10] Lou, like John J., or "Jamie" as she liked to call him, was a great riding enthusiast. On one occasion she had participated in a buffalo hunt far out on the Kansas prairies. She remarked at the time that the vast herds of buffalo were all moving south, and here she heard the legend that no plainsman had ever seen buffalo moving northward.[11]

Sometime between May and September of 1865 the warm friendship Ingalls held for Lou turned to love, and he wrote her a formal letter of proposal.[12] Lou accepted his proposal of marriage, and plans for the wedding were undertaken. In the meantime, however, Ingalls' parents had heard rumors of their son's contemplated marriage. They wrote a letter of cautious inquiry, and Ingalls responded by saying that a letter was on its way which included a small picture of Miss Chesebrough, "my probable wife." He also wrote a description of her "general style, a delineation of her character, and a catalogue of her virtues." In an almost flippant manner he closed his letter by stating that he supposed his parents "might be interested somewhat of this latest accession to the family circle." He related how he had ordered his wedding suit and in returning with it "some godless miscreant, moved and seduced by the devil, stole the pantaloons from the case." He was grateful, however, that the "claw hammer" coat and white silk vest were spared. He told how he had obtained the services of a local "Dutch tailor" to work on a pair of substitutes "for the purloined inexpressibles" with the hope that the ceremony would not be delayed as a result of the theft. "I propose to be married," he exclaimed, "even if I have to adopt the Georgia custom of a pair of spurs and a shirt collar *solus*." He announced that the "interesting event" was set for 7 P.M., Wednesday the twenty-seventh of September, 1865.[13]

Their marriage had originally been scheduled for an earlier date, but for unexplained reasons Mrs. Chesebrough, Lou's stepmother, had asked her daughter to postpone the wedding.[14] Perhaps as a result of his disappointment over the delay, Ingalls decided to journey up the Missouri River in August of 1865. From the upper river he planned to cross Iowa, then go up the Mississippi River and return to Atchison by way of Lake Superior, Chicago, and St. Louis. He planned to be gone approximately three weeks and promised his parents that he would write to them en route.[15] After Ingalls' return to Atchison, Mrs. Chesebrough, for equally inexplicable reasons, withdrew her objections to the wedding and gave her permission and best wishes to the overjoyed Lou and Jamie.[16] The ceremony was performed in the Chesebrough home, and Lou's sister, Fanny, was simultaneously married to Andrew Hughes in a double ceremony presided over by Bishop Thomas H. Vail, of the Episcopal Diocese of Kansas.[17]

The response of Ingalls' parents to his wedding was overwhelmingly enthusiastic. Frequent references to his marriage and his excellent choice of a wife fill the letters that he received from home. "Mother is more and more enraptured with Lou," his father wrote, and, "she seems to think she is an uncommonly womanly woman."[18] Other expressions such as "Isn't she a darling" and "Mother is quite as much pleased as I am," all bear testimony to the elder Ingalls' enthusiasm.[19] Jamie, in describing his bride to his parents, claimed that she was "as high as my shoulder; weighs 125 lbs or thereabouts; sound as a partridge and healthy as a thorough-bred race horse." He also commented that the wedding preparations were made by Mrs. Chesebrough against his wishes, but he was "obliged to submit."[20]

The newlywed Ingalls and Hughes couples traveled to St. Louis on their wedding trip. Upon their return to Atchison, the Ingallses began housekeeping in a small place on Q Street between Sixth and Seventh streets.[21] The house was very small, and it stood by itself near a ravine. A spring flowed in the ravine, from which they pro-cured all their water. Their house had three rooms and a lean-to for a kitchen and a small porch over the front door. It was modest, to say the least; the kitchen walls were not even plastered. In spite of the humbleness of their home, however, they did have a Negro servant named Tilly. Tilly had been a slave in Kentucky prior to the Civil War. Lou described her as a "faithful servant and quite a good cook," although she quickly added, "I, of course, made the cakes, desserts, etc. etc."[22]

This first house was adequate for a married couple, but as they awaited their first-born, Ellsworth, the house was judged to be too small. Shortly before his birth they moved to another house on South Third Street at the corner of S Street, overlooking the Missouri River. This house was also rather small, but there was a possibility of adding on, which would relieve their former crowded condition. The area of the yard embraced about one-half of a city block. Third Street, which fronted their property, at that time was only a "paper street," thus there was no thru traffic nor any nearby neighbors. It had the seclusion of a place in the country. It was here that all eleven of their children were born, with such additions being made to the house as the needs of a growing family dictated.[23]

Ellsworth made his arrival on June 18, 1866. In close order, ten additional children were born to the Ingalls household: Ruth, in 1867, who was one of John J.'s favorites. She died at the age of six and one-half, a loss from which he never really recovered. Ethel, in 1868, who lived longer than all the rest. She passed away in 1958. Ralph, in 1870, who grew up to be a handsome, adventurous soldier and sailed to the Philippines during the extended guerilla warfare there near the close of the nineteenth century. Addison, born in 1872, whose sudden death at the age of four and one-half also nearly broke the hearts of his parents. Then there was the lovely Constance, born in 1873, who passed away just eight months before her father, at the age of twenty-six. Sheffield was born in 1875, and reached the highest political plateau of any of the Ingalls children when he was elected Lieutenant-Governor of Kansas. Then there was little Faith, who was born and died on the same day, May 25, 1877. Faith was followed by Marion, who was born in 1879. She grew up to become a lovely woman. Next there was Muriel, born in 1881. It was Marion and Muriel who proved to be blithe spirits in the Ingalls home and who were affectionately referred to by John J. as the "M and M" sisters. Lastly there was little Louisa, born in April of 1883, who died just four months and one day later.

Lou was twenty-three when her first child was born, and her last was born just three days before her fortieth birthday. Eleven children in seventeen years. If numbers were essential to the building of a dynasty, then the Ingalls foundation was firmly laid. The Ingalls family occupied the same home until it was mysteriously destroyed by fire in 1888, by which time it had become a rambling structure and a storehouse of memories.[24]

Less than a year after their marriage Mrs. Ingalls narrowly escaped death. The Central Branch Railroad was being built at the time—and construction trains were continuously moving over the tracks within the city limits of Atchison. Lou was about to cross the tracks when a train frightened her horse. The horse shied, wheeled around, and overturned the buggy in which she had been riding; and she was pinned beneath it. Nearby workmen immediately rushed to her aid, and fortunately she was not seriously injured, although she stated that she "was dreadfully bruised—one side was black"[25]

Marriage and children did not preclude Ingalls' continuing interest in politics and commercial affairs. His letters to his parents are replete with comments on the leading figures and issues of the day. To Ingalls, Edwin M. Stanton, the Secretary of War, was "the most reckless old despot in the land at the present time . . . and I am inclined to think the people will bring him to his senses before the close of the administration."[26] As for his old nemesis Pomeroy, Ingalls periodically modified his earlier views and once even described him as a man of initiative and intelligence. Perhaps his views were modified by the fact that Pomeroy had just arrived from the East with nearly two million dollars for the railroad link, and the first engine and cars were to arrive in a few days.[27] Prosperity, like politics, makes strange bedfellows. Also on the prosperous side of the ledger was news that Atchison was soon to have a "National

Bank" with capital of two hundred thousand dollars, which Ingalls believed would give impetus to business.[28] His overall optimism in these early years of his married life led to his claims that Atchison was destined to be a great city and that "unless some unforeseen disaster occurs, I think we shall win the race."[29] In a note of nostalgia, however, he was moved to comment on the dying, indeed dead, town of Sumner. He told of visiting the place and of how the old "Sumner House" was being torn down. The reusable material was being brought to Atchison for use in construction there. He took a last walk through the old building and bade it farewell as his "earliest home in the West with feelings of pervading regret," although he claimed that the retrospect "was not wholly unpleasant, nor entirely cheerful."[30]

For amusement Ingalls preferred the circus above every other form of entertainment. He once lamented that the rain had canceled a circus performance and claimed that he felt "a great deprivation, for I have an uncontrollable passion for such performances, which I gratify by habitual attendance upon all the shows that visit the country."[31] The opportunities for such shows were not overly abundant, and this unfortunate cancellation proved especially irksome to Ingalls as he believed it "held out the most seductive and fascinating programme of gymnastics and equestrian feats."[32]

By the late summer of 1866 Ingalls' father, Elias, was warming to the contest between President Andrew Johnson and the "radicals" in Congress. He remarked that he was "getting a little warmed up" and obviously disapproved of the position his son had taken in the matter. "I see you have taken your position, perhaps the best you could do there," he wrote, "but Andy will win. Had you come out in his favor it might have paid tho in a minority."[33] A few months later Ingalls also referred to the national problems, as well as the local problems then current and concluded that "between grasshoppers, reconstruction, disordered currency, tariff, deranged trade, defunct industry and infernal weather, it seems as if the country was clean given over to the adversary."[34] He found one exception to this dreadful state of affairs, however, remarking that the law business was excellent. In fact, business was so good that his spring docket was full.[35] He also referred to his "usual fate"—"successful when I don't expect it, and beaten when sure of victory." He thus surmised that "law is anything but a positive science."[36]

Ingalls' love for Lou increased as time progressed, and after two years of marriage he had concluded that love was something more than a transitory affection. His abiding love for Lou was evident in his remark that "age cannot wither her, nor custom stale her infinite variety."[37] Their first daughter was born during the second year of their marriage. Ingalls described her as "a fine fat healthy miss of 10½ avoir dupois," and her mother, he gratefully acknowledged, was doing well. "We have named the stranger 'Ruth,'" he wrote to his father, "after your mother, and hope she may inherit the virtues as well as the name of that excellent woman."[38] As the family grew, so did responsibilities; whether the added responsibilities of children was the cause or not is a moot point, nevertheless the fact remains that Ingalls required considerable medical treatment at various times for a stomach disorder and a general nervous condition.[39]

The political campaign of 1868, like that of 1866, received ample attention from Ingalls. He wrote his father that the "Grant and Colfax Headquarters for this country are established in one of my office rooms, and we intend doing some yeoman work in the canvass." He claimed to have started "on the warpath" and that he was speaking and writing on all "proper occasions." He believed that the "soldiers and warmen" were breaking ranks and "coming over to us" daily, because "the rebels showed their hands too soon."[40] Whether, as Ingalls put it, the "showing of hands" was a factor or not, Ulysses S. Grant won a close victory over the Democratic candidate Horatio Seymour, and Ingalls was able to revel in the knowledge that the "political zion" was in friendly hands.

The four years of Grant's presidency were as inauspicious for Ingalls as they were for the Republican party generally. There were in Ingalls' case, however, some minor successes and a promise of things still better to come. Before Ingalls had been married four years he had become a father three times. His wife had borne him one son and two daughters, Ellsworth, Ruth, and Ethel. Each child in turn stirred Ingalls to believe that the latest offspring was destined for a noble and great life, perhaps after the fashion of his imaginery "Crichton." The children were in no way looked upon as a burden, but were reared with love and affection and welcomed to the family circle as another promising addition to the Ingalls "dynasty." After four years of married life their home life had settled down to a stable routine, and Lou became a master of domestic particulars. Throughout her married life of nearly thirty-five years she kept a diary.[41] The one known extant diary is for the year 1869, and on the title page, inscribed in Ingalls' hand, are the words: "Anna Louisa Ingalls From Her Husband, Jan. 1, 1869, Nulla dies sine linea [no day without a line]."[42] The diary relates the daily routine of the Ingalls family. Lou and Jamie frequently spent the evenings in the parlor, where she often played the piano with more bravado than skill. It was not uncommon for Ingalls to join his wife in song, and as a duo they sang their favorite songs of the day. At other times Jamie would lie on the sofa with his head in Lou's lap, while she read to him or stroked his hair. Their domestic life was generally uncomplicated and happy during these years of their marriage.

Ingalls' office routine usually required that he leave the house around 9 A.M. He would return for lunch around noon. On some days he would not return to the office until 2 P.M. and generally came home for the day around 5 or 6 P.M., unless detained for a specific reason. Frequently he surprised Lou with presents, such as jewelry, an article of apparel, or a book. For the children he would bring a toy, a pair of shoes, or perhaps a trinket. On Sundays the entire family often attended the Episcopal church, where Lou was a charter member.[43] On occasion, however, they might attend the Presbyterian church. In all, Lou was far more faithful in attendance than her husband, who as an adult never "professed" religion nor joined a church. However, the parish records of Trinity Episcopal Church in Atchison list Ingalls as the head of the family and indicate that he had been baptized sometime in the past. Although Ingalls spoke of Trinity as "our" little Trinity Church, he was not a member in the formal sense.[44] In Lou's only extant diary she made mention of the baptisms of Ruth and Ethel and other religious events of significance.

Jamie was coddled by his wife like one of the children, especially when he was ill. If he came home from the office with a headache, which he occasionally did, she would give him a massage with a hot towel brush, put him in bed, and "cover him up warm." To Lou he was "poor darling" when he felt badly, and there is every indication that Ingalls delighted in this sort of attention. Lou was in many ways a sentimentalist, recording such events as Ruth taking her first steps, Ethel laughing out loud for her father for the first time, or noting that she had caught Ellsworth scrawling in her diary. The books she read were carefully noted, which, for 1869, included "Bonninni's *Life of Napoleon*" and "Parton's *Life of Aaron Burr*." In community service Ingalls kept busy in such matters as school meetings and civic affairs in general.

In spite of the happiness of their marriage, the Ingalls' domestic life was not without its quarrels. There are frequent references of Jamie or Lou getting "cross" with each other. Mrs. Ingalls frequently cried at the slightest "upset," and after a domestic difference of opinion, she would often go out to the stable before Jamie left for the office and kiss him goodbye. After "scolding" him on one occasion, she mentioned feeling "repentant" and asked his pardon, after which she "sealed it with a kiss." On still another occasion she told of how one evening they sat down together and discussed their "mutual shortcomings." There seems to be no doubt that the love shared by Jamie and Lou was profound and beautiful. Her diary is filled with touching scenes of their love for each other, and Lou confided on one page of her diary that she could forgive Jamie of "anything but not loving me." Each night the toddlers, Ellsworth and Ruth, were sent downstairs for a good-night kiss from their father; then Mrs. Ingalls would tuck them in bed and hear their prayers as soon as they were old enough to recite. If Jamie came home late at night, she would be out at the stable to meet him with a lantern. If he traveled overnight or was away for several days, she impatiently waited for the mail and cried if an expected letter did not arrive.

Before she was twenty-six years old, Lou had all her teeth removed and remained in virtual seclusion for approximately three months while she waited for her false teeth to be fitted. Such was her social consciousness. Mrs. Ingalls' friends in 1869 included Fanny Neal and Ella Hubbard, who were perhaps closer to her at this time than any of her other friends. Mrs. Ingalls always had domestic servants to look after the children and to do the heavy housework. She was therefore free to visit her friends and to be active in the social affairs of the town. In spite of her close friends and domestic servants, however, she always complained of feeling "troubled and worried" whenever her husband was away. On one such day, which was also dark and cloudy, she wrote that she hoped Jamie "will never go away again." Aside from her very close friends, Lou also had numerous other friends. This circle included Mrs. Benjamin F. Stringfellow, Mrs. George W. Glick, and Mrs. Peter Byram. It is worth noting that Mrs. Ingalls' personal friendships with these and other ladies was never affected by political matters, even though her husband and the husbands of her friends might be bitter political or even personal enemies. Ingalls never seemed to mind that this situation existed, although he would deliberately drop a slur or a "dig" in their presence if an opportunity were available.

Ingalls in many ways was a demonstrative person, while in other circumstances he might be almost completely withdrawn. On one occasion he was walking down an Atchison street and Lou recorded in her diary that "Jamie . . . kisses me on the street." This is not the kind of conduct that Ingalls approved of in others and only serves to show that he might behave in an unpredictable manner. Ingalls always kept "spirits" in the house and even made his own wine, assisted by his wife. Apparently he believed in the medicinal qualities of whiskey, for he once administered a sizable dose to their Negro servant Mary's grandmother, who was feeling ill. This use of alcoholic beverages was never carried to excess, and Ingalls himself denounced drunkards but not drinking. He opposed prohibition laws, claiming that drinking, like many other matters, was a personal concern and should not be regulated by legislation.

Although Ingalls was "hot and cold" with respect to Samuel C. Pomeroy, he did not neglect his political bows to him and was careful to attend a reception for him on the evening of June 25, 1869. Mrs. Ingalls described it as a "pleasant evening," adding the comment "my husband looks splendid." Their affection for each other was such that they were able to enjoy each other's company without boredom. For example, they frequently would sit on the porch of their home on hot summer evenings simply "watching the Missouri shore and the boats." Or perhaps they just sat silently, while Lou listened to Jamie scratch a pin on the railing. Rather than being considered boring or dull, such unpretentious pastimes proved mutually enjoyable.

A highlight for Lou in the summer of 1869 was a visit from her sister, Fanny, and her baby who now lived in Denver. Even little "Worth" was "delighted with his cousin." A lonely September, however, resulted from the fact that Jamie and little Ellsworth left for a trip to Boston and Haverhill, Massachusetts. In response the elder Ingallses planned a trip to Atchison the following spring.[45] Elias Ingalls wrote that perhaps he might like Atchison so well that they might wish to spend the remainder of their days in the vicinity.[46] Lou also remained considerate of her mother and took pains to remember her in special ways, such as sending fruit or food baskets on occasion. Lou was in general a considerate person, and no better example of her kindness can be cited than the circumstances surrounding the birth of Mary's illegitimate child and Lou's care and concern for both mother and infant. Mary, a Negro girl, was one of her domestic servants, and for several days after the birth of Mary's child, Lou served the meals, changed diapers, and in general cared for Mary and her baby in a most affectionate manner. The household servants were always held in high esteem by the Ingalls family, and the favorite of all the Ingalls' domestic servants over the years was "Uncle Pendleton," a Negro. He served the Ingalls for many years as a trusted servant and guardian of the children. It was he who would go to fetch the children late at night and bring them home safely from a party or whatever social function they might have been attending. He was a familiar figure around Atchison for many years and could usually be seen driving the family buggy with one or more of the Ingalls children seated by his side. When he died in 1887, Ingalls himself delivered the eulogy; and he later claimed that from the time of Pendleton's death his own luck went bad.[47]

As the years slipped by, Ingalls became more prominent as an attorney. As a consequence he was engaged as one of the attorneys to defend General Philip Sheridan, who was being sued in the United States Circuit Court at Topeka for twenty-five thousand dollars.[48] The suit was being pressed by an alleged cattle thief whom Sheridan had arrested and then sent out of the Indian country.[49] Ingalls' father, like his son John J., quickly saw the significance of the case and told his son that it would have national interest and would, no doubt, be reported in the papers throughout the country.[50] At last, or so it seemed to Ingalls, fate was on his side, and he was gaining a measure of prominence which could conceivably lead to his attaining his perennial ambition of rising to some high political office. As it turned out, however, Ingalls received virtually no publicity whatsoever. Nevertheless, legal success and political ambitions were only a part of Ingalls' goals. He dreamed of founding a dynasty as a more permanent living monument to his name. In a letter to his father, Ingalls urged him to leave New England and move to Kansas. His argument was based on the fact that the Ingalls ancestry had scratched out a bare subsistence for two centuries "among the barren ridges of New England" and it was now time that they turned their backs on an unpromising land to one of promise. Ingalls held a profound conviction that "we" shall found a family "powerful in wealth, numbers and intelligence, that shall rule among men and become conspicuous in the great future that lies before us." He continued by pointing out that "such is my hope, my ambition, my immoveable belief. It may not come to me, for I must lay the foundation and work at the roots of things, but my descendants will rear the superstructure and crown it with my memory." In summation, Ingalls argued that "it would be fitting and appropriate that you should transfer your own remaining labors to that land which is to be the theatre of the future development of your family, lending the emulations of your virtues, and the inspiration of your example, to those to whom you have given life, and in whose success you might find the consolation of your declining years."[51]

After this appeal Ingalls outlined the glowing prospects for Atchison. He spoke of the construction of the railroad between Atchison and Topeka and its supposed beneficial results. He also mentioned the proposal for a bridge across the Missouri River at

Atchison, the progress of construction on the Atchison and Nebraska Railroad and of the Central Branch Railroad pushing westward up the Republican River. There was also a railroad under construction which would link Atchison with Lawrence, and then in turn Atchison would have a connection with the Galveston route to Texas; and when all this was finally accomplished, Ingalls concluded, "There will be no other point to which we can build."[52] Thus Ingalls' vision embraced limits of development which would make Atchison the pearl of the plains. He believed that Atchison would outstrip all her rivals and predicted that by 1876 her population would be twenty-five to thirty thousand people. Atchison had no rivals according to Ingalls, who believed that Leavenworth, St. Joseph, and Kansas City were all declining, "exhausted" by their past efforts. He declared that these towns were burdened with monstrous debts and that railroad developments were cutting them off on all sides "and centering directly toward Atchison." Ingalls' faith in his claims was so great that he was investing to the extent of his capital and credit in the hope that two more years would "make a spoon or spoil a horn."[53] Ingalls' father, in spite of the persuasive argument of his son, chose to remain in Massachusetts.

As a lawyer Ingalls occasionally gained favorable notice and was able to "cross fencing sticks" with some of the best in the business.[54] His dreams and aspirations gradually appeared more promising. Lou shared her husband's ambitions. She claimed that when she thought of his potential and the great promise of his life, she was willing to be patient and submit to any present problems, trusting that the future "held better things."[55] If public acclaim and a high political office were "better things," then their hopes were perhaps closer than they realized. By 1872 Ingalls could be described as living comfortably, though he was by no means a man of wealth. He described their Thanksgiving of 1872 in a letter to his father, and after disclosing a sumptuous menu, concluded with the comment that they did not suffer "in our cabin upon the frontier in the far west."[56]

Turning to a field in which he was not entirely an amateur, Ingalls assisted in the launching of a new periodical known as the *Kansas Magazine*. Ingalls contributed two essays and several poems to this publication. The essays were entitled "Catfish Aristocracy" and "Blue Grass."[57] These prose compositions gained a measure of fame for Ingalls that his earlier efforts had failed to secure. "Catfish Aristocracy" was a parody on Jonathan Gardner Lang, better known as "Shang." Shang was perhaps the last person to remain a resident of the defunct and destroyed town of Sumner, and he enjoyed referring to himself as the "Mayor" of that place. In "Catfish Aristocracy," Ingalls used Shang to epitomize the fate of all those who "dwell along the creeks and upon the bottoms." Ingalls' facetious thesis was that bottoms or low lands produce an inferior race and culture, and conversely, highlands produce a noble race and a loftly civilization. The bottom-dwellers were the "catfish aristocrats," and Kansas had an abundant supply of such persons.

Shang had been befriended by Ingalls, who enjoyed accompanying this member of the "aristocracy" on his frequent "jugging" excursions on the muddy Missouri River.[58] After Ingalls moved to Atchison and settled down to married life, Shang used to come frequently from his Sumner residence to peddle vegetables, fruits, walnuts, and hazelnuts at the Ingalls home and in Atchison generally. Mrs. Ingalls claimed that he rode a little calico pony, without a saddle, and that the tips of his huge feet dragged the ground. She also stated that he was very fond of children, "who regarded him with a speechless wonder," no matter how many times he appeared in Atchison.[59]

After "Catfish Aristocracy" was published, Mrs. Ingalls claimed that "two young friends" of her husband got Shang drunk and read Ingalls' description of Shang to him from the essay, pointing out that he was the man being described. Mrs. Ingalls then gave the following account of Shang's reaction: "Lang [Shang] mounted his pony and already crazed with whiskey, he dashed madly for the Ingalls home. He entered the driveway yelling that he had come to shoot Mr. Ingalls." She went on to relate that their servant, Pendleton, told Shang that Ingalls was in Seneca and would not return until the next day. Shang, however, sat down on a well-curb and vowed he would wait. Ingalls was actually visiting friends in the neighborhood, and fearing that he might return momentarily, Mrs. Ingalls tactfully told Shang that if he believed the story was about him, he was justified in being "not only angry, but very angry." She invited him into the kitchen and prepared him some supper. When Ingalls returned, he found Shang laughing, with all traces of his anger now gone as the result of a hearty meal and the wit of his hostess.[60] Ingalls further alleviated the distress of Shang's sensitive soul with a side of bacon and a sack of flour.[61]

The thesis of "Blue Grass" also dealt with the problem of environmental determinism. Ingalls claimed that the importance of food for human consumption was collateral in importance with the general environmental conditions. "What a man, a community, a nation can do, think, suffer, imagine or achieve depends upon what he eats," wrote Ingalls. "Bran eaters and vegetarians," he continued, "are not the kings of men. Rice and potatoes are the diet of slaves. The races that live on beef have ruled the world, and the better the beef the greater the deeds they have done."[62] If beef were important, then so was grass; thus, seed the country down to Blue Grass, and you would produce superior beef and consequently a superior race. To substantiate this claim he referred to the Blue Grass country of Kentucky as having been "the arena of the most magnificent intellectual and physical achievement in the world." In further corroboration of this statement, Ingalls cited Henry Clay, fast horses, and beautiful women as proof enough.[63] The poems he contributed to *Kansas Magazine* appeared under the pseudonyms of T. Donneley and P. Flannigan and did not merit the attention given to his prose. The overall importance of the publicity Ingalls received from these publications was significant not only to his literary career, but it also gave impetus to his long-hoped-for "legitimate aspirations." The United States Senate was just one of those aspirations, and this one he was about to achieve.[64]

The years from 1865 to 1873 were indeed interim years. They were years in which Ingalls patiently and persistently laid the foundations for his dreams both of founding a dynasty and of attaining high political office. Had Ingalls been a member of Congress in these years of reconstruction, he would have been a "radical." On other major political matters of the period, such as "hard" money and civil-service reform, he differed with his party's position. In spite of differences with his party, Ingalls regarded himself as a "Republican-Republican," and as such he was ready and waiting to carry the political banner that was about to be dropped by the Republican incumbent, Senator Samuel C. Pomeroy.

6

A NEW SENATOR FOR "HAPPY-LAND-OF-CANAAN"

The winter of 1872–1873 was politically momentous for Kansas in general and Ingalls in particular. Samuel C. Pomeroy was completing his second term of office as United States Senator from the Sunflower State. For years Pomeroy had been subject to frequent attack as a man generally corrupt and unfit for public office. In spite of the rising tide of criticism, however, Pomeroy was willing to "forgive" his critics and once again enter his name on the political list as an incumbent seeking re-election.

Mark Twain and Charles Dudley Warner used the 1873 U.S. Senatorial contest in Kansas as a cornerstone in cataloging the corruption of the period in their novel, *The Gilded Age*. It takes but little perception to peel away the thin veneer of disguise in order to recognize "Senator Dilworthy" as the incumbent U.S. Senator Samuel C. Pomeroy and "Mr. Noble" as Kansas State Senator York, who "exposed" Pomeroy. All this took place on January 29, 1873, at "Saints Rest" (Topeka), "Happy-Land-of-Canaan" (Kansas).[1]

This period in the nation's history was generally notorious for its corruption. Henry Adams singled out the period as one which was "poor in purpose and barren in results."[2] Matthew Josephson denounced it in his best seller *The Robber Barons*.[3] Republican Presidential victories from 1876 to 1892 in each instance failed to carry a majority vote, and only in 1880 did the Republican nominee receive a plurality. Godkin concluded that democracy had become identified with property rights, rather than human rights, and consequently little was accomplished in the area of social reform.[4] The Republican party might boast that it had "saved" the Union, but there were those who stated with equal fervor that in so doing it had emasculated the Constitution. The Republican party of this era, however, frequently equated party loyalty with national patriotism and charged the Democrats with treason. Such charges and counter-charges were exemplary of the political climate that characterized the age.

In this era of national reconstruction, political questions loomed larger and more complex. Reconstruction embraced more than the traditional notion that it was principally involved with the problem of "reconstructing" the defeated Confederate States of America. The aftermath of the Civil War and the succeeding period of "reorienta-tion" posed problems whose "solutions" stamped an impress not only on the South, but on the nation as a whole, North, South, and West. Ingalls appraised these developments with a singleness of purpose and did not "dabble" in political theory or the constitutionality of the many facets of Reconstruction policies. He viewed the two major political parties as being interchangeable with the armies of the Union and the Confederacy. The political parties, Democratic and Republican, and the sections of the country, North and South, were, in Ingalls opinion, opposing armies. The Republicans had won, and therefore the case was closed; for to the victors belonged the spoils, and in this case the "spoils" meant the political predomi-nance of the Republican party over the Democrats.

In writing to his father in June, 1872, Ingalls stated that he pre-sumed that his father would "hail with delight" the opportunity to vote for Greeley, and quickly added, "As for me and my house we are going for Grant."[5] Ingalls was a partisan to an ultra degree. He once wrote that "the independent non partisan has no place in American life. He is a hypocritical, sanctimonious, canting parasite, usually infesting the party in power, and belongs in the same cate-gory as those creatures employed by oriental despots to guard their harems. Every man ought to be a partisan," he continued, "& if he believes he is right he will be. He ought to be a partisan in religion, morals, education as well as politics."[6]

By September, 1872, Ingalls reported to his father that the Kansas political scene had become "rather lively" and that he had been elected president of his Congressional district convention which had met in Lawrence on September 4.[7] In the same commu-nication he claimed that he could have been nominated for Congress by acclamation, but he chose to defer, stating that at one time he thought that the convention would nominate him in spite of his protests. He enjoyed his ability to overcome such a "temptation," commenting that "it isn't often that a man has a chance to put such a bauble aside, and still more seldom that he has the fortitude to do so, especially when a nomination is equivalent to an election."[8] There is no need to guess at Ingalls' reason for rejecting this political "bauble." In succinct terms he penned the epitaph of the incumbent Senator: "Pomeroy's term expires this winter and he cannot be reelected." Ingalls claimed that a "strong feeling" was developing in his own favor as Pomeroy's successor to the Senate and remarked that several counties had promised him support. He was biding his time in September, as he put it, "looking over the field to see what the prospect is."[9] If the chance to replace Pomeroy looked good, Ingalls did not intend "to lose it by inaction." Pomeroy, on the other hand, was confident of his reelection. In a hasty note penned to Samuel N. Wood, Pomeroy asked Wood's aid in the approaching election by stating, "I am expecting to be elected . . . if you can't do that [help me] don't help my opponents—*For I am going through.*"[10] In a more polite tone Pomeroy also wrote Ingalls and requested him to join "several of our Atchison friends who are coming over to aid me by their influence in this election." The letter concluded, "With Sentiments of esteem."[11] In spite of Pomeroy's entreaties and his apparent confidence of being reelected, events were to take place that would prove disastrous for him and shocking to the state and nation. In Topeka, on the eve of the Senatorial election, the assembled legislators were addressed by Governor Thomas A. Osborn. His remarks were brief, but strongly suggestive. He assured the legislators that he did not want to be "understood as sanctioning the reports that have been so generally circulated of the wholesale purchase of our Legislatures, in our former elections." Nevertheless, he concluded that "it would be idle to deny the existence of such reports" and cautioned his "sheep," as a good shepherd should, to " 'abstain from all appearance of evil?' "[12]

In the smoke-filled rooms secret political caucuses were being held and powerful forces were working for Pomeroy's defeat. Of the men who figured so prominently in bringing about this result, none was more conspicuous than Senator Alexander M. York from Montgomery County. Other persons who figured prominently in the anti-Pomeroy movement included W. A. Johnson, B. F. Simpson, and J. C. Horton. The exact relationship of Ingalls to this anti-Pomeroy group is still uncertain. On the night preceding the election Ingalls telegraphed his wife in Atchison that he had been unanimously nominated for the Senate by the anti-Pomeroy caucus. He claimed that fifty-seven votes were pledged for his election and that his supporters were optimistic.[13] The Topeka *Commonwealth* later claimed that Ingalls had been nominated because he was the best compromise candidate and not because he was either the strongest or most popular figure on the scene.[14]

January 29, 1873, was the day of the election, which was made dramatic, even for a Kansas election, by the action of State Senator York. The election procedures previously agreed upon required the clerk to call the roll, after which each legislator in turn was to rise and vocally cast his vote. When York's name was called, he arose and addressed the presiding officer, the assembled legislators, and the uninvited guests in a most startling manner. He claimed that he had secretly visited Pomeroy's quarters in the Tefft house on the previous Monday night and that in the course of this interview his vote was bought for the sum of eight thousand dollars. He stated that two thousand dollars was paid to him at the time of the interview and that five thousand dollars was delivered to him the following day, with the balance of one thousand dollars to be paid after he had cast his vote for Pomeroy. In a dramatic conclusion York is alleged to have said, "I now in the presence of this honorable body hand over the amount of $7,000 just as I received it, and ask that it be counted by the secretary. . . . I ask, Mr. President, that that money be used to defray the expenses of prosecuting the investigation of S. C. Pomeroy for bribery and corruption."[15] York went on to add that he had not exposed Pomeroy in the interest of any other candidate, "but in behalf of the outraged and long-suffering people of the commonwealth."[16] Needless to say, pandemonium broke out. Pomeroy's supporters sought to delay the vote until Pomeroy had been given a chance to defend himself, which would have been both ethical and in keeping with jurisprudence. However, their efforts to secure a delay were overcome by the argument that delay would only give the "corrupt" and "contemptible" Pomeroy the opportunity to marshal his forces and gain reelection. In the subsequent balloting Ingalls polled one hundred and fifteen out of the one hundred and twenty-nine votes cast and was duly elected as a United States Senator for Kansas.[17] The outcome of the election was never in doubt once the voting had gotten under way. There were charges and countercharges in the days following this stunning display of "Kansas political bushwhacking."[18]

Pomeroy was brought to trial in Kansas on the charge that he had attempted to corrupt a public official, but the court entertained a motion for a nolle prosequi. The motion was granted, and Pomeroy was discharged from any further action in the matter so far as Kansas was concerned.[19] Further investigation awaited Pomeroy in the United States Senate, and there Pomeroy "demanded" that a committee be appointed to investigate the charges so recently made by York. The results of the Senate investigation were inconclusive. Pomeroy's supporters claimed vindication, while his enemies claimed that a "Scotch-verdict" had been rendered—guilty but not proven.[20]

Ingalls' election was regarded by many to be just as startling as Pomeroy's defeat. Ingalls had not been what could be described as an overwhelming political success prior to his election to the United States Senate. By no calculation could he have been counted among the politically prominent men of Kansas, yet he had triumphed over his supposedly stronger rivals. Whether a "deal" was made to assure his election is still an unanswered question. Certainly rumors were flying, to such an extent that Ingalls took it upon himself to write a long letter to James A. Garfield, explaining the circumstances surrounding his election. He began by explaining to Garfield that his election was assured after the first ballot on the twenty-eighth of January. "I knew nothing of the York business," he continued, "till the joint session was about to meet, & was not then informed who was to make the disclosure. I have never met Mr. York and do not now know him by sight. I reserve the expression of my judgement upon his act till I can see you." In summary Ingalls stated, "I presume you are well enough acquainted with some phases of Kansas politics to require no caution about giving credence to the injurious rumors which are so industriously circulated."[21] Some of the "rumors" circulating had it that Pomeroy was "framed" and that Ingalls was a party to this action. To quell such unholy conversation the Kansas Senate, with the House concurring, passed a resolution in which they stated their "unbounded faith" in the new Senator-elect, claiming further that they believed him "incapable of using unfair or corrupt means to further his own interests, or of conspiring against another person in order to elevate himself."[22]

The press generally gave favorable notice to Ingalls' election and hailed it as an indication that Kansas was cleaning up its political corruption. On February 6, 1873, the *Nation* stated that Ingalls appeared to possess a good character, but quickly added, "Of course any product of the Kansas Legislature must, for a while, be regarded with suspicion."[23] On March 1, 1873, *Harper's Weekly* claimed that Ingalls was the author of a denunciatory article about Pomeroy which appeared in the Leavenworth *Daily Conservative* of April 11, 1861. In this article, alleged to have been written by Ingalls, Pomeroy received a scathing rebuke as an inept and unworthy public servant. *Harper's* went on to add a comment about Ingalls' character and stated that "those who know him well are most confident that his election marks the overthrow of the old era and the beginning of a better."[24] The *New York Times,* however, took a different view of Ingalls. In short they accused him of being generally corrupt and guilty of bribery.[25] Ingalls was deluged with personal messages of congratulations. Included among the numerous pieces of mail was a letter from United States Senator Phineas W. Hitchcock from Nebraska, who had been a classmate of Ingalls' at Williams College. The letter read in part as follows: "You have the genius that can with the opportunity which is now offered you reasonably aspire to anything. Welcome and hail."[26] Ingalls' wife, however, made a matter-of-fact entry in her diary on January 29, 1873, the day of his election: "Coldest morning of the season. Busy all forenoon. Mr. Schofield brings dispatch announcing James' election to the Senate. Friends call all afternoon offering congratulations."[27]

Assuming that Ingalls' election was untainted by corruption, the question that undeniably presents itself is, What brought Ingalls the fame and following to secure his election? Representative selections of articles from the Kansas and Missouri press indicate that his literary talents were largely responsible. The most pronounced claim of this sort is found in the introductory remarks of the book *The Writings of John James Ingalls* and is quoted here: "John J. Ingalls . . . became United States senator because he wrote 'Catfish Aristocracy' and 'Blue Grass.' "[28] William Elsey Connelley penned this poetic phrase, which smacks more of enthusiasm than accuracy. Nevertheless, other sources made similar claims. On January 30, 1873, both the Kansas City *Times* and the Lawrence *Journal* cited Ingalls' literary ability as an important contributing factor in his election to the Senate. On January 31, 1873, the Topeka *Commonwealth* declared that "Mr. Ingalls owes his success more to his connection to that publication [*Kansas Magazine,* where his "Blue Grass" and "Catfish" essays were first published] than to any other one thing which entered into the contest." Whether the claims of the press were true or not, it is interesting to note the emphasis placed on his literary talents.

Atchison celebrated the victory of its "adopted son" by holding a "Complimentary Banquet" at the Corinthian Hall on February 12, 1873.[29] Ingalls, his family, and much of Atchison made the most of it. In April, Ingalls was feted at a banquet given at Leavenworth in his honor. In addressing his audience he assured them that all political factions were now united in the interest of bringing prosperity to the state. The high point of his address was his commitment to the creed promising that "honesty is not hereafter to be unprofitable."[30] But Ingalls had enemies in Atchison as well as throughout Kansas. Bitter rivalries were to characterize his relationship with several of his fellow townsmen throughout the remainder of his life.

Ingalls was thirty-nine years of age when he went to the nation's capital as a Senator-elect from Kansas. He was enthralled with Washington City and described its beauties and its dynamic nature in glowing terms: "Washington looks charmingly. I think it is the most delightful city I ever knew. . . . there is a prevalent air of activity, thrift and enterprise which is like an inspiration. The great size of the public buildings: the luxurious elegance of the grounds with their masses of color, their shaven lawns greener than emerald: the odor of box, balsam and pine: the great trees that brood with impenetrable shade upon groups of idlers in the wandering path: the fountains sending their flashing spray into the sunlight to return into the pools that seem like liquid sunshine below: all contribute to form an impression that no other city to me has ever produced. Add to this the association arising from the consciousness that here is the nation's mysterious life: that here its vital currents coalesce & return again to the remotest extremities: that ambition looks hither as its proudest goal: that here are all the possibilities of wealth, power, pleasure, culture, in their most intense expression and the dramatic effect is complete."[31] Such a description conveys a fascination and affection for Washington that was to continue throughout his tenure there as a United States Senator.

Aside from his delight with Washington, Ingalls had little to report in his domestic correspondence the first few months on the political scene. One intriguing exception, however, is an interesting reference to Senator Charles Sumner of Massachusetts, whom Ingalls greatly admired. Sumner had taken the floor of the Senate with "his negro bills, and various sentimental schemes for the amelioration of the condition of mankind." On the same evening the Negro troops gave Sumner a serenade "by a most execrable band" right under his, Ingalls', window. Sumner came out on his steps and in a few sentences "reiterated the creed of so many years." And then, in a melancholy summary, Ingalls concluded that there was "something grand about the old fellows' [sic] devotion to an idea, once so potential, but about which the world now so little cares."[32] Negro civil rights were as iridescent as ever, and within a few months Sumner, their champion, would be dead.

By November of 1873 Ingalls was making preparations for the arrival of his wife and two of his children. He rented a suite of rooms with a southern exposure looking directly out upon "Senator Sumner's Castle" and beyond to the still uncompleted Washington

Monument, and thence out upon the Potomac River and the hills beyond.[33] As a young, ambitious Senator, Ingalls was very much concerned about not only the proper kind of residence but also about his own personal appearance. He was especially sensitive about the impression that he made on the other Senators and the crowds in the galleries. He reassured himself, after a careful comparison, that his wardrobe was already "better than the majority of the members" and that "it was not well to be *too* fine."[34] He was not able to live as sumptuously as he might have wished, explaining to his wife that his income came solely from his Senatorial salary, which amounted to approximately five hundred and fifty dollars a month the year round. His own personal expenses took about one hundred and seventy-five dollars a month, leaving a balance of three hundred and seventy-five dollars for the support of his family in Atchison. He claimed to be so busy with his duties as Senator that there was no time to secure any extra "honorariums," and this, coupled with his confessed lack of frugality, added to his financial problems. One of his consistent problems was his financial affairs. He had a near-morbid fear that if anything happened to him, his family would not be properly cared for. He confessed to his wife that if he were only rich, it would relieve him of one great dread of death that always haunted him. "I feel I could break into a bank or commit a crime," he continued, "if I could only feel that you were safe and happy as long as you lived, after I am gone."[35]

In spite of the strain on his income, Ingalls maintained his Washington suite of rooms plus his home in Atchison. On January 1, 1874, Mrs. Ingalls and the two youngest children arrived in Washington, leaving the four older children behind in Atchison in the custody of friends.[36] These first exciting weeks in Washington were marred by the greatest personal tragedy Ingalls ever encountered. His six-year-old daughter, Ruth, suddenly became quite ill, and telegraphic information advised Ingalls and his wife to return to Atchison at once. Then word quickly followed that Ruth was improving, but mother and father decided to return to Atchison in any event. En route to Kansas they received a telegram in Chicago telling them that Ruth had suffered a relapse and had quickly and quietly died. The grief of the parents, especially that of Ingalls, can hardly be exaggerated. Throughout his life he made dozens of references to his "own dear sweet Ruth," and the tragedy of her death left an emotional scar that time could not efface.[37] Ingalls' father wrote a tender and consoling letter, claiming that time would be beneficent and that someday this tragedy "will be so mellowed and softened that it will be a cloud with a golden lining."[38] Ingalls himself did his best to console his wife. A few weeks after the death of Ruth he wrote Lou and asked her not to "upbraid" herself for being absent at the time of Ruth's illness. And then from the depths of his soul he poured out his love for his wife in these words: "You seem more dear and sacred to me because you bore in your womb and gave birth to that dear child that has preceded us to the world beyond. Let us cherish her memory as an additional tie if such were necessary to unite our souls in a bond that shall strengthen with time and be perfected in eternity."[39] A few weeks later he again referred to Ruth's death, making the hopeful yet melancholy comment that "she is spared all the wretchedness and misery of this tragedy which we call life." In summary, he expressed his love for Lou, saying, "We must love each other more because we loved her so much and so live as to meet her in that world whither she has gone to herald us and give us companionship when we come."[40]

To all public appearances, Ingalls did not betray his grief, in fact he plunged himself into the thick of his Senatorial responsibilities. His parliamentary skill was quickly recognized, and frequently he took the Vice-President's chair temporarily and presided over sessions of the Senate. He often wrote letters during the dull moments of the proceedings, and while presiding one cold March day, he wrote about the recent death of Senator Sumner, his funeral, and the resultant loss to the Senate and nation.[41] Ingalls had attended Sumner's funeral, which he described in great detail:

> The Great Senator was borne to the Capital at 9, and placed beneath the canopy in the Rotunda, in a square casket upon a black base, and covered with the rarest and costliest flowers—lilies, violets, japonicas, smilax, camelias in wreaths, garlands, crosses, with evergreens prophetic of immortality. A dense surge of humanity moved endlessly through the corridors, aimlessly, curiously, black, white, ragged, unkempt, chilled with the cold blasts, and filing past the cold, livid, discolored face that lay beneath the transparent glass like a drowned man under the ice. There were no tears. The scene was heartless. Loud talk, vain babbling, and senseless laughter echoed through the stony thoroughfares; and still the throng surged on and on, without beginning and without end.
>
> The Senate galleries were densely packed at an early hour. Tier above tier, it was a solid mass of faces, relieved against the dark drapery behind—at 12 the Senate was called to order, the journal read, and some formal

business transacted. We were presented with black gloves and crepe on the left arm. Soon the House of Representatives were announced and took their places on the south side of the chamber; then the representatives from Massachusetts with their families as mourners, noticably old Ben Butler with his wife, a tall, graceful striking looking woman with aristocratic features and bearing; then the Chief Justice and associate justices of the Supreme Court in their black gowns; then the officers of the Army and Navy; the diplomatic corps in plain dress, headed by the formal courtier, Sir Edward Thornton; then President Grant and his cabinet, who sat by the head of the coffin, the silver mountings of which shone through the mass of flowers. The President was dressed in plain, dark clothes, and sat as expressionless as stone, sometimes drumming his hat upon his knee.

The scene was exceedingly impressive, and the solemnities were austere, consisting only of prayer and selections read from the Scriptures. At 10 minutes past one the Amen was pronounced, and the House, the Court, the President, and the guests retired slowly from the chamber, and the Senate adjourned till Tuesday noon.

In conclusion Ingalls wrote, "I send you some violets from a great purple mass crowned with white that exhaled their fragrance in the dim chamber that shall know him no more forever. Keep them as a memento of a Great Life that has ended today."[42]

Within a year of taking his seat in the Senate, Ingalls had lost his little daughter Ruth, and now the hero of his youth was dead. On the heels of these tragic events, Ingalls was obliged to begin the process of mending his political fences in Kansas. Albert H. Horton and C. G. Foster were competing for the political appointment to a federal judgeship in Kansas, and Ingalls was caught between the conflicting ambitions of these two men. He explained to his wife that Horton could not be appointed "for many reasons," but chiefly because the "delegation was against him upon general grounds." Then, too, Horton was made less attractive because Pomeroy had "meddled" in the matter. President Grant, on the other hand, was opposed to Foster. Ingalls finally secured Foster's appointment, but in the face of what at one time appeared to be overwhelming odds.[43] A few days after Foster's appointment Ingalls wrote his wife inquiring about Horton. He had not heard from him lately, and he feared that "his love has grown cold." In an almost taunting fashion he asked, "How does he bear his discomfiture?"[44] Although Ingalls had worked in Foster's behalf, he claimed that he was aware of the fact that Foster did not like him and never had. Nevertheless, Ingalls had worked for Foster's appointment to placate an unnamed, powerful political opponent. In a boastful fashion Ingalls claimed that he was "a power at Washington" and that he was being congratulated for his skill and energy in overcoming obstacles that at one time seemed insuperable.[45] As a matter of fact, no stone was left unturned in Ingalls' quest to become politically powerful. He even encouraged his wife to make friends whenever possible to counter his own inability to play the role of the glad-handing, back-slapping friend of the people, a role that he loathed.[46]

Throughout the remainder of the spring term of 1874, Ingalls' star steadily climbed. When Congress adjourned, Ingalls returned to Atchison as a model of young, dynamic leadership in the political affairs of the state and nation. He had been appointed a member of three standing committees, namely Indian Affairs, Pensions, which he vigorously promoted, and Education and Labor. He had introduced numerous bills in his first year covering a wide range of subjects, such as bills to regulate mineral lands, to organize the Territory of Oklahoma, for relief of settlers on homesteads and pre-emption lands, for the carrying of freight and passengers on the Union Pacific Railroad, to incorporate the Colorado Irrigation and Land Co., to enable New Mexico to become a state, to amend the bankruptcy act, to amend the Pacific Railroad Act, to abolish the board of Indian Commissioners, as well as a resolution in memory of the late Senator Charles Sumner. In addition he had presented the Senate with a petition from a group of women in Kansas who sought the right to vote. He introduced a bill for the benefit of "loyal" Creek Indians and supported Colorado's effort to enter the Union.[47] In all he had "done his homework" in behalf of the people of his state and nation. Within a few weeks of his return to Atchison, however, Ingalls was required to fight for both his personal and political survival. On August 6, 1874, the Kansas City *Times* printed a brief notice under the heading "The Ingalls Exposé." The notice claimed that on the following day it would prove Ingalls to be a totally corrupt man, unfit for public office, in fact unfit to be at large in society. On August 7, as promised, the *Times* ran a fifteen-column story under various headings and subheadings, such as "Ingalls— The Would-be King of Kansas Politics." The article accused Ingalls of everything but decency. Among the numerous accusations was the claim that Ingalls had lived in adultery with a Mrs. Benedict at Sumner, Kansas, after first breaking up her marriage. It was alleged that Mrs. Benedict had borne a child by Ingalls and that Ingalls had bribed her into silence. It was also claimed that Ingalls was a bigamist. The *Times* claimed that he had married an unidentified woman in Sumner and that when he tired of her, he sent her out of the Territory. Not content with these charges, the *Times* continued by claiming that Ingalls had tricked his mother-in-law, Mrs. Ellsworth Chesebrough, out of the inheritance that she had received upon her husband's death and then claimed that he had "turned her out in the cold."

In addition to assassinating his personal character, the *Times* also attacked Ingalls' political life. It claimed that he had deliberately miscounted the votes in the 1861 Senatorial election, giving Pomeroy the election to the United States Senate. Also the *Times* claimed that Ingalls took part in the York exposé of Pomeroy in 1873, and then it summarized its attack by listing no less than ten additional charges, all of which attacked Ingalls' sense of honesty, his integrity, and his general fitness to hold public office. On the same day, August 7, 1874, the Fort Scott *Daily Monitor* listed these charges in brief. The *Monitor* took a different position, however, and claimed that "however corrupt Ingalls may have been in his past political life, the charges against him are feebly put and a large portion of the evidence very unsatisfactory." The *Times*, in making its accusations, had claimed that it had in its possession personal letters purported to have been written by Ingalls and that it would release these letters to the general public in due course. The highly "touted" evidence was never made public.

Ingalls reported the episode to his father, claiming that the publishers of the *Times* were "confederate democrats" who were his bitter personal enemies. He related that he had been advised to take no notice of the story except with a "rawhide" and that a number of Atchison citizens had offered "to get up a monster indignation meeting." Ingalls refused this offer, claiming that contempt and indifference would cut deeper. He told his father that he had anticipated such an attack for several months and that his accusers had offered to "fix things up," if he would give one of them a special mail agency in the state. He rejected their offer in his "mild gentle way," then threatened to "kick the entrails out of the fellow if he ever came within reach." In a final attempt to bribe Ingalls the threats were repeated three days before the "exposé" was printed. Ingalls told his father that it was all a mess of lies from beginning to end, but conceded that the whole affair was irritating, "but so are the grasshoppers."[48] Grasshoppers soon die or disappear, and so did the *Times*'s accusations against Ingalls; but as a plague of insects can damage crops, the accusations had also left their scars on Ingalls' reputation.

By October, following the August "exposé," Ingalls was on the political stump in southern Kansas, "preaching the gospel of Republicanism in the waste places of our political Zion," as he liked to put it. Once more he referred to the "villainous onslaught," but claimed that his enemies had not done him much harm.[49] His return to Washington created no unusual attention, and with a sigh of relief Ingalls claimed he saw no evidence of aversion on any side.[50] The *Times* attack had sputtered out and Ingalls' seat was not in jeopardy. He had weathered his first severe political storm.

7

EXONERATION
THROUGH VIGILANCE

The fact that his reputation had
been slightly tarnished did not deter Ingalls from aspiring to still
higher political office. When he returned to the nation's capital in
the winter of 1874, he prepared to "make a racket here in Washington, so as to become National." By so doing he hoped to enhance his
political prospects. But in the last analysis he believed his future
success depended on the subtle power called fate, "which makes or
mars the fortunes of all."[1] He did not leave all to fate, however, for
he boasted that by a judicious use of patronage he had created a
formidable following all over the state among the newspapermen
and leading men of both parties.[2] He described the opening session
of the Senate in December of 1874 with enthusiasm. Mrs. Grant,
the wife of the president, was present, looking "as dowdy as usual."
Vice-President Henry Wilson was presiding, Roscoe Conkling was
in his seat, "cleaning and paring and filing his finger nails." Ingalls
claimed that Conkling spent enough time on his "digits" to groom a
race horse. John Sherman, John Logan, and the other "magnates"
were all in their seats; and Ingalls jubilantly anticipated the opening
of the "show."[3] The Congressional session was socially launched
with a reception at the Executive Mansion in January of 1875. President and Mrs. Grant played host and hostess to the diplomatic corps,
army and navy officers, finely dressed ladies and their male companions, elegant in their white chokers and "steel pen" coats. Ingalls
moved easily in such circles and enjoyed writing colorful descriptions of such proceedings for Lou, in order that she might be kept
well informed of the "haute" culture of the Washington social set.[4]

These first months in Washington were invigorating for Ingalls, and he wrote voluminously of the events, places, persons, sights, and sounds that he encountered in this dynamic city. The population in 1870 had exceeded 100,000 for the first time, and Washington had not yet become an urban sprawl with its accompanying anonymity. In spite of being the seat of government, it retained something of the "folksy" atmosphere typical of small-town America. The Library of Congress held less than 300,000 volumes; the Capitol rotunda was lit at night by 3,000 gas jets; Ford's Theatre was serving as the Army Medical Museum; the Smithsonian Institution consisted solely of the original red-freestone building with its numerous towers; and the shaft of the Washington Monument was still unfinished, Ingalls being a member of the Congress that appropriated the funds for its completion. The major streets were serviced by "horse-car" routes, and during the rainy season the "streets" became a sea of mud. This is the Washington that greeted Ingalls and charmed him so. This early exuberance led him to design a coat of arms and a motto which he used on his stationery for a time. The symbol was an eye, with the letter "I" in the background. The Latin motto, translated into English, read, "He conquers who is vigilant," or as Ingalls facetiously put it in "cockney," "vigilance wins," or "vigilance vins," or as the Dutchman would say, "look a leedle out."[5] Ingalls was unaware that his motto was prophetic. Before his first term closed, he was called upon to do much more than "look a leedle out" in order to save his political life.

Ingalls' preoccupation with the political and social scene in Washington did not preclude his interest, though often a disdainful interest, in religion. He frequently attended either the Episcopal or Presbyterian church. Once he rather surprisingly claimed to feel better for having attended.[6] On the next Tuesday, Ingalls called on President Grant. He reported that he was received cordially, but noted that Grant was "looking very heavy, dull & gross this season. Evidently drinking a great deal and showing it badly."[7] In spite of the stimulation of audiences with the President and the swirling pace of Washington society, Ingalls pined for his family. "I would like to gather you all round the library fire this bitter night and talk over the affairs of the day," he once wrote, "and discuss with you the name of the new girl baby that you say is coming."[8] In the margin of this letter a penciled note states, "This was not a girl, but Daddy." "Daddy," in this instance, proved to be Sheffield Ingalls, who later gained considerable renown in the field of Kansas politics, most notably as Lieutenant-Governor. Ingalls' love for his family once more induced him to make preparations for them to come to live in Washington during the sessions of Congress. The advantages for

Lou were pointed out with the explanation that in Washington she would have more leisure for society and enjoyment and politics.[9] Not all was enjoyment for Ingalls, however, who bitterly complained of "office-seekers and place hunters" who literally haunted him from morning till night. He confessed his annoyance, but boasted that he listened with patience and answered with courtesy.[10]

Interestingly, Ingalls rarely discussed key political issues in letters to his wife. For example, he hardly even noted the Panic of 1873 and its subsequent impact on the nation's economy. He made no reference to the "Salary Grab" Act of 1873 or to the repeal of major portions of it. Although he spoke of Grant, there is no mention of his fiscal policies with respect to the resumption of specie payments and the issuance of legal-tender notes. Nor does he mention such controversial issues as the "Whisky Ring" conspiracy. In fact Ingalls seemed reluctant throughout his Senatorial career to speak out, privately or publicly, on the major issues of the day. There were some exceptions, such as virtually any "bloody shirt" issue, the cause of silver, black civil rights, the "democracy" (Democratic Party), the idea of continentalism, and England as our "natural enemy." He was also always ready to extol the virtues of Kansas. However, he was never a powerful voice insofar as major pieces of legislation were concerned.

The adjournment of the Forty-third Congress was greeted by Ingalls with mixed emotions. He described the closing sessions as ending in an uproar and confusion indescribable. In fact the tumult was so great that Vice-President Wilson summoned Ingalls to preside and then quietly retired to the privacy of his room. It was during these last days of the session that Ingalls first saw "old Andy Johnson," as he called him, and reported to his wife that the former President was greeted with applause.[11] In summing up his own progress during the recent session, Ingalls claimed that he had been "generally successful" and had been well recognized on committees.[12]

The impending national election of 1876 was already casting its shadow, and Ingalls, feeling "generally successful," looked forward to the outcome with optimism. He referred to the elections of 1874 with the remark that "The fond parent [electorate] having a year ago caressed its Republican child with a trunk strap, now takes its Democratic offspring by the scruff, shakes it till its bones rattle and kicks it down the back stairs." And then in direct reference to Rutherford B. Hayes's political prospects he claimed that "it will not be a miracle if Governor Hayes is the next President."[13] As for his own aspirations, he claimed that Kansas might well present the name of her favorite son for Vice-President, meaning himself of course. He admitted that this would be a gratifying, though empty, gesture and stated that he preferred to remain a Senator "for the present."[14] When 1876 rolled around, Ingalls still claimed that he cared nothing about the Vice-Presidency, but "should Blaine be nominated, it would not be unlikely that I should receive the second place."[15] For someone who was not interested in being Vice-President, it is interesting to note that Ingalls counted on Kansas, Nebraska, Missouri, Arkansas, Indiana, Illinois, and Massachusetts for convention support for the nomination to the Vice-Presidency.[16] Ingalls counted on Blaine's support largely as a result of his wife's close personal friendship with Mrs. Blaine.

As the fall elections of 1876 approached, Ingalls predicted that the Republicans would triumph. He reasoned that the "Republicans saved the country and they will rule it till the war is forgotten. The heroes and principles of the Revolution controlled the nation till the war of '12 [1812]. The victors in that war ruled the country till the Mexican war, and the triumphant policy in this contest maintained the supremacy till the Civil War broke out. We are in the direct line of succession and our dynasty will not perish."[17] As a member of this dynasty, Ingalls claimed that he omitted nothing that would contribute to his own and his party's success. He treated everybody affably, went about among the people, answered all his mail, and endeavored to so demean himself that people would respect him and take pride in him.[18]

As a public figure Ingalls was always self-conscious about his personal appearance, and he was particularly pained that he was so thin. He regarded this as a personal handicap, and in spite of all his efforts he was never able to put on any appreciable amount of weight. "If I could get fat," he once wrote, "I would live on milk to the exclusion of everything else."[19] In 1876 he gave up drinking and smoking in an attempt to gain weight, but he was never able to get above one hundred and forty pounds.[20] He was particularly upset when his wife sent him a clipping which described him as a man who looked like a clergyman. Ingalls replied, "Could any description be more insufferably disgusting! 'Slim, with a pleasant smile, and the aspect of a minister of the gospel!' What a cursed irony of fate. . . . That is precisely the type of man that I loathe, detest and abhor at sight!" In a pleading fashion he begged his wife for suggestions as to just how he might "disguise" himself and facetiously asked, "How would a costume made of Persian rugs become me?" And then in conclusion he exclaimed, "I wish I weighed four hundred pounds, with a paunch so big that I could not see within five feet of my toes."[21] Apparently Ingalls believed that a fat politician "pulled more weight at the polls" than a skinny one.

Ingalls did not receive the nomination for Vice-President in 1876. Whether this was because Blaine failed to secure the Presidential nomination is not known. If this proved to be a disappointment, it was only slight in comparison to the grief he felt at the loss of his four-year-old son, Addison. Having lost his beloved six-year-old daughter, Ruth, in 1874, he now lost the pride among his sons in 1876. He described his son's death in a letter to his father, stating that "he died Sunday night at 11 o'clock, in peace. He was the noblest and most promising of my sons, as Ruth was the most lovely and engaging of my daughters. There may be some consolation for such inexplicable afflictions," he wrote, "but I have not discovered them. . . . His affection for me appeared to be the supreme law of his being. His illness was brief and comparatively painless. He recognized us, and his attendants, just before his sweet soul vanished into the unknown." And then in conclusion Ingalls wrote, "Yesterday beneath the clear sky that brooded above us like a covenant of peace, we laid him to sleep beside his sister to wait the solution of the great mystery of existence when earth and sea shall give up their dead. That I may meet him again in the great hereafter is a profound aspiration rather than a living faith, but if eternity will release its treasures, sometime I shall claim my own."[22] Certainly this lovely tribute dispels any illusions that Ingalls was a "cold and heartless" man, as some of his contemporaries claimed.

In the wake of this tragedy Lou became seriously ill. Her illness led to the premature birth of a baby girl who died within hours of her delivery. Little Faith, the new-born infant, was laid to rest with the other departed Ingalls children, and Lou began a long period of convalescence. In time she regained her health, but her illness left her permanently lame, with a stiffened joint of the right knee.[23]

In the very midst of these personal tragedies Ingalls had been obliged to campaign in behalf of the slate of Republican candidates in the momentous elections of November, 1876. Subsequent to this he became deeply involved in the disputed electoral returns with respect to the Hayes-Tilden fiasco. He was appointed a teller on the part of the Senate, and being in this position, he was able to go "behind the scene" in his observations of the proceedings. In fact he later published his account of the events under the title "Stormy Days of the Electoral Commission."[24] As a result of this experience he surmised that it was unlikely that there had ever been an absolutely "square and honest" Presidential election, at least not since the time of George Washington.

A few months prior to his campaign for reelection Ingalls wrote to James A. Garfield and requested him to "write a little notice, a hands breadth long, saying in a few words what you can about my Republicanism and my capacity for public office and the gratification that would be felt upon my return, and have it printed editorially in some Ohio paper & send me a copy for prints here." In turn Ingalls claimed that when Garfield became a candidate for President, he would "pull Kansas voters for *you*."[25] No doubt Ingalls was willing to accept aid from those who might be in a position to advance his own political fortunes and would probably have invited the help of even President Hayes, whom he once described as "the most pitiably helpless, feeble-mushy tea custard executive that has ever been in power since this government began." Ingalls claimed that he really felt sorry for him, stating that he "should as soon think of kicking a canary bird."[26] Hayes had a redeeming quality, however: he was a Republican.

Ingalls speeded up the pace in his campaign for reelection. During his first term in the Senate he introduced a total of 214 bills. He had been a member of five standing committees, the committees on Indian Affairs, Pensions, the District of Columbia, Education and Labor, and Privileges and Elections. During the second session of the Forty-fourth Congress he had been chairman of the Committee on Pensions. The bulk of the bills that he introduced were related to his committee assignments, and this was especially true of pensions. Special pension bills composed the lion's share of his proposed legislation. There were, nevertheless, many bills of a more important nature. Included among the more significant ones were his proposals attempting to extend time to preemptors on public lands, to secure appropriations for the protection of navigation of the Missouri River near Atchison, to secure corporate approval for mining and irrigation projects in Colorado, and to provide for the adequate care of Indians in the West. In addition there were dozens of bills of a local nature designed to secure appropriations for Kansas. He had also commented on scores of bills proposed by others. He soon gained a reputation for being excellent in debate, a skilled parliamentarian, and a master of sarcasm and was generally regarded as a man who possessed a keen and analytical mind. This was the reputation that he was making in Washington, but his Kansas constituents could not be expected to delight in Ingalls' personal triumphs, even though they might indirectly aid Kansas. Apart from distributing pensions and patronage, Ingalls could not claim the authorship of any measure of particular magnitude, either for Kansas or the nation.

On February 15, 1878, Ingalls made one of his most important speeches during his first term in the Senate. It was in regard to the silver question. This topic touched not only Kansas but the entire nation. It can be argued that Ingalls, who advocated free silver, was appealing for Kansas votes by proclaiming a monetary policy which the farmer and laborer were demanding. The logic of his speech, however, indicates that Ingalls believed that the gold standard, coupled with the relatively constant supply of gold, was the greatest enemy of the public credit. In denouncing the gold standard, Ingalls made a dramatic appeal by claiming that gold "is the most cowardly and treacherous of all metals. It makes no treaty that it does not break. It has no friends whom it does not sooner or later betray."[27] Ingalls concluded that silver money was an "American idea" and that silver was the "money of the people."[28]

John A. Martin, editor of the Atchison *Daily Champion,* backed up Ingalls' views in an editorial which he published on February 17, 1878. Martin claimed that the West needed financial consideration and reasoned that if the West was to be helped, her resident debtors must be helped. He also claimed that the continued development of the West was essential for the nation's progress; therefore the Western debtors must be helped, and free silver would help them.

In the meantime ex-Senator Pomeroy was renewing his interests in the approaching senatorial contest. Ingalls brushed aside any threat that Pomeroy might pose, and assured his father that "Kansas will sit down on him, Pomeroy, in November, so heavily that he will try no more experiments with the moral sense of a great people. His pretensions are everywhere regarded as a stain upon the honor of the State."[29]

Ingalls entered the fall campaign of 1878 and concluded his "canvass" of the state early in November. He regarded his own prospects for reelection by the Kansas legislature as being very good, but at the same time he claimed that he was indifferent about the result. In fact he confessed with a sense of shame that he was unable to generate any real enthusiasm during the campaign.[30] The fall elections were carried by the Republicans, and Ingalls returned to Washington to await developments prior to the balloting of the Kansas legislature for United States Senator, which would take place in January, 1879. If Ingalls had been apathetic and unenthusiastic in the recent campaign, it was at least partially compensated for by the enthusiasm of his wife. She kept abreast of the latest developments on the Kansas political scene and relayed all her information to Ingalls in Washington. As the time for the senatorial balloting drew closer, she anxiously wrote him that Pomeroy was busy in his own behalf and concluded that "The old man [Pomeroy] is certainly making a desperate effort to rally."[31]

When the balloting for Senator began, no less than eight persons received votes during the first roll call. On this first ballot Ingalls had twice as many votes as his closest rival, but he was unable to muster a majority. Not until the fourth ballot was he able to defeat his former friend, Albert H. Horton, and then by only a scant six votes.[32] The contest had been a bitter one, and Ingalls was subjected to malicious attacks. Among those who particularly attacked Ingalls was John Guthrie. Nevertheless, Mrs. Guthrie called on Mrs. Ingalls and begged her not to let the antagonism of their husbands interfere with their friendship, and indeed it did not.[33] Ingalls' enemies were not content to allow him to gain the laurels of victory unchallenged, and they threatened to expose him as a man who had resorted to bribery to gain his recent election. In fact his antagonists hatched a plot similar to the one so successfully executed against Pomeroy in 1873. Ingalls related some of the incidents of their plan in an undated letter to his father in which he claimed that "Playter got Hossack drunk and induced Hossack to sign the paper alleging that he had been offered a thousand dollars to vote for me."[34] Ingalls claimed that Playter attempted to use the signed document to blackmail him for money which Playter needed to get out of financial difficulty. Ingalls reported that Playter offered to let him have the incriminating paper for a "loan" of six thousand dollars, and when he declined, Playter boasted that he could easily find "a party" that would give him even more money than he had asked of Ingalls. Ingalls then related that Playter had tried to sell the paper to his (Ingalls') friends, and being unsuccessful, he returned it to Hossack. The paper was later presented to a special committee of the Kansas legislature appointed to investigate the charges against Ingalls, but the paper was finally discredited.[35] The special committee, after taking exhaustive testimony, reported that it was "unable to find testimony proving or establishing the crime of bribery or corruption against any of the late candidates for U.S. Senator" and reported that in its opinion "further sessions of this committee will not result in any benefit to the people of the State."[36]

Ingalls' enemies were not content with this outcome and consequently carried their charges into the United States Senate. They prepared a "memorial" and presented it to this body, repeating all their earlier charges with additional embellishments.[37] The "memorial" was prepared and submitted by F. S. Stumbaugh, Samuel A. Riggs, and W. C. Webb. The Vice-President, William A. Wheeler, presented the memorial to the Senate, where it was referred to the Committee on Privileges and Elections. After a considerable delay, Vice-President Wheeler laid a letter before the Senate, which was from F. S. Stumbaugh and L. F. Eggers, dated March 26, 1879. Included with the letter was the report of the Special Committee in Kansas regarding the election of Ingalls. The letter urged the Senate to look into the matter. This request was also referred to the Committee on Privileges and Elections, and Ingalls, who had been appointed to this committee, discreetly declined to serve on it. Finally Senator Eli Saulsbury of Delaware, who was chairman of the Committee on Privileges and Elections, presented a resolution from his committee calling for an investigation of the charges that were made against Ingalls in the memorial. An investigating committee, including a stenographer, a clerk, and a sergeant-at-arms, with power to administer oaths and take testimony, was requested in the resolution. In addition, a subcommittee was authorized to go to Kansas and investigate the charges there also. The investigation was also directed to continue its work throughout the Congressional recess period.

The resolution was delayed from coming to a vote by Senator Donald Cameron, who claimed that Ingalls wanted to answer the charges prior to the investigation. Ingalls was not present at the time, and the resolution was put aside until he had been given an opportunity to speak. The next day Ingalls was present and was given the opportunity to make a reply to the charges. Ingalls, however, declined to speak, and the resolution was promptly approved.

Witnesses were summoned to Washington to testify, and some had to be placed under arrest in order to secure their presence before the Senate. Among those arrested were J. V. Admire, E. B. Purcell, George T. Anthony, Leonard T. Smith, and Levi Wilson, all of whom were from Leavenworth, Kansas, and all of whom had failed to appear in response to subpoenas of the investigating committee taking testimony in Kansas. After exhaustive testimony had been taken concerning Ingalls' election, the case became increasingly frustrating and inconclusive. Ingalls, in referring to the investigation, reported that having once been exonerated, he expected to be so again.[38] He commented on the Senatorial investigating committee and claimed that "egged on by the Democratic press," it had delved into the charges. Hossack, who was the main line of attack against Ingalls, was described by the defendant as "a weak worthless fellow, but who was elected [to the Kansas legislature] as a friend of mine and pledged to my support. He was in my caucuses, and of course there was no need of buying him."[39]

In the meantime Pomeroy was doing his best to "pull the skids" from under Ingalls. In a letter to P. H. Coney, he accused Ingalls of "*delay*," claiming that this was the first time that a man so assailed "confessed his guilt by dodging—excusing—and delaying action!!!!" In summary Pomeroy called for the "skillful" use of the statements of the witnesses against Ingalls, stating that "skillfully arranged . . . they can be woven into such a chain, as to bind the strongest man."[40] Ingalls proved to be stronger than the strongest man, and by October, 1879, he wrote his father that the investigators were now on the defensive. He stated that "Judge Horton left town yesterday P.M. secretly for parts unknown, and a banker of Manhattan, who is proved to have been furnishing money to beat me, also absconded and cannot be found. We have got the felons," he wrote, "and I propose to show them no mercy. They have been fooling around the wrong end of the mule."[41] A few months later Ingalls reported that "everybody is now fully satisfied as to the nature of the war that has been made on me." He claimed that the case would soon be closed, and he once more cited the discomfiture of his antagonists. A witness against him at Topeka had committed suicide, Playter had fled to "parts unknown," another who testified against him was gored to death by an elk, and the hair had fallen off the back of the head of one of the attorneys of the "memoralists." To all this Ingalls commented, "The devil will claim his own."[42]

On February 17, 1880, two reports from the investigating committee were submitted to the Senate, a majority and a minority report. The majority report claimed that "the testimony taken by the committee proves that bribery and other corrupt means were employed by persons favoring the election of Hon. John J. Ingalls to the Senate to obtain for him votes of members of the Legislature of Kansas in the senatorial election in that State. But it is not proved by the testimony that enough votes were secured by such means to determine the result of the election in his favor, nor is it shown that Senator Ingalls authorized acts of bribery to secure his election." The majority report was submitted by Senators Eli Saulsbury of Delaware, chairman, Benjamin H. Hill of Georgia, Francis Kernan of New York, James E. Bailey of Tennessee, George S. Hareston of Alabama, and Zebulon B. Vance of North Carolina.

The minority report was submitted on the same day as the majority report, and it stated, "We concur in part of the report [the majority report]. We exonerate Mr. Ingalls from any complicity with improper practices. We also find that the result of the election was not accomplished by such practices. We think that, when the report goes further and finds that persons favoring Mr. Ingalls' election were guilty of such practices, it should in justice state what was clearly and unquestionably proved, that such means were employed in opposition of his election." The minority report was submitted by Angus Cameron of Wisconsin, John A. Logan of Illinois, and George F. Hoar of Massachusetts.[43]

Ingalls was not proved guilty of bribery or corruption, but his "vindication" was open to question. He had not suffered Pomeroy's fate of January, 1873, and though "bloody," he was not beaten. On March 6, 1880, Ingalls returned to Atchison to make what was supposed to be a conciliatory speech, in the hope that deep wounds within the Republican ranks would be bound up and would begin to heal. The speech was well advertised, and the railroads provided free transportation to those who wished to journey to Atchison from the surrounding area. The speech had been scheduled for Corinthian Hall, but the crowd was too great, and Ingalls agreed to address the throng, estimated at 10,000 persons, from the balcony of the old Otis House, later named the Byram Hotel. Instead of being conciliatory, as he had agreed to be, Ingalls lashed out at his recent antagonists, especially Albert H. Horton, and railed in his magnificent rhetoric for two hours. Although the crowd was surprised, it cannot be said that they were bored. Having vented his wrath, Ingalls calmly retired to the privacy of his home, relieved now that the "devil had received his due."[44] Ingalls' vigilance, coupled with the questionable veracity of his accusers, had been sufficient to exonerate him; and in his Otis House speech, Ingalls rhetorically laid his political enemies to rest!

8

SENATOR INGALLS
IN WAR PAINT

Although Ingalls had been "vindicated" of the charges of bribery and corruption, he began his second term in the Senate under a cloud of public suspicion and personal depression. He vented his wrath, not only on his personal enemies, but upon Atchison. In short, he was engaged in a private war. He did little by way of accomplishing anything for Atchison, and in fact appeared to be rolling "political plums" in the direction of other Kansas towns. In the spring of 1880, John A. Martin, editor of the Atchison *Daily Champion* and a perennial booster of that town, took it upon himself to write a "personal" letter to Ingalls inquiring into his inaction insofar as Atchison was concerned. The case in point concerned a public building via federal assistance, and Martin's query was simply, Why did not Atchison get this building? Martin came bluntly to the point and told Ingalls that he thought Ingalls was doing "this city [Atchison] and its people gross injustice in the criticisms you make upon it and them." Martin went on to say that he was not questioning Ingalls' loyalty to Atchison and pointed out that the town and its people had been conspicuously and faithfully loyal to him. Nevertheless he did criticize Ingalls by pointing out that he was being unfair to hold the community responsible for the acts of a few individuals. In support of this statement, Martin called attention to the fact that Ingalls had "much sincere friendship" in Atchison and that the *Champion* had continuously expressed its good will and its confidence in his vindication.[1]

The whole affair was no doubt as unpleasant to Ingalls as it was to those whom he had offended. On one occasion he had written that he would like to take a long sea voyage where he would not see a letter or paper for months. He confessed, however, that his private and public responsibilities would not permit this, and concluded that he would continue as usual.[2] The next political battle shaping up was the impending Presidential election of 1880. James A. Garfield, Ingalls' former college classmate and distant relative, had been nominated by the Republican convention that had convened in Chicago in June. Ingalls appraised Garfield as "rather mushy and lacking in spine," but quickly added that he thought he would be better than Hayes, who had earlier pledged not to run for a second term.[3] Ingalls also mentioned that he had been requested to campaign in several states, but had declined, claiming that he preferred to "stick to Kansas."[4] This may or may not be true considering the fact that Ingalls' own political fortunes had so recently been tarnished.

Garfield triumphed over his Democratic rival, Winfield S. Hancock, by a close popular vote but with a comfortable 214 to 155 electoral margin. His administration was barely under way when he was struck down by an assassin's bullet, and after lingering for weeks, he succumbed to his wounds and died on September 19, 1881. The death of Garfield left a profound impression on Ingalls, which found expression in a letter he wrote to his father. He described the "tragedy of July," the month Garfield was shot, and claimed that it seemed incredible that within three months "the chosen ruler of a great nation has been buried amid the grief of all the civilized world, and that the trial of his assassin was proceeding in sight of the capitol from which the remains of the victim were so lately borne to their last repose." And then, in almost caustic fashion, he stated that "the moralist and the philosopher might find abundant food for thought, nor could the cynic restrain his sneer at the spectacle presented by the thoughtless throng of ambitious aspirants who have so readily transferred their allegiance to the new President who sits in the Council Chamber so lately vacated by the dead." In mocking conclusion he wrote, "The emptiness of fame, the hollow mockery of friendship, the vanity of ambition, the ruthlessness of power, the insignificance of man never had a more striking illustration. 'The King is dead! Long live the King!' "[5] Nevertheless, Ingalls surmised that in spite of the "wretchedness of humanity and the evils of human life," there was something attractive about existence. He described the "good" things of life as taking place when the digestion was good, the nerves calm and steady, then it was pleasant "to eat a good dinner, to get a little drunk, to smoke a cigar, to talk with bright men and women, to drive in the woods, to stroll in the sun, to get into a row occasionally if you can be on top, to sleep and to wake, to play with children, to read good books, and wonder what life means, and to what it leads, how we got here and where we are going: a perplexing riddle which has not yet been solved."[6]

Ingalls did not even mention the perplexing problems festering within his own party. He considered himself a "Republican's Republican," but he never committed himself in the "Stalwart" and "Half-Breed" feud going on in the party. He was always an admirer of Blaine; based on this, then Ingalls would appear to lean towards the "Half-Breed" wing of the party. To confuse any conclusion that might be drawn here, however, is the fact that Ingalls also admired Chester A. Arthur, Garfield's successor, who was definitely a "Stalwart."

Ironically, Arthur's administration held the happiest memories for the entire Ingalls family. Ethel Ingalls wrote that President Arthur always felt that the White House should belong to the people, and thus Mrs. John J. Ingalls, as well as many others, had the privilege of showing her friends through the historic mansion at any time she wished, providing only that she notify the housekeeper of her coming.[7] President Arthur's sister, Mrs. Mary McElroy, was the official hostess and was known for her gracious manners and her "perfect dinners."[8] Ingalls personally admired Arthur, and once after calling on him at the executive mansion, he exclaimed, "What a splendid animal he is and what clothes he wears! It must be a luxury to be so handsome, high colored and strong."[9]

During the Arthur administration Ingalls gained increasing public attention. Not all of it proved favorable. His mastery of the art of sarcasm in debate made more enemies than friends, while creating a sense of awe in both. D. W. Wilder, editor of the Hiawatha *World*, once wrote him that "since Lane [Senator James Lane] died I suppose you and I have said more mean things than any other Christians in the State. We have thought that they were almighty keen, and so they were." And then, in a moment of sentimentality, Wilder concluded, "But one word of kindness is worth them all. I tip my beaver, and wish you all prosperity. 'Blue Grass' appears this week, and what an amazing essay it is! All Kansas in a chapter."[10] In debate, Ingalls had a way of drawing his enemies into a vulnerable position. The *Nation* commented on this by referring to a discussion going on in the Senate with regard to the "Chinese Bill." Senator James T. Farley of California had denounced the Chinese as "a horde of loathsome lepers." Ingalls simply asked, Why, if the Chinese were so repulsive, did the people of California insist on employing them? The *Nation* remarked that "the California

Senator found this a very hard question to answer."[11] Ingalls' taunts and his often vitriolic sarcasm became both his strengths and his weaknesses. He seldom took the middle ground. He was inclined to annihilate critics, whether friend or foe, and compromise in debate was to Ingalls a form of surrender. He developed the reputation of being a "cold," withdrawn person, and not without reason. He loved solitary rides or walks in the woods, where he was able to withdraw from the "natural enmities" of mankind. On one such solitary ride, which led him south from Atchison to the ruins of Sumner, he commented that he could not define "the subtle and exquisite pleasure which these lonely rides in the forest confer."[12] Once, just prior to making a speech in Ottawa, Kansas, he exclaimed, "I am scared and sick, wishing I were safely under the trees at Reresby [a wooded area south of Atchison]. You don't know how I suffer and in what misery I am. I was wishing all the morning that the train would run off and break my leg, or crush me into pulp, so that I could be taken home in a sack."[13] These comments appear to be needlessly morose, especially when it is considered that they were written to his wife whom he loved beyond question. Just a few months before, he had written to her claiming that she was "the best and bravest and noblest woman I ever knew! What *should* I have done had I been mated to one of these selfish, helpless, shallow creatures. . . . I shudder at the thought. . . . The longer I know you the more I appreciate you and you have had so much to endure! So much separation! So much heart ache and grief and desolate loneliness. Why have we been parted for an hour!"[14] Ingalls' fluctuating disposition and ultra sensitivity produced extremely divergent attitudes. He was either "up" or "down," he either loved or hated.

Politically, Ingalls could also be found on either extreme of those issues he cared to concern himself with. On one occasion the Senate was engaged in debate over the Desert Lands Bill, and Ingalls, quite properly, pointed out that the region under consideration was not desert as that term usually applies. He illustrated by declaring that these "desert" lands had for countless generations supported immense herds of bison, elk, antelope, and smaller animal life. He concluded his argument by referring to the Great Plains as a pastoral region, claiming that these plains should have been reserved as public domain to be used as the great pastoral region of the continent.[15] Ingalls is essentially repeating the argument of William Gilpin as to the potential of the Great Plains, but his extremism, if it can be called such, was his much-too-tardy argument that it should be the nation's "common pasture."

Civil-service reform was the political craze of the age, and in typical extremist form, Ingalls opposed it vehemently. Matthew Josephson, in commenting on the bill for civil-service reform, stated that both parties claimed credit for the act, except for a few candid voices, such as that of Senator Ingalls of Kansas. Josephson saw Ingalls as opposing it on the grounds that it was a "subterfuge through which each side hoped to cheat the other."[16] In a speech that Ingalls made at Williams College, as reported in the *New York Times*, he attacked civil-service reform as "un-American." The *Times* concluded its coverage by denouncing Ingalls, along with hostile critics of civil-service reform, for "gliding off into safe generalities."[17] In short, Ingalls was being accused of being emphatically opposed to a piece of legislation on generalities and not facts. A charge that was repeated frequently.

Ingalls' political "creed" is also very general, at least if you can believe the *Times*. The *Times*, purportedly quoting from a letter that Ingalls was supposed to have written to the Honorable J. Ambler Smith of Washington, D.C., and dated at Atchison, Kansas, on July 2, 1881, carried the following as a quotation from that letter: "I would say that my creed is simple. I believe in the universal diffusion of political rights, accompanied by sufficient guarantees for the protection of life, the security of property, and the preservation of personal liberty."[18] Whether the quotation is accurate or not, the fact remains that Ingalls was a political generalist, but then so were most politicians of that day, and this. His claim to political fame rested upon his brilliance as a political opponent. He was seldom an advocate of significant, constructive legislation. Perhaps this is explained in part by the fact that it is generally easier to oppose than it is to support, whatever the issue.

As a general rule, Ingalls held more men in contempt than in good stead, and one man who was particularly obnoxious to him was Senator Horace A. W. (Haw) Tabor, the "Colorado millionaire." Ingalls described Tabor in loathsome terms, claiming that a "fouler beast was never depicted. . . . Such a vulgar ruffianly boor you never beheld; uncouth, awkward, shambling, dirty hands and big feet turned inward: a huge solitaire diamond on a sooty bony black-smith finger: piratical features, unkempt, frowsy and unclean: blacked with disease—he looks the brute he is. He was stared at with curious but undisguised abhorence."[19] In the same communication he commented on other "fallen angels," pointing out that "Don" Cameron was going bad "at a hand gallop," with the added remark that he had been drunk for the past ten days and was approaching "delerium tremens." He named half a dozen others among his Senate colleagues, claiming that they were "inflamed or besotted with whiskey half the time." Such behavior prompted Ingalls to remark that he was not sure but what prohibition was "salutory" after all, even though he opposed it.[20]

One person who remained a steadfast friend of Ingalls', and definitely not to be counted among the "fallen angels" of the Washington social set, was Madeleine Vinton Dahlgren. She was the widow of the Swedish-American Admiral John Adolph Dahlgren of the United States Navy. He had invented the smooth-bore gun that bears his name, but which was more commonly called the "soda-water bottle" by people of that period. She befriended the entire Ingalls family and frequently had them as weekend guests at her summer home at Boonsboro, Maryland, which she called South Mountain House. She liked to invite "brilliant assemblages from the world of fashion, arts and sciences" to her home, and in such company Ingalls seemed to find pleasure.[21] Life afforded its brighter moments during these intervals, and at such times Ingalls was a charming, brilliant, and pleasant conversationalist, in sharp contrast to the image of him so frequently presented to the public and his public image, which became increasingly identified with his attacks upon his colleagues in the Senate. The *Nation* carried an almost blow-by-blow account of a verbal feud that Ingalls once had with Senator Joseph E. Brown of Georgia. Apparently Brown had inserted a sentence in the *Record* which changed the entire substance of the preceding debate between himself and Ingalls. Ingalls called this "falsifying and forgery" and claimed that "while he was perfectly willing to submit to the daily fortunes of debate, he wished to be secure from the 'Parthian arrows which a flying enemy may dispatch from the safe ambush of the printing office.'" He summarized his contempt for Brown by comparing him to a "thug stabbing a sleeping enemy,"[22] a "Uriah Heep of the Senate, as the Joseph Surface of American politics, as a sniveling political Pecksniff."[23]

If the foregoing appears to be strong language, it is only modest compared to the choice epithets Ingalls reserved for Governor John P. St. John of Kansas. The Republicans in 1884 nominated the "Plumed Knight," James G. Blaine. President Chester A. Arthur, the "Stalwart," had been unacceptable to the Republican nominating convention. This filled the Ingalls family with mixed emotions, for they considered both men as close personal friends. In the meantime, Governor St. John became the candidate of the Prohibition party, Benjamin F. Butler was the Greenback-Labor candidate, and the Democrats nominated Grover Cleveland. The contest was extremely close, with Cleveland winning in the electoral college by 219 votes to 182 for Blaine. In the popular-vote column, Cleveland had only 29,214 more votes than Blaine, out of more than 9,729,000 votes cast. Butler polled 175,370 votes, while St. John polled 150,369 votes. A slight shift, amounting to no more than six hundred votes, would have pulled New York State's electoral votes from Cleveland to Blaine. Ingalls never forgave St. John for "defecting" from the Republican party and claimed that "had the Republican votes cast for St. John been given to Blaine, he would have been elected in 1884.[24] He elucidated further on St. John's character by stating that he had, since the election, lived without labor and acquired wealth with no visible means of support other than serving as an "apostle of temperance" and the enemy of railroads. Ingalls concluded that there was no conclusive evidence that St. John "had thirty pieces of silver, but it shifts the burden of proof."[25]

The campaign had been degenerative in many respects. The "Mulligan letters," of 1876, shed unfavorable light on Blaine's questionable business dealings while serving as Speaker of the House, and the Democrats made political hay with them. The Republicans countered with the charge that Cleveland had fathered an illegitimate child, which Cleveland admitted. The "fatal" infamy of the campaign, however, was when the Reverend Samuel D. Burchard referred to the Democratic party as the party of "Rum, Romanism, and Rebellion." Many attribute this statement, which was not refuted by Blaine, as the reason that Blaine lost New York state, which was the Irish-American stronghold. Blaine later conceded that this cost him the election; however, Ingalls preferred to release his "Parthian arrows" at St. John of Kansas and to place the blame on him. Regardless of who took the blame for the defeat of Blaine, it could not efface the fact that Ingalls would soon be serving under a Democratic chief executive. In Ingalls' eyes the Confederates had captured the nation's capital.

9

FROM POLITICAL TRIUMPH TO A "TURNIP CRUSADE": THE THIRD AND FINAL TERM

Ingalls' immediate political fortunes brightened with his reelection to the Senate for a third term without the serious difficulties of his preceding election in 1879. He remained in Washington while the balloting took place in Topeka, and on January 27, 1885, his wife telegraphed him the news of his victory. Ingalls immediately responded, writing that his first emotion upon hearing the news was a feeling of "devout and reverential gratitude to the Great Being that had so strongly guided and directed" his footsteps. He thanked this "Great Being" for guarding and protecting him from the "machinations" of his enemies, from the consequences of his own sins and errors, and from evil passions, so that he could once more attain "this great and unprecedented honor, almost without effort, device or contrivance." Ingalls' delight in his victory was not altogether selfish, for he expressed an understanding of how much this must please Lou, his wife. He concluded that his "unchallenged" victory was a blessing for their children, who would now be able to say that Kansans had refuted the former accusations made against their father.[1] His success at Topeka was the result of a joint effort, for it was Lou who managed his canvass there. He praised her efforts in his behalf and humorously concluded with the comment "I fear you must be intending to set up for yourself in politics!"[2]

The enthusiasm generated by his election to a third term must have prompted Ingalls to exaggerate a bit in a speech he made at a commencement exercise in 1885.[3] In his address he claimed that among all the acknowledged leaders of the past quarter-century, none was favored by birth or fortune. He referred to Lincoln the rail-splitter, Grant the tanner, Vice-President Henry Wilson the shoemaker, Garfield the canal boy, and then named Thaddeus Stevens and "Phil" Sheridan, with the claim that "all sprang from obscurity to renown." In summary he stated that "the gilded youth of 1885" would not be the leaders and rulers of the Republic in the next century. Such leaders, he said, "will come from the field, the farm, the workshops." It is difficult to understand Ingalls' intent at this point, for if he was addressing a college class, obviously they would not be the "rail splitters—tanners—shoemakers" and such, whom Ingalls looked to for leadership in the next century. Also, if the road to success as a national figure was to be found in the meek and lowly tasks of life, why was Ingalls so insistent that his own children secure a college education and shun the "base" and mean tasks in life? It seems apparent that Ingalls was making use of hyperbole, a device he frequently employed to move his listeners.

In spite of Ingalls' elation over his own election, the inauguration of the Democrat Grover Cleveland cast shadows over his personal triumph. Ingalls viewed the election of a Democratic President as being comparable to Jefferson Davis taking the Confederate oath of office on the Capitol steps in Washington. Nevertheless, he attended the inaugural ceremonies and described the proceedings to his wife on the following day. "Cleveland was inaugurated yesterday with no cosmic convulsions so far as I can discern," he remarked. "The earth continues its revolutions and the elements are undisturbed," adding, "Cleveland has a hard mug. He looks like a tough citizen who has left off drinking none too soon. His visage is scarred and seamed by the passions and not by thought." Ingalls conceded, however, that Cleveland was a "strong, self-poised, confident man, with evident complacency in his demeanor, who will do as he pleases with little regard for the consequences either to himself or others." In commenting on Cleveland's inaugural address, Ingalls pointed out that he used no manuscript, having only a small slip of paper concealed in his hand, "about as big as a visiting card," and on this were "catch-words." Cleveland's ability to speak in this manner, "without hesitation" and in such a presence, was an indication to Ingalls that Cleveland possessed both intellectual power and discipline.[4]

Cleveland's inauguration was, in effect, the battle cry for Ingalls to attack this man "possessing every acknowledged disqualification" for the Presidency, a statement he was later to have printed and publicly circulated. The first year of Cleveland's administration was relatively peaceful, insofar as Ingalls was concerned, but by March of 1886 the antagonists had begun to parry. With respect to domestic issues there was the problem of what to do with the growing surplus in the Treasury. Ingalls generally regarded such monies as useful in making "patronage payments" to Union Civil War veterans. During his eighteen years in the Senate, Ingalls introduced hundreds of private pension bills and several public pension bills. Patriotism, and particularly party loyalty, were characteristics Ingalls generously rewarded. This issue would generate into a major political battle before Cleveland's term was out, and he and Ingalls would soon prove to be diametrically opposed as the crisis peaked. In the course of this controversy, Ingalls attacked General John C. Black, the Pension Commissioner, for impeding the passage of private pension bills. This charge was only the beginning. He went on to accuse Black of securing for himself a $100-a-month pension which he did not deserve. However, Ingalls was reminded by Senator Vorhees that the pension to Black was granted while Ingalls was serving as the Senate chairman of the Committee on Pensions. Ingalls responded to this by claiming that Black's claim was now known to be fraudulent. Ingalls declared that only deserving soldiers should be pensioned and that Black was woefully lacking in this respect.[5] This kind of exchange was not uncommon and frequently degenerated into a mutual name-calling contest, as exemplified by the following: The Senate was debating an oleomargarine bill, and Senator Miller of New York slandered Ingalls by referring to him as a "peddler of quack medicines at a country fair." Ingalls replied in kind and more.[6]

Cleveland, however, in a gesture of political peace-making, apparently tried to curry Ingalls' favor, and on March 6, 1886, he sent Ingalls a note asking his opinion concerning the postmaster's job in Atchison. Both H. Clay Park and W. W. Cochrane were under consideration, and Cleveland asked Ingalls if he had a choice between the two. Ingalls ignored Cleveland's courtesy, and shortly thereafter he attacked Cleveland in his famous, or infamous, "Mugwump" speech.[7] Mrs. Ingalls later claimed that in her opinion, her husband made a fatal political mistake when he delivered his attack on Cleveland. She pleaded with him not to, but he ignored her counsel. Later she claimed to believe that it was one of the causes of his defeat in the Senate. As far as she knew, there was no provocation for Ingalls' vicious attack.[8] It seems that the fact that Cleveland was a Democrat was actually in itself provocation enough. An interesting incident, however, may also be associated with Ingalls' animosity towards Cleveland. The story is related by Mrs. Ingalls that Marion, their six-year-old daughter, became very fond of President Arthur, and when the Republicans refused to nominate him for President in 1884, she claimed that she "was no longer a 'Publican' but had gone over to the Democrats."[9] After his election Cleveland learned of this incident and invited Mrs. Ingalls and Marion to call on him at the White House, which they did. In the course of this visit with Cleveland, Marion's "conversion" to the Democratic party was discussed. Mrs. Ingalls pointed out that Marion was only a child. "All the better," replied Cleveland. "When she grows up she will probably lead some fine young man in the right path." Marion had been out of the room during this portion of the conversation, but now at Cleveland's request she was brought into the room. Cleveland kissed her, and since it was February 10, and near Valentine's Day, he gave her the prettiest valentine he had. Marion soon grew as fond of Cleveland as she had been of Chester A. Arthur, and she promptly named her cat Grover.[10] The next day Cleveland wrote a personal letter to Mrs. Ingalls, enclosing his official calling card for Marion, which had a picture of the Executive Mansion and was personally autographed. The letter itself expressed Cleveland's feelings: "Hoping that in spite of her good mother, it may tend to confirm her in the democratic faith. I am yours sincerely, Grover Cleveland."[11]

Cleveland's encouragement must have borne fruit, for Marion remained a Democrat from that day on, a fact that Ingalls never graciously accepted. It was shortly after this interview that Ingalls delivered his "Mugwump" attack on Cleveland from the Senate floor.[12] The attack was centered on Cleveland's plan for civil-service reform, nevertheless Cleveland was the real target of Ingalls' verbal blast. Ingalls denounced the entire Democratic platform, claiming that "their Shibboleth is civil service reform."[13] Then warming to his task, Ingalls went on to add that, "These political epicenes, without pride of ancestry or hope of posterity, chant in shrill falsetto their songs of praise of nonpartisanship and civil service reform, and apparently have been selected as the harmless custodians of the conscience of the national Executive."[14] In summarizing his reasons for opposing civil-service reform, Ingalls argued that the Republicans and Democrats had always acted upon the principle that the party in power should control appointive offices. Ingalls believed that this was a good policy, as those who did not hew to a party were "canting parasites." Finally, he used Cleveland as a poor example to push for civil-service reform, claiming that Cleveland did not get interested in this "reform movement" until after he had distributed patronage.[15] In defense of Cleveland, it would hardly have been possible for him to have done otherwise, for the appointments to office could not wait the one, two, or more years it might have taken to get such a measure through Congress.

Following Ingalls' attack on Cleveland, the *Nation* published an article entitled "Offensive Partisanship." The article denounced Ingalls' "blind partisanship" and his use of such terms as "eunuchs" as being uncalled for. The *Nation* predicted that if the Republican party hoped to return to power, "it will not be done by ridiculing reform, and by solemnly resolving to vote for the devil if he be regularly nominated, but by recovering the ancient Republican respect for political liberty and independence." *Harper's Weekly* also carried a caricature of Ingalls, entitling it "The Personification of Manliness and an august body of the United States Senate." A note beneath the picture concluded, "His speech would have been more appropriate for one of their secret sessions."[16]

In spite of his attack on Cleveland in March, in June of 1886 Ingalls was invited, via a personal note from Cleveland, to attend a White House reception. Not to be "outdone in courtesy," Ingalls went and claimed that he was "invited behind the throne," but declined. He noted Cleveland's appearance with the remark: "Poor Cleveland mopped himself incessantly and the perspiration ran down his mustache like the ointment down Aaron's beard."[17] In spite of this courtesy, Ingalls did not stop his attacks on Cleveland, in fact he intensified them.

Although he received a bad press occasionally, Ingalls was mentioned, along with Senator George F. Hoar, as a leading candidate for the position of president pro tem of the Senate. The position meant an increase in salary from $5,000 to $8,000 per year, and both Senators were eager for the prize. Although the *Times* had been critical of Ingalls, it conceded that he would be a good choice, primarily because he had "a voice that can be heard in every nook and cranny of the chamber."[18] In the next issue, the *Times* declared Ingalls to be the more "progressive" of the two. Apparently the Senate concurred, for Ingalls won rather handily. The *Times* summarized by claiming that Ingalls could do the job well enough, but closed by inferring that no one really cared.[19]

Ingalls claimed that he had been hesitant about accepting the nomination, but had consented, realizing that such an honor would be "a good reply" to all those who in the past had been critical of his prowess as a Senator, especially the Topeka *Capital*.[20] Then, too, he was replacing the influential Senator John Sherman, whose term in the Senate was to expire on March 4, 1887. Sherman's resignation as president pro tem took effect at 1 P.M. on the twenty-sixth of February, with Ingalls becoming his successor in that office immediately after the resignation.

The position of honor that he now held came in spite of the fact that he had once more launched a scathing attack on Cleveland. He claimed that "the nomination and election of Grover Cleveland have made the pretensions of any American citizen to the Presidency respectable." Speaking specifically of Cleveland, he went on to say, "There is no man in this country whose ignorance is so profound, whose obscurity is so impenetrable, and whose antecedents are so degraded that he may not justifiably aspire to a Presidential nomination—by the Democratic party."[21] This vitriolic attack came just one month and three days after Mrs. Ingalls had received a gracious note from Mrs. Cleveland, asking for her assistance at a White House reception, and it was deeply embarrassing to Mrs. Ingalls.[22]

Ingalls' feud with Cleveland was probably as costly to himself as it was to the Democratic President. It consumed both his time and energy, and at the conclusion of a session of Congress in February, 1887, he wrote his wife that the end of a Congressional session was always depressing to him, "as I recall how little I have done compared with what I had hoped to accomplish and how swiftly and inexorably my life is vanishing away."[23] Ingalls spoke these repentant words at a time when his political career was approaching its climax.

In 1887 the Irish question was being debated in the United States at large and also at the local level. In Kansas, Chase County was the scene of considerable oratory concerning the overall Irish question, that is, rent reform, land reforms, and home rule. In 1884 the Irish settlers of Chase County organized a Robert Emmet Club, which met annually until 1891. Kansas politicians found it expedient to make ingratiating speeches to local ethnic settlements, and Frank Doster, a young attorney from Marion, Kansas, addressed the local chapter of the Irish National League of Chase County on December 10, 1885. Doster was later to become a leading Populist spokesman.

In 1887 the local Irish league secured the speaking services of "an exile's daughter," Mrs. Mary Elizabeth Lease, who gained fame for admonishing farmers to raise more Hell and less corn. She did so well that a repeat performance was requested, and on March 4,

1887, she addressed the Emmet Day celebration in Chase County. She was hailed as the leading woman orator of America.[24] On April 12, 1887, an Irish anticoercion meeting was held in Topeka. Several public figures made addresses, including Ingalls. In November another such state meeting was held, again in Topeka, and this time it was presided over by Chief Justice Albert H. Horton, Ingalls' intraparty nemesis. Ironically, people of differing political positions found themselves united on the Irish question, at least at the state and local levels. Even Ingalls and Lease were united on this question, and the old axiom that politics makes strange bedfellows was never more aptly demonstrated. Ingalls, however, was always ready to twist the "Lion's tail" and did so again in a speech contained in the *Congressional Record*. He referred to England as a "ruffian and coward, and the bully among the nations of the earth" and much more. All of this was said in consequence of the seizure of American vessels by the British as a result of Cleveland's termination of the Canadian fisheries feature of the 1870 Treaty of Washington. Ingalls had proposed coastal defenses as a first line of defense against any naval threat from England.[25] Although his defense scheme was subject to criticism, he was praised for his anti-British stand by Mrs. Lease and was commended by both houses of the Kansas legislature.[26] But in spite of praise and commendation, Ingalls did not propose the kind of constructive legislation that both he and his critics seemed to desire. His role persisted along the old partisan political paths—attack your enemies, at home and abroad, and appease your constituency.

By the fall of 1887, Ingalls was a nationally known figure and was styled famous or infamous, depending on one's politics and general point of view. Ingalls gained additional notoriety in an article that he wrote for *The Forum*, which was published in the September, 1887, issue under the title "The Sixteenth Amendment." Ingalls had never favored woman suffrage, and in this article he set down some of the reasons for his objections. He argued first that suffrage was not a "natural right" and that the question was not one of "intelligence or morals," but that suffrage was a privilege. Taking a page from Thomas Hobbes's *Leviathan*, Ingalls claimed that all government rested ultimately on force and that "the state had always confided control and direction of its powers to those who could enforce its decrees." His logic was simply that women, who were the "weaker sex," should not be permitted to enact laws that they would be unable to enforce. This was a poor argument, so far as the women were concerned, and especially for Susan B. Anthony. Earlier, after a suffrage bill was killed in the Senate, Ingalls remarked, "Miss

Anthony I understand is particularly malevolent toward me, though I did not say one word in the debate, and announces that she intends to canvass every legislative district in Kansas to prevent my return to the Senate!"[27]

In pressing his opposition to female suffrage, Ingalls went on to add that Thomas Jefferson was mistaken in believing that numbers should prevail against "intelligence, duty and justice," and claimed further that Jefferson "had no conception of the moral forces which give a nation strength, duration, and grandeur." In elaborating even further, Ingalls termed the Declaration of Independence a piece of "fallacious rhetoric." In regard to the late Civil War, Ingalls declared that the South had been "logical" in its political stance, "but force was ultimately right." This is, obviously, just another way of saying that might is right, but how Ingalls was able to assume that "might" embraced "intelligence, duty and justice" remains a moot question. In summarizing, Ingalls claimed that politics were "the metaphysics of force." He also claimed that by 1900 the nation's "surplus population, no longer having the fertile area of free land over which to diffuse itself," would accumulate in cities. The rich, he predicted, would become richer and the poor become poorer, and eventually the "middle class" would disappear. Using a quasi-Darwinian theme, he closed his argument by claiming that "there is no legislation that can annul the ordinances of nature, or abrogate the statutes of the Almighty."[28]

Ingalls' article posed many difficulties. How could he be so opposed to female suffrage, while at the same time being a champion of Negro suffrage? Why was one a "natural right" and the other an "abrogation of the statutes of the Almighty?" Or how could Ingalls endorse a representative form of government, based on universal white-male suffrage, when in truth he was echoing phrases from Hobbes and from Tacitus, who believed in a government of senatorial aristocracy? All of these inconsistencies only point up the often-frustrated, crossed-purpose thinking which so frequently characterized Ingalls, not only in political matters, but also in economics and theology as well. This article, in large measure, provided ammunition for his political enemies. On August 30, 1888, the "Union Labor State Platform" was printed in the Topeka *Daily Capital*. Section ten of that platform contained a denunciation of Ingalls' philosophy of government, "That the just powers of the government are not derived from the consent of the governed but rest upon force." The platform claimed that Ingalls' views on government were "treason to our republic," and concluded further that "John J. Ingalls [was] a traitor unfit to represent the state of Kansas." Such complaints were to become more frequent as Ingalls' third term in the Senate began drawing to a close.

Once more Ingalls turned his attention to Cleveland. One particular feature of Cleveland's policies that Ingalls detested was his lower tariff proposals. Ingalls claimed to believe that Cleveland was dead wrong in this policy and that if it were adopted, the American laboring man would suffer. He promised that it would be a major issue in the Presidential campaign of 1888, and in this respect he was most certainly correct.[29]

The most vicious of all Ingalls' statements about Cleveland were yet to come; these appeared in the June, 1888, issue of the *North American Review*. The Ingalls article was entitled "Fetichism in the Campaign." Cleveland was thoroughly castigated. "He has no perceptible connection with the category of accidents to which his elevation is due," wrote Ingalls, and he claimed that Cleveland's enjoyments "were those which are found in the unrestrained indulgence of the appetites and passions, and his chosen associates were the companions of his orgies." Finally Ingalls referred to Cleveland as a "vacant mass," but conceded that his election was actually good for the nation, for it had proved to the people their capacity for self-government.[30] In conclusion, Ingalls plead for Negro suffrage, particularly in the South, a theme that he was to intensify in his remaining time as Senator.

In spite of Ingalls' hostility toward Cleveland, he was friendly to some members of Cleveland's cabinet, particularly Thomas Bayard, Secretary of State, and William C. Endicott, Secretary of War. Even among these friends, however, Ingalls could not resist making use of his verbal barbs. On one occasion they were having lunch together at Harvey's fish house in Washington, D.C., and were engaged in eating oysters. Bayard remarked that oysters were good brain food and that they were gathered by the bushel in Delaware. "You don't grow any in Kansas do you?" he asked. "No," replied Ingalls, "I suppose they grow only where they are most needed."[31] After leaving the Senate, Ingalls revised Luther Stearn Cushing's book entitled *Manual of Parliamentary Practice*, a more tangible result of his long career as a Senator, and something quite apart from his sarcasm.[32]

A tragedy which struck Ingalls a severe blow was the destruction of his home in Atchison by a mysterious fire in January of 1888. W. A. Croffut, a Washington neighbor of Ingalls', described the Senator's reaction to the news that his home was destroyed. He claimed that Ingalls remained calm upon receiving the news at a Senate committee meeting, and that he silently folded up the dispatch, placed it in his pocket, and went on about the business at hand. He also described Mrs. Ingalls' reaction, quoting her as saying from behind a smile, "I do not say, like the defeated General, 'all is lost save honor,' but when I look around on my seven children and my husband all alive and well, I do feel like saying with something of a sense of triumph, 'all is not lost by a good deal.'"[33] Croffut claimed that Ingalls lost 15,000 books, which comprised his personal library, besides valuable papers and autograph letters from distinguished men and women.

Carrie Mize, an Atchison friend of the Ingallses' wrote of the fire, stating that some books were saved as well as some furniture and that all the pictures were saved, plus many of the children's things. Mrs. Mize summarized with a description of what remained: "Only the tall chimneys like mournful sentinels looking down on the ruins of one of the hightest [sic] homes I ever knew. . . . Your desk was saved, and I believe papers saved."[34] When Ingalls returned to the ruins of his home, he described the scene as follows: "Peter was raking the lower drive as I approached the ruins of our home and the sun shone through the dim mist upon the azure bluffs and the shining river, as though earth had never known a tragedy nor human life a woe."[35] After the fire, Ingalls purchased the Oak Ridge house in southwest Atchison upon his wife's recommendation, as Ingalls himself had not inspected the premises prior to its purchase.[36]

Shortly after the loss of his home, Ingalls launched an attack on Senator Daniel W. Vorhees of Indiana and thus added to the ignominious reputation he could never completely escape. It is interesting to notice that Ingalls became verbally volatile after almost every personal frustration. Ingalls had been arguing for the dependents' pension bill which many Democrats opposed. In his discourse he denounced a number of Democrats, including General George B. McClellan, who was the Democratic Presidential nominee in 1864. Ingalls cited McClellan's claim that the Civil War was a failure, and then said that if this were so, it was because McClellan had spent two years trying to make it so. Some time after his attack on McClellan, Ingalls was called from the Senate chamber on business, and while he was absent, Senator Vorhees denounced Ingalls for attacking McClellan. Ingalls learned of this in the newspaper the next day, April 26, 1888. Shortly thereafter Ingalls announced that he would make a reply to Vorhees on May 1. On the specified date Ingalls delivered a speech which lasted for two hours. Among other things, Ingalls claimed that "all guerillas and bushwhackers, the men from the Union States who entered the Confederate service for plunder—in war cuthroats, in peace horsethieves—were Democrats." When Ingalls concluded, Vorhees rose and taunted Ingalls' sparse war record and likened him to "a mountain which labored and brought forth a mouse." He went on to claim that Ingalls was "politically dead and was walking around to save funeral expenses," and concluded that Ingalls had been born with "inaccuracy marked upon him."

When Vorhees sat down, Ingalls rose to reply. He first apologized for his "inconspicuous and obscure" war record, but reminded his listeners that however feeble those efforts might have been, they were always on the side of the Union. He then produced a letter written by Vorhees to a Confederate brigadier general, in which Vorhees had recommended a Mr. Francis Sharp for an appointment as a brigadier general in the Confederate Army. The letter stated, "I take this occasion to say that his sentiments and my own are in close harmony." The disclosure of this letter, and its public reading, struck Vorhees like a bolt of lightning. He was unable to regain his composure and was led from the chamber mumbling, "The dirty dog, the dirty dog."[37]

Some time after this episode, Ingalls wrote to his wife complaining that he was "always vexed about the Vorhees incident." He claimed that he regarded it as one of the "least creditable" actions in his career and that it was remembered more than any other thing he had done. Ingalls concluded that "all the good work I tried to do is forgotten and that discreditable event is preserved."[38] And, indeed, the Vorhees event did stamp a stereotype upon Ingalls as a man of mean scruples. Ingalls' sarcasm and vindictive nature, which characterized his public life, is revealed again in a comment he once made to Senator Don Cameron of Pennsylvania. Cameron had made some critical remarks about Ingalls, and in retaliation Ingalls replied that there had been but two great men from Pennsylvania, Albert Gallatin from Switzerland and Benjamin Franklin from Massachusetts. Cameron fell into silence.[39]

Regardless of a rising tide of criticism, Ingalls' name began to be mentioned as a possible Presidential candidate for 1888. As early as March of that year, Ingalls wrote his close friend P. I. Bonebrake, claiming that the mention of his name as a candidate had been "wholly involuntary." Ingalls claimed that he had taken no part in instigating such a move, although he conceded that he would "appreciate the honor." At the same time he stated that he had no desire to be President, nor did he expect that he ever would be. Nevertheless, he hoped that the Republican convention would "go in any direction that may be thought best after full and free conference with an interchange of opinion."[40] From February of 1887 through

June of 1888, newspapers such as the Washington *Post,* the New York *Sun,* the Topeka *Commonwealth,* and a whole host of smaller Kansas newspapers discussed Ingalls' potential candidacy at the impending nominating convention.[41] Eugene F. Ware even telegraphed Ingalls a rather strange endorsement which read, "If anything should happen to that man that has that neck, the people of the country will observe that you're on deck."[42] The man with "that neck" was not identified. When the Republican nominating convention actually got under way in Chicago in June of 1888, Ingalls referred to the proceedings from Washington, D.C., where he had remained, and remarked that he supposed Marion (his seven-year-old Democratic daughter) probably did not care to know what was going on in a "Republican Convention."[43]

Ingalls did not figure as a prominent contender for the nomination at Chicago, which was obtained by Benjamin Harrison. In commenting on the behind-the-scenes struggle that had taken place at the convention, Ingalls told of John Sherman's disappointment at not securing the nomination. He related how Sherman had called on him in the Vice-President's chamber and had confided to him that New York and Pennsylvania had agreed to support him after two ballots for Harrison had been taken. Ingalls pointed out, however, that Harrison had risen too fast and that Sherman's last chance was gone, for at his age there would be no other opportunity.[44] Although Ingalls made no comment concerning his own disappointment at not receiving the nomination, Mrs. Ingalls wrote her husband, expressing relief that he had not been nominated and claiming that she feared the Republicans would march to "sure defeat." She commented that the "times are all out of joint" and encouraged her husband to arouse a little bit of the "old enthusiasm" by becoming active in the campaign.[45] The very next day she once more expressed relief that Ingalls had not been nominated and rejoiced that Blaine and Sherman were "snowed under." Apparently her former "love" for Blaine had grown cold. In conclusion, she claimed that she aspired to no higher office for her husband than the one he held, for "representing Kansas in the Senate is honor enough," she exclaimed.[46]

Prior to the November elections, Ingalls was interviewed by Blakely Hall of the New York *Sun.* Ingalls was pleasantly surprised both at Hall's complimentary remarks about him and the striking appearance that Hall presented. In all, Ingalls regarded it quite an honor to be interviewed by a man who had interviewed "Bismarck, Gladstone, and all the great English and American Statesmen."[47] In the same communication, so filled with praise for Hall, Ingalls verbally poked at one of his favorite targets, Grover Cleveland, commenting that "both parties are afraid of each other and of Cleveland, though it would seem as if his capacity for mischief was exhausted."

In order to assist in ending Cleveland's "mischief," Ingalls was promptly at the polls in Atchison on November 4 to cast his vote for Harrison. While waiting to do so, his vote was challenged by Ben Early, who claimed that Ingalls was no longer a resident of Atchison, since he had not been in town since the previous Christmas, and since his home having burned, he had no residence he could claim in Atchison. Ingalls reported that no doubt Early had been "set on by the Guthrie gang," but that there was a general clamor of protests at Early's action by the citizens who were standing by and that Early finally withdrew his protest as a result of the taunts from those present, who shouted "shame!"[48]

After Harrison's narrow margin of victory in November, Ingalls wrote E. A. Augier, claiming that the Republican administration would be delinquent if it did not insist on the equality of all citizens before the law, and "demand explicit and conclusive assurances of justice." Ingalls claimed to believe that the election of Harrison was a mandate for civil-rights guarantees for all citizens and that unless such a policy were pursued by the Harrison administration, the Republican triumph would be "empty and barren."[49] This statement is in keeping with Ingalls' earlier civil-rights stance, however the closeness of Harrison's win may have prompted a new burst of enthusiasm for civil rights in order to assure that next time there would be more registered Republican voters.

A few weeks before Harrison's inauguration, Mrs. Ingalls also took it upon herself to offer a suggestion to the incoming administration. She wrote a short letter to Harrison, expressing an interest in who was to be appointed Commissioner of Pensions. In short, she asked that the appointment be given to a Kansas man, for Kansas—who had an "eighty-two thousand Republican majority—should receive some recognition, and then *too*," she added, "she is known as the soldier state." Mrs. Ingalls claimed that this was a suggestion rather than a request and was made "entirely *on my own* account." In a final appeal she stated her belief that the Harrison administration would "be a blessing to our country."[50] *Harper's Weekly* concluded otherwise, and in an article entitled "The Drift of Parties," claimed that the despotism of the Republican party was absolute; among the conspicuous representatives of corruption and despotism they named Ingalls and half a dozen other well known Republican leaders.[51] The following month *Harper's Weekly* again denounced the Republican party and with it Ingalls, lamenting that the Republican party used to be "'the party of great moral ideas'" but that this was no longer true.[52] It is doubtful that the barbs of *Harper's Weekly* prompted Ingalls to launch a moral crusade; nevertheless, the fact remains that on January 23, 1890, Ingalls delivered one of his more-famous Senate speeches, which was entitled "Fiat Justitia." The speech grew out of a debate over a bill introduced by M. C. Butler of South Carolina (Negro Deportation Bill S-1121), which provided that any Negro person from any Southern state could move anywhere in the United States at the expense of the Federal government. A sum of five million dollars was to be set aside for this purpose. Ingalls saw this as a Southern conspiracy to remove the Negro from the South by a program of "voluntary" migration. He protested strongly and argued that this was not the solution to the Negro question. Ingalls claimed that the solution lay in the South extending the vote to the Negro and allowing the Negro the opportunity for self-improvement. "Mr. President," said Ingalls, "I confess with humiliation that to this nullification of the Constitution, to this abrogation of the social compact, to this breach of plighted faith, this violation of the natural rights of man, the people of the North have apparently consented. . . . The word of promise that was given them [Negroes] by the North has not been kept." In summary, Ingalls appealed to the South to "try the experiment of justice. Stack your guns, open your ballot-boxes, register your voters, black and white," he exclaimed, "and if, after the experiment has been fairly and honestly tried, it appears that the African race is incapable of civilization, if it appears that the complexion burned upon him by a tropic sun is incompatible with freedom, I pledge myself to consult with you about some measure of solving the race problem; but until then nothing can be done."[53] No doubt Ingalls had political interests in mind, but he also held a genuine esteem for the Negro people. This does not mean, however, that he regarded them as racial, social, or political equals.

Although *Harper's Weekly* had called for a moral crusade by the Republicans, in Kansas there was a different plea. In a series of articles published in the Topeka *Daily Capital*, Ingalls was roundly denounced because he was not doing anything for the farmers.[54] While Ingalls was being denounced by the *Daily Capital*, he was almost simultaneously being honored by the Senate; and on March 12, 1890, he wrote that "the Senate decided that my office of President pro tem is permanent until another is elected."[55] A few days later Ingalls offered an amendment to the Sherman Anti-Trust Bill, then under consideration. His amendment was designed to curb "futures" and "options," however the amendment proved to be a virtual copy of an amendment that had been introduced earlier in the House by Representative Benjamin Butterworth of Ohio. Ingalls attempted to explain away this rather embarrassing predicament by explaining that Butterworth's amendment "seemed to me to carry out more clearly and more accurately and more thoroughly than anything I had seen the purposes I had in view."[56] Ingalls' amendment failed to carry. It was probably a political device to appease the agrarian forces then gathering strength, but it was of no avail.

At the time that Ingalls' "political pot" was virtually boiling, for good or bad, he granted the now-famous photographic interview to the New York *World* on April 30, 1890. In the course of this interview, Ingalls claimed that "the purification of politics is an iridescent dream. Government is force. Politics is a battle for supremacy. Parties are the armies. The Decalogue and the Golden Rule have no place in a political campaign. The object is success. To defeat the antagonist and expel the party in power is the purpose." After comparing political leaders with army generals, Ingalls went on to add that "the commander who lost the battle through the activity of his moral nature would be the derision and jest of history."[57] In conclusion, he claimed that the "modern cant" about political corruption proceeded from "tea-custard and syllabub dilettanteism and frivolous sentimentalism." The public response was immediate and angry, perhaps because Ingalls' statements on politics were so widely circulated. Actually in substance Ingalls' remarks were essentially the same as those he made in his article "The Sixteenth Amendment," which was published in the *Forum* in 1887. Discontent with Ingalls was gaining momentum. Populism was on the horizon, Ingalls' third term was drawing to a close, and the Farmers' Alliance forces were determined that it would be his last.

The nation was approaching its "awkward age." It was straddling a transitional fence in the process of changing from an agrarian society to the urban-industrial America of today. There was more at stake than just politics and power or economics. The changing face of America was contorted by the agonizing struggle for a particular way of life. Grangers and Alliance members, in short, the Midwestern and Southern farmers of the nation, gave birth to one of America's epic third-party movements. In May of 1891, in Cincinnati, Ohio, "The Peoples Party" was born and baptized. Laborers were included among its ranks, but it was primarily an agrarian political crusade that reached its climax when many of its principles were fused with those of the Democratic party, most notably under the leadership of the "Great Commoner," William Jennings Bryan, of Illinois and Nebraska.

Some see this struggle in Marxist class-struggle terms, however, this seems to overcomplicate the real problem. Rural America's way of life was being threatened by the new technology and by the urban-corporate forces that wielded increasing political and economic power. Farmers did not understand the new economics, and neither did Ingalls. Farmers wanted their way of life represented, and Ingalls was accused of representing the very forces that the farmers feared.

About this time the *Times* printed an article accusing Ingalls of plagiarism. It had picked up its story from the Baltimore *Sun* of January 27, 1890. The *Sun* story claimed that Ingalls' "Fiat Justitia" speech had been plagiarized from John Philpot Curran, being taken from page 163 of a book entitled *Justice and Jurisprudence*. There is reason to believe that there could be substance to the report. In checking through personal papers of Ingalls, one finds speeches clipped from magazines or newspapers, in which names and places are crossed out and Kansas names or places, usually, inked or penciled in. Assuming that Ingalls delivered these "speeches," then certainly he was guilty of plagiarism on occasion.[58] All these factors combined to work to the detriment of Ingalls' future political prospects. The Kansas Democratic platform devoted article eleven to the *World* interview, denouncing the "iridescent dream" speech, in general, and Ingalls, in particular.[59] Also the *Nation* denounced Ingalls' "iridescent dream" speech and its implication that this constituted the proper moral code of ethics for American politics.[60] As the criticisms mounted against him, Ingalls became increasingly cognizant of them. His first reference to the possibility of his "retirement" from the Senate was contained in a letter written to his wife on July 4, 1890: "Should I retire from public life," he wrote, with reference to their cost of living, "it will not cost so much and we can be quite comfortable."[61] In August of the same year, Ingalls wrote to his close friend P. I. Bonebrake, commenting that the Republican prospects were poor but not hopeless. He referred to the Farmers' Alliance as the "enemy" and claimed that its strength was unknown —"a secret organization based upon discontent, bound by oath, led by malevolent and vindictive conspirators, who have everything to gain and nothing to lose in the conflict." Ingalls cautioned that the impending campaign was not one which should be based on "fire works, oratory and brass bands," but should be "business from the start."[62]

Apparently Ingalls and the Republicans did not start their

"business" early enough, for the results of the November elections in Kansas found a predominance of Alliance men and anti-Ingalls legislators elected to the Statehouse. The Senate, however, remained predominantly Republican, as this was an off year for Senate elections.[63]

On February 19, 1890, the *New York Times* claimed that Ingalls was "On Trial For His Political Life." The story claimed that state officers of the Farmers' Alliance had sent Ingalls a letter asking him to define his position on various trusts and combines. They asked, Did he intend to help break the power of exchanges? Would he assist in suppressing option dealing? Would he pass stay laws and redemption laws? The *Times* believed that these were questions that Ingalls could not answer. The article went on to claim that Ingalls could not possibly define his position to the satisfaction of Kansas farmers.[64] In July, 1890, Ingalls was attacked by Kansas State Senator J. W. Rush as a man who did not keep his word. The specific accusation involved patronage, and Rush claimed that Ingalls promised several men the same job.[65]

In August, 1890, Ingalls was once again attacked by the *Times* in an article entitled "Thrifty Senator Ingalls." The substance of the story was that Ingalls was investing heavily in certain "pet" Kansas banks. Ingalls was named as a director of the Hays City and Lacrosse banks and as president of the Atchison Trust and Savings Company. In addition he was named as a director of the Southern Kansas Mortgage Company. The *Times* made its boldest charge when it claimed that "iridescent John J.," as it called him, had had an investment of about $10,000 in the Abilene Bank of Lebold, Fisher, and Company, since 1887. The bank was under investigation, and President C. H. Lebold stated that between July, 1887, and October, 1889, he had discounted Dickinson County farmers' paper at 18 percent, having received the money to engage in this operation, so he claimed, from John J. Ingalls, who then received and held the paper. The story went on to claim that Ingalls was "robbing the hard-working citizens of the State" by shaving their notes. His wealth was estimated to be one-half million dollars, with a monthly rental income of $500 and with $40,000 having been invested in real estate during the past twelve months.[66] On September 20, Ingalls denied the story.[67] Nevertheless, whether true or false, such accusations seriously impaired Ingalls' chances for reelection.

After the November elections, in which the Alliance made sizable gains, the *Nation* denounced Ingalls as a corrupt man and claimed that "his most conspicuous characteristic as a debater is his foul mouth." The *Nation* then hopefully suggested, "It will be an incalculable gain to the moral atmosphere of the Senate chamber to have this vulgar ranter tipped out of its Chairman's seat."[68]

Noting the gains of the Alliance in Kansas, the *Times* spoke hopefully of Ingalls' defeat and stated that the Senate "could not, from its present membership, [of Senators] lose a worse one."[69] Former President Cleveland publicly wished for his defeat, declaring Ingalls to be the "vilifier of everything Democratic."[70] Again in December the *Times* headlined an article as follows, "The Decree Has Gone Forth That the Senator [Ingalls] Must Go." The story pointed out that only a few years earlier Ingalls had been the idol of Kansas, but that now "Ingalls is cold, selfish, and unfeeling. . . . He is an intellectual firefly, shining occasionally, but with no warmth in his fitful glances of light, and yet the very men who aided in making him what he is now denounce him as a viper and a monster."[71] Nevertheless, Ingalls was not inclined to surrender without a fight. In a letter to J. W. Steele, Ingalls spoke of the approaching Senatorial contest and claimed that everything "*depends.*" "If the short dance continues [the Alliance]," he wrote, "and the expectation of a political Messiah is not repressed, it goes one way. If the frenzy subsides, it goes the other. . . . The programme is to butcher me to make a Roman holiday. If this is carried out, I should like to have friends there to see that I fall gracefully at the base of Pompey's Statue, and that the folds of my toga are properly disposed." If he won, however, Ingalls thought that it would also be agreeable to have friends present, "to watch the contortions of the other fellows." In any event, Ingalls professed a feeling of tranquility, "with a heart for any fate." In conclusion he prophetically wrote, "I have had my day, and am content."[72] Ingalls' letter closed on a note akin to despair, but it was not indicative of a spirit of utter defeatism. On January 14, 1891, Ingalls delivered one of his more memorable Senate speeches, entitled "The Image and Superscription of Caesar." In this speech Ingalls attempted to "correct" the interpretations made in his "iridescent" statements in the New York *World*. Ingalls claimed, in effect, that politics could be purified, but not by the "elixir of civil-service reform," or "by the bacilli doctors of politics." Ingalls went on to claim that he was, in his "iridescent dream" comments, merely describing a condition and not inculcating a doctrine. Nevertheless, Ingalls reverted somewhat to his "eye for an eye" doctrine by stating that if an enemy smote him on one cheek, he would attempt to smite his enemy "under the butt end of his left ear" if he could. "If this be political immorality," he roared, "I am to be included among the unregenerated."[73]

Following this explanation of his unfortunate New York *World* utterances, Ingalls then devoted the bulk of his speech to the cause of "free silver." He pointed out that money was merely the "creation of law," therefore the law could implement a policy of "free silver" as surely and as safely as the existing gold-standard policy. Furthermore, he argued, this would create an elastic currency which he claimed would benefit the debtor-farmers and -laborers.[74] This was, no doubt, a belated gesture in the direction of the discontented elements in Kansas. It was too little and too late to snatch an Ingalls victory from the jaws of defeat. Nevertheless, the Atchison *Daily Globe* as late as January 26, 1891, claimed that "there is not only a ray of hope, but a chance of victory."[75]

The *Times* claimed that if Ingalls lost the election he would test the validity of the vote in an attempt to retain his seat.[76] On the eve of the election the *Times* reported that there was such intense suspicion in Topeka that each Alliance legislator was being watched by three "emissaries" from his own county. It was reported that Jerry Simpson had revealed that Ingalls money had been circulated among them, but that they pocketed it without any intention of voting for him. The article summarized the impending proceedings by pointing out that Ingalls had lost the confidence of the people of Kansas, and that they therefore had elected a legislature largely upon the issue of his defeat.[77]

On January 27, 1891, the Kansas legislators gave William A. Peffer, editor of the *Kansas Farmer*, ninety-eight votes and Ingalls fifty-eight votes, with eight votes scattered among three other United States Senatorial candidates. The final count gave Peffer one hundred and one votes and Ingalls fifty-eight votes, with six votes scattered among three "favorite sons."[78] After the vote of January 27 was taken, an "enthusiastic old granger" rose and moved "that as the decalogue and golden rule had a place in politics, the house adjourn until two o'clock."[79] Of all Ingalls' public statements, none recoiled on him as did the "iridescent dream" comment. On January 31, 1891, the *Literary Digest* picked up a story that appeared in the New York *Evening Post* on January 27, 1891. It was a commentary on Ingalls' defeat. The story claimed that he had little opportunity to employ his "immoral tactics to secure his re-election," pointing out that every "Alliance" member of the legislature had three bodyguards, day and night, consequently they could not be bought. In conclusion the *Digest* satirically commented that "no statesman of our time has ever had to battle for political existence against such fearful odds."[80] On February 5, 1891, the *Nation* heaped insults upon Ingalls, referring to him as a "charlatan and demagogue" and indeed claimed he had been such "during the last few years."[81] No doubt such derisions hurt Ingalls' sensitivities, but he maintained a kind of stoic humor throughout this period of derogatory publicity. On February 8, at the height of such criticisms, he wrote his wife inquiring, in a facetious kind of desperation, as to the whereabouts of his "ecru drawers." They had disappeared, he claimed, "gone from my gaze like a beautiful iridescent dream."[82] History leaves no record of their having ever been found.

Not all the political epitaphs of Ingalls were critical by any means. Walter Wellman, in a syndicated column, claimed that Ingalls was "the first orator of the Senate." The article claimed that Ingalls was much better as an opponent than as an advocate, stating that Ingalls lacked sympathy and could never stir an audience to tears or compassion. He was much better at arousing distrust, exciting ridicule, and inducing contempt.[83] On February 13, 1891, the Atchison *Daily Globe* carried an article written by a "Washington special correspondent," entitled "Ingalls and Newspapers." The article claimed that Ingalls was very fair to newspaper men and was not shy in asking favors in return.[84] On February 21 the *Globe* carried another article by Walter Wellman, entitled "Ingalls Loss in the Senate." Wellman more or less inferred that Ingalls was "the" person Washington tourists wanted pointed out, and that with his loss, the Senate would lose "much of its attractiveness." Wellman expressed the hope that "Judge Peffer" would, in his way, prove to be just as "interesting."[85]

On February 20, 1891, Ingalls resigned as president pro tem. On March 10, 1891, he left Washington, D.C., to return home via a trip to his parents in Haverhill, Massachusetts. He took one long, last look at the city he loved so well and gazed for an especially long time at Capitol Hill. As his mind became flooded with memories, he wrote of them to his wife: "A tumult of vague memories agitated my spirit as I thought of the vanished years, and the incidents of my career so intimately associated with the scene, so soon to disappear, its triumphs and defeats, its sorrows and its exultations, all ended now like the annals of a dream."[86]

Whether dream or nightmare, Ingalls' career as an elected public servant had come to a close. He described himself as the "innocent victim of a bloodless revolution—a sort of turnip crusade, as it were."[87]

10
THE
COUNTRY GENTLEMAN

There were many who took at least partial credit for Ingalls' defeat, and among these was Mary Elizabeth Lease. She was quoted as saying, "We, the women of the Farmers' Alliance, defeated John J. Ingalls."[1] She went on to claim that Ingalls was a smart man: "He must be a 'smart man' to be the consummate rascal he has made of himself."[2] Perhaps in the last analysis, though, Ingalls was his own worst enemy, particularly with respect to his unbridled tongue. His own defeat, however, in no way deterred Ingalls from giving political advice. He warned that the Republicans must not ignore the free-coinage issue or they would lose in 1892. He also advised the Republican party to revise its views about the tariff, claiming that it was unfair to the producer and consumer and was favorable to merchants and manufacturers. His tariff position was currently in sharp contrast to what it had been when he was so critical of Cleveland's tariff stance, and as on so many occasions, Ingalls was found closing the "political barn doors after the horses were out." In summary, he claimed that Cleveland would be nominated by the Democrats regardless of his position on the important issues.[3]

After his "retirement" from the Senate, Ingalls occasionally referred to himself as a "farmer" or "country gentleman."[4] He owned a sizable farm in Walnut Township in Atchison County, Kansas, and here he hoped to make improvements that would afford him the modest luxury of living out his years as a "country gentleman," with time for leisurely reading and writing. Although Ingalls never actually made a home for himself on this Walnut Township farm, he did see to it that extensive improvements were made upon it and took care so that only a "proper" tenant leased the land.[5] According to Ingalls, he never lived the coveted life of relative seclusion and quiet because "destiny decided otherwise."[6] The Creator must have smiled on Ingalls, for he was contacted by "some New York millionaires" a few days after being defeated in his bid for a fourth term in the Senate, and they made him an attractive offer to "take charge" of a newspaper which was intended to rival the New York *Herald*. Ingalls wrote his wife about the proceedings and claimed that he had been offered a salary of $25,000 per annum if he would accept the challenge. Ingalls refused their offer, but related how the same men then proposed another paper to be called *Truth*, which was to be issued weekly. This time the "New York millionaires" asked Ingalls to accept an annual "engagement" to write for this paper, as Ingalls put it, "anywhere I might be, on any subjects I chose, at my own terms." Ingalls replied that he wanted to see how the first issue looked, and if it was "cheap" or "flippant" and "insincere," he would decline their offer. Ingalls was then given $500 by these same "millionaires" to write some contributions for the first issue. Then he was asked if he would spend a year abroad and write his impressions of social, political, and economic conditions there as compared with those in the United States. This information, in turn, would be used as the basis for a book dealing with European legislative and parliamentary methods as contrasted to those of the United States Congress. Ingalls claimed that this seemed more attractive, but still he did not give his assent. He claimed that he did not want to leave Kansas, as it would look as though he had remained there only because he was in the Senate. In summary, Ingalls related how Blakely Hall had told him that he, Ingalls, was the most conspicuous figure in the nation today (1891) and that more people were interested in what he had to say on public questions than any other man in the United States. Hall also told Ingalls that his recent political defeat had only served to elevate him in public estimation and interest. To all this Ingalls wrote, "This made me smile incredulously."[7]

On February 25, 1891, Ingalls sent his wife the first number of *Truth*, which contained his picture and some of his compositions. In an accompanying letter, Ingalls related how the proprietors of *Truth* had offered him more than his Senatorial salary had been to contribute two or three articles a month on any subjects he cared to select. Blakely Hall assured Ingalls that the paper was financially sound, as the promotors had deposited $100,000 in the bank "to make it sure of success." Again Ingalls declined any contractual agreement.[8] On March 7, 1891, the Atchison *Daily Globe* carried a summary of one of Ingalls' *Truth* articles. In his *Truth* essay Ingalls attacked the naval policy of defending the coastal regions with warships. Ingalls claimed that shore fortifications were superior for coastal defense, stating that technology made ships both too expensive and all too suddenly obsolete. In summarizing his line of argument, Ingalls stated that "our only enemy is England and she is under bond to keep the peace." On March 13, 1891, the *Globe* carried a reply to Ingalls' naval commentary by a Captain Richard W. Meade, who, it was said, "handles the Kansas ex-senator without gloves." Meade claimed that Ingalls had not been keeping up with the times.[9] He pointed out that Ingalls was making analogies between 1861 and 1891, and that things in 1891 were "vastly different." Meade argued that a navy was needed to defeat a navy, no matter how small the antagonist's navy might be. To illustrate this he claimed that the South, during the Civil War, never had more than six cruisers, yet the damage that they were able to inflict on the Union was immense. Meade argued that Ingalls had conceded this when he mentioned the fact that Great Britain compromised on $15,000,000 "in payment of the score." If Ingalls came off second-best in this verbal encounter, he fared better in literary circles, for his essay "Blue Grass" was receiving a revival of attention and was being reprinted in installments in the Atchison *Daily Globe*.[10]

Ingalls continued to express his views on matters of public interest and commented that the Farmers' Alliance, which had swept him out of office, was more powerful than the East realized. He compared it to the Republicanism of 1856, and 1860, in its intensity and popular appeal. He believed that if the two parties, Democratic and Republican, would "adjust" their platforms, the Alliance people would return to their former political alignments.[11] Unfortunately he had not "adjusted" in time to save his own seat in the Senate.

Although Ingalls never formally contracted to be an employee of the periodical *Truth*, he did continue to submit articles to it, for which he was paid handsomely. In April, 1891, he received a letter from Blakely Hall, who had become the editor of *Truth*, with a check for $1,000 for three articles and a poem entitled "Opportunity." Hall requested Ingalls to do six more articles, and he once more sought to encourage Ingalls to become an employee of the periodical on an annual basis, and once more Ingalls declined any formal commitment.[12] The poem, or sonnet, "Opportunity" received almost immediate international recognition.[13] The opening line expressed Ingalls' profound wish for, rather than his confirmed belief in, man's opportunities: "Master of human destinies am I!" The lesson contained in its substance proclaimed that opportunity comes but once, it does not wait, and if rejected, returns no more.[14] Perhaps

Ingalls, in his declining years, was growing more pessimistic, for certainly as a younger man he did not believe that life afforded a person but one chance or opportunity. In 1871 he had written an enthusiastic letter to his father in which he claimed that opportunities were infinite: "We are very apt to feel as though everything had been accomplished, when we contemplate the results of past efforts, forgetting that opportunity is infinite. To the sagacious, today has as many chances as yesterday and tomorrow more than both."[15] Ingalls' father, on the other hand, had once remarked that opportunity was, perhaps, limited. "I now see," he wrote, "that there is an opportunity given to most every man to gain a position—but in most cases the present absorbs the future."[16] Near the close of his life Ingalls regretted ever having written "Opportunity" and said, "I hate the sight of it. I am sorry I ever composed it!" He concluded that he must have repeated it five hundred times in response to requests for autographed copies of it.[17]

Apparently Ingalls found it necessary to find several sources of employment now that he was "a statesman out of a job," a term the *Times* employed to describe the ex-Senator and a term he used about himself.[18] In consequence of his "unemployment," Ingalls joined the Chautauqua lecture circuit, making his debut June 30, 1891, at Glen Echo, New York. The title of his address was "The Problems of Our Second Century." He warned of paternalism in government and once more used the old cliché that if all the money were divided equally, after six months some people would be rich and others poor. Above all this, Ingalls cautioned, "there would be heard again the voice of the irrepressible reformer earning his livelihood by the perspiration of his jaw rather than by the sweat of his brow." He summarized his opinion about reform by stating that the rich and the poor were what they were because the "Creator" willed it so.[19]

In another lecture engagement Ingalls stated that he favored prohibition, while admitting in the same breath that he drank. He claimed to favor woman suffrage, again an about-face to his earlier position, and urged every man *and* woman to be a political partisan. Next he sounded seemingly racist tones by praising the nation's Anglo-Saxon Pilgrim Fathers, who, he claimed, first fell on their knees, then fell on the aborigines, and later their descendants fell on the Chinese. "The name of the Anglo-Saxon is Eli," he said, "for he gets there. The name of all the other races is Dennis, for they all get left."[20] He pressed his argument by warning that it was currently being proposed by reformers that the men who had "failed shall take charge of the things of those who have been successful.' "[21] He then related how, as a young man, he had succeeded. "I took my gripsack and diploma and went West to grow up with the country. I am now a statesman out of employment."[22]

By late summer of 1891, Ingalls was scheduled to lecture in a number of states, including some in the South. He was to speak in Atlanta early in August, and he wrote his wife that he dreaded the undertaking, but like the "old French soldier," he claimed, "My body trembles at the dangers into which my undaunted soul is about to bear it." And then, in conclusion, Ingalls remarked that it was "odd how little control we have over our own destiny," declaring that he was driven by an unknown force much as a horse is guided by his rider. His nostalgic hope was expressed in the comment "Sometime I hope to be in the saddle myself."[23]

In his journey through the South, Ingalls remarked that Tennessee, in particular, was composed of a people and a region which bore the marks of privation and destitution. He described the soil as poor, the crops "scanty," the cattle wretched, and "the people forlorn to the last stage of apparent ignorance, shiftlessness and degradation." He described the whole aspect of the country, as "forbidding and depressing."[24] No doubt, Ingalls' dislike of this paid public-speaking circuit contributed to his melancholy description of Tennessee. In one forlorn letter to his daughter Ethel, he wrote of his lecture tour and mentioned that it paid well, but that "being of a monastic and secluded temperament, the publicity and agitation are intolerable."[25] One can only wonder why Ingalls consistently sought positions in life that required him to be a public figure. Perhaps his earlier reference to being "driven by an unknown force" exercised greater control over Ingalls than might be normally expected and his claim should not be dismissed lightly. On one occasion it was rumored that Ingalls would be appointed to a cabinet post, to which he replied, "My dear sir, I am getting too old to go to Washington to be a private clerk for President Harrison."[26] In the same vein, he declined an invitation to speak in behalf of New York Republicans on the grounds that they were too fond of Tammany and "decent Republicans" would not come from outside to help.[27] Perhaps in these instances Ingalls was at least momentarily "in the saddle."

In December of 1891, Ingalls' father, to whom he had been very close, passed away. Also his Kansas Senatorial colleague, Preston B. Plumb, died. He praised both at their passings and pondered his own remaining time on earth.

With the advent of January, 1892, speculation began to rise as to whether Ingalls would seek election again, either as Senator or as a Congressman at large. The Atchison *Daily Globe* paid Ingalls an elaborate compliment for having secured a new post-office building for Atchison, claiming that the building would always be a monument to Ingalls' personal popularity with the "powers at Washington." The article concluded by claiming that Ingalls was especially deserving of praise since "Atchison was not strictly entitled to an appropriation."[28] In February the *Globe* referred to Ingalls as belonging to the "young crowd of old soldiers," a compliment with an undesirable twist to it as Ingalls' war record had been something less than enviable.[29]

As the Republican political bandwagon began to gather speed in readiness for the summer conventions and the fall elections of 1892, Ingalls valiantly tried to keep pace. Early in March he addressed a Republican rally in Topeka, Kansas, in which he replied to his Republican critics in general and his Democratic and Alliance opponents in particular. He was particularly annoyed that people had questioned his Republicanism, a criticism which dated back to the Civil War era when he twice campaigned on a "Union" ticket. He told his audience that he did not propose to have his Republicanism questioned before the people of Kansas and furthermore that he had been a Republican "before these defamers were born. I will be one after many of them are dead." Ingalls blamed the East for the Republican defeats of 1890 and referred to himself as a "western Republican." He continued by telling his audience that he was such a "Republican-Republican" that he even voted for Governor St. John for a third term. The substance of Ingalls' defense before his critics was that he was and always had been a true Republican, that he favored restricted immigration and high protective tariffs and that although he was not a female-suffrage politician, he had never made war on the suffrage movement. He also facetiously claimed that he was a prohibitionist, but would not shun the help of those who drank a glass of beer.[30]

Early in March, 1892, Ingalls addressed the Kansas League Club Convention in Topeka and complained of not receiving Republican support in 1890. Some went so far as to claim that there was a move on to put Ingalls on the Republican ticket for Vice-President "as a trumpet over the Kansas Republicans, who, they say, are responsible for his undoing." Such a move never really got off the ground. By May of 1892 the *Globe* was asking the inviting question: Was Ingalls available for Congressman at large? Furthermore, the *Globe* suggested that Ingalls was too good a Republican to refuse a party call.[31] A few days later the *Globe* claimed that Ingalls was as popular as ever with the people of Kansas, but added, "The wolves are against him." The paper went on to point out that when "Ingalls was proposed at Hutchinson yesterday to head the Kansas delegation to Minneapolis, a scene of the wildest enthusiasm followed. The rules were suspended, and the nomination made by acclamation."[32] In spite of the "wild enthusiasm," it was George T. Anthony who was nominated for Congress, not Ingalls.[33]

The Atchison *Daily Globe* boomed Ingalls, as chairman of the Kansas delegation, for chairman of the National Republican Convention which was to meet in June.[34] When the convention convened, the *Globe* devoted considerable space to "Ingalls Ovation at National Convention." The article claimed that Ingalls' appearance there "was the signal for the greatest demonstration of the day."[35] The *Globe* described the ovations given to other Republican leaders, but concluded that "the Kansas man attracted the greatest attention in today's meeting."[36] Regardless of the accuracy of this statement, it was William McKinley who was elected convention chairman. Once more it seemed as though Ingalls' popularity was more or less the result of a kind of traditional enthusiasm which did not necessarily denote confidence in Ingalls' leadership. The close of the Republican National Convention in June of 1892, for all practical purposes, also marked the close of Ingalls' political prospects, although there were sporadic signs of an Ingalls political revival in 1895 and in 1897.[37]

Immediately following the Republican National Convention, Ingalls decided to sail for Europe. He boarded the *S.S. Ems* on June 25, 1892. It is doubtful that the trip overseas, which lasted approximately three months, was an attempt at "escapism." It should be recalled that earlier the periodical called *Truth*, had urged him to journey to Europe and to write his impressions for publication. Whether he went to Europe under contract with *Truth*, however, is not known. Ingalls' first letter en route to Europe was dated June 25, 1892, on board the *S.S. Ems*, at sea.[38] Three days later Ingalls wrote a detailed report of his sources of income and general financial condition. He listed seventeen pieces of property that he owned in Atchison, whose rentals brought in $5,568 per annum. Also listed were eight vacant pieces of property which Ingalls calculated should bring in $2,380 per annum. If all his Atchison property were rented, therefore, Ingalls hoped to realize an annual income from them of $7,948.[39] In addition to his income from property, Ingalls included the income that he should realize from his "Kansas Trust & Banking Company stock and salary," which should bring in $1,200 per annum. He also hoped to make another $1,200 per annum from his "Small Hopes Mining Stock." Ingalls also stated that if the money he had on hand were to be properly invested, it would bring in another $1,000 per annum. In summary, Ingalls concluded that these sources of income, coupled with what he could earn, "ought to make us all comfortable."[40] A conservative estimate of Ingalls' average annual income from writing and speaking would be at least $10,000 per annum and probably two or three times this amount in some years. In 1892 this would have made a family, even as large as Ingalls', "comfortable."

While on board ship, Ingalls had considerable time for thought. He commented on the "technical" progress of man and predicted that in another four hundred years man would travel through the air a hundred miles an hour and communicate "constantly with the population of other planets."[41] On July 3, 1892, Ingalls caught his first sight of England, which filled him with emotion. He wrote, "I was moved with emotions unutterable as I beheld for the first time those historic shores upon which Caesar gazed, and every conqueror since, and which William Chesebrough [his wife's forefather] and Edmund Ingalls watched as they sailed away to found homes for their descendants, in the savage wilderness of America."[42]

Although Ingalls reached England first, he saved his tour of that place until after he had toured Europe. His first descriptive comments were made about Germany. He was duly impressed by the figures that crowned the domes of the large buildings in Berlin and commented that the figures were generally gilded, "which give them an aspect of splendor and opulence quite unconceivable." He remarked that he had once tried to have the "Statue of Liberty" on the United States Capitol dome gilded, but in vain. "I was wiser than I knew," he concluded.[43]

On the journey between Berlin and Dresden, Ingalls described the countryside as being composed of "gloomy plantations of stunted pine much like the country between Andover and Middleton" in Massachusetts.[44] In Dresden, Ingalls visited a museum where Napoleon's saddle and boots were on display, and he confessed "with shame and humiliation of spirit" that he admired Napoleon's saddle and boots more than Raphael's Madonna of San Sisto.[45] His travels carried him to Vienna, where he found that the women were well dressed, stylish, pretty, well shod, and looked like Americans.[46] The busy, happy pace of Vienna caused Ingalls to exclaim that he wished he were young again. However, he morosely concluded, "but I never was young!"[47]

Ingalls visited Rome next and gave a detailed description of his position in and impressions of the piazza that faced St. Peter's Church.[48] He was fond of visiting the famous churches and chapels of Europe, and while in Rome, he visited the "Sixtine" and Nicolas chapels in the Vatican.[49] From Rome, Ingalls traveled to Milan and drew an analogy between the landscape en route and that of the Kansas prairies. He thought the landscapes were similar, but he confessed he was partial to Kansas.[50] He also commented on the region around Pisa, taking note of the famous leaning tower, but giving more attention "to the splendid background of mountains and magnificent plains."[51] He took pains, while in Italy, to view da Vinci's famed "Last Supper," which he described as a "stained and faded wreck on a dingy wall."[52] Regarding his European tour thus far, Ingalls concluded that "Rome ought to be reserved for the last. There is nothing more." His enthusiasm for St. Peter's made all other structures seem insignificant. He was not impressed with the exterior view, but he described the interior as surpassing "all superlatives of splendor. . . . If you would take the Marble Room and the Presidents' [in the United States Capitol] that we brag so much of and multiply them by ten thousand you would not have a fraction of what the church contains," he wrote. "I was tempted to kiss the bronze toe of the Apostle that is worn down smooth by the osculation of his worshippers but I did not," he continued, "though I touched it reverently." Ingalls' fascination with St. Peter's caused him to bribe one of the guards so that he might descend into the grotto containing "the sacred dust" (of Saint Peter) and the original copper sarcophagus in which he was interred.[53] In the same commentary, Ingalls again referred to Napoleon, whom he now described as a man who had "a superfluity of what in the U.S. is called gall."[54]

In the cathedral of Milan, Ingalls encountered Eugene Ware, the Kansas poet who had gained fame through his book of poems entitled *The Rhymes of Ironquil,* and his wife. Ingalls commented that they had not seen him and that he (Ingalls) had been tempted to slip away quietly and then in Kansas sometime comment to Ware that he "saw him at his devotions and did not wish to disturb him." Ingalls chose to attract their attention, however, and commented that they had had a very pleasant talk about Kansas affairs, and that Ware thought the approaching Kansas elections would be a repetition of the Glick (Governor George Glick of Kansas, a Democrat) affair and that he (Ware) was not going to take any part in it.[55] From Italy, Ingalls journeyed to Lucerne, Switzerland and here he encountered ex-Governor Leland Stanford, whom Ingalls described as being in very poor health.[56] It was while he was in Lucerne that Ingalls learned of the death of his brother, Francis T. Ingalls, who was a Congregational clergyman and president of Drury College in Springfield, Missouri. In his notebook Ingalls wrote, "The news of my brother's departure shocks and depresses me—Saw the announcement in my *Herald* 8th."[57] In a subsequent letter to his wife, Ingalls paid the highest tribute to his dead brother, claiming that "I think I never knew a man whose future I should have less doubt [about] than his—I never heard a harsh or impatient word or thought from or with him, that I recall, and upon his memory there is no scar, nor stain nor blemish."[58]

On August 11, Ingalls was in Paris, and as if by an unknown magnetism, he found himself standing before Napoleon's tomb. His mood stirred him to write, "I think I am more profoundly impressed here than even in Rome . . . [here there are] mute memorials of the supreme glory of that stupendous career."[59] While in Paris, Ingalls met several other acquaintances from the United States, notably a Mr. Montgomery, who conveyed greetings from "Andy" Hughes of Denver, Colorado, who was Ingalls' brother-in-law.[60] Also while in Paris, Ingalls visited the famed Moulin Rouge and went to the "infamous" Red Mill to view the performances there. He described the Red Mill as supposedly a very wicked place but actually "rather a tame variety show with high prices for beer, poor singing, worse dancing." The "midnight performances" he described as "degrading."[61]

From Paris, Ingalls traveled to London, a city which, like Rome, enthralled him. His notebook is crammed with descriptions and impressions of that great city. He spoke of the "great hall of Westminster" as the most magnificent of all and commented that visitors were required to leave their bags and packages outside, for fear of dynamite.[62] While in London, Ingalls encountered an old and bitter enemy in the person of Albert H. Horton. Ingalls described their meeting by commenting that Horton had called at the hotel to pay his respects, but that he was out at the moment. Ingalls returned just as Horton was completing a brief note, which he was going to leave, saying that he had called.[63] They exchanged pleasantries and traded "interesting gossip," and their unexpected meeting was enjoyable. Ingalls claimed that Horton's visit was no more surprising than if he were to encounter his grandfather's ghost.[64]

Ingalls was pleasantly surprised by his impression of Englishmen. He had historically held an animosity towards England as America's "natural enemy," but he admitted that Englishmen were not at all as he had imagined them. In fact he described Englishmen as quite "pleasant and friendly."[65] Regarding London in particular, Ingalls concluded that it was "the" place to see and a place in which to learn and find enjoyment. In fact he claimed that London was better for these things "than all the other cities I have seen combined."[66]

Early in September, 1892, Ingalls started on his return trip to the United States. Perhaps en route he wrote an essay entitled "Observations by the Way." In this essay he concluded that English and European railroads were of superior construction compared to those in the United States. In addition, he commented on trains, coaches, classes of travel, depots, customs regulations, hotels in Rome, Milan, and Florence, and many other details recalled from his travels throughout Europe. He concluded that English was becoming the universal language. Once more he wrote that if a man could visit but one foreign city, "he had better go to London—whole civilization, are [sic] science and humanity can be studied here. Epitome of the progress of human race—not from the exterior—artistically attractive."[67]

Upon his return from Europe, Ingalls found himself in considerable demand both as speaker and author. By January of 1893 he had begun another lecture tour, which once more carried him through numerous states, and once more he complained of this most miserable manner of making a living. On one occasion he described his feelings by saying, "I can't like it, and were it not for the compensation I would never again appear upon stump or platform."[68] Why Ingalls persisted in doing that which he detested is explained best in his own words: "It is strange how my path has always been prescribed for me in life, against my will and inclinations: how I have drifted into activities that are repulsive, and occupations that I detest. A lover of peace, quiet, seclusion and solitude, happiest always among my books or in the forest. I have been impelled by destiny to continually confront great masses of people in a function that I abhor. Of course, in a way, I consent, I might decline, but it is made so much more to my interest to follow these vocations that there is really no choice. Between earning a thousand dollars a week one way and a thousand dollars a year another, there is not much room for argument, and one must sacrifice inclinations to interest."[69]

There is no doubt that Ingalls' interest in his family and their material welfare overshadowed his other "inclinations." On still another occasion Ingalls claimed that his life on the speaking circuit was much like that of an actor, except that he had no company, wore no costumes, and carried no scenery. His "routine" consisted of being escorted by a committee through the side entrance to the stage, where he made his "salutation," was applauded, "declaimed" for an hour, bowed amid applause, retired, and then prepared to move on to another town and go through the same routine.[70] One particular complaint that Ingalls repeated was in regard to the terrible hotel accommodations. Burlington, Iowa, provided a typical illustration. Ingalls described the hotel there as being so bad that it was almost good. The room was unpapered, and the sooty walls were fissured with zig-zag cracks in every direction, so much so that Ingalls likened them to a railroad map of Kansas. The windows were dim with grime, and the woodwork was unpainted. A rusty sheet-iron stove "shaped like a fat hog" occupied one corner, and beside it, on the carpet amid the floor sweepings, was a pile of wood. "The creaking bed smelt like a setting hen's nest and the soggy 'comforts' settled down on me," he wrote, "like an ancient poultice." The dining room was choked with the grease from the kitchen griddles, while a slovenly waiter brought him "a fluid extract of cascara diluted with turpentine [coffee]." After an interval of "silent prayer," he procured two flapjacks, which filled the "aching void."[71] Thus Ingalls poignantly illustrated his usual discomforts as a traveling orator of the "gay" nineties.

An unusual "honor" came Ingalls' way when a sketch of his likeness as President of the Senate was placed on exhibit at the Chicago Exposition of 1893.[72] Ingalls was not overly pleased with this dubious distinction of being on public display, nor was he overly enthusiastic with regard to other features of the Exposition. The "Congress of Beauty" contained no beauty, in Ingalls' estimation. He called it "the worst and cheapest fake of all the fakes in the Midway." It smelt like an "international cesspool," he wrote, "and the forty representatives of the female loveliness of the world were the foundered graduates of the variety shows and beer gardens of the stockyards district."[73] In this manner Ingalls paid "tribute" to the supposedly most attractive feature of the Exposition.

In 1893 Ingalls wrote a lengthy essay for *Harper's Monthly*, entitled "Kansas, 1541–1891."[74] *Harper's* had requested such an essay from Ingalls back on January 12, 1888, and H. M. Alden, the editor at that time, was willing to pay Ingalls five hundred dollars for it.[75] Alden paid Ingalls a further compliment by asking for any suggestions that would be of use to him editorially.[76] The *Harper's* article was actually the beginning of the acceleration of Ingalls' literary career. For the most part, however, Ingalls kept to the speaking circuit as his major source of income.

In 1894 he revisited Middleton, Massachusetts, the site of his birth. In a small notebook he sketched a diagram of the house of his birth, indicating the room in which he was born.[77] By that time the Flint Public Library stood on the site of his childhood home, a fact which Ingalls noted and wrote on the back of the picture of the

Middleton house that hung in his home at Oak Ridge.[78] He also located his grandfather's anvil in Middleton and had it shipped to Atchison as a sentimental gesture.[79]

Again, in 1894, Ingalls referred to his dislike of the speaking circuit, but commented in his pocket notebook that he did not have enough money due to the depressed state of business, therefore he would continue the circuit. He mentioned also that his speaking engagements had been more numerous than ever before and that his present tour carried him from Colorado to the Atlantic and from Duluth to Georgia. With regard to political office, Ingalls scribbled the following: "No I have no purpose nor inclination to return to public office in any capacity. I have had my day. I am not indifferent to the honor, the rewards and the splendid [?] of public life but I have had my day." And then the rather strange remark: "To a man of ambition and sensibility, no spectacle is so intolerable."[80] One can only speculate about whether these remarks were sincere or merely a draft for a public statement.

On October 24, 1894, Ethel Ingalls became the first of the Ingalls children to marry. She was married to Dr. Edward Giles Blair at Trinity Episcopal Church in Atchison.[81] Ingalls had learned of the impending wedding the previous June, and in a long letter to Ethel he reluctantly approved her choice. Ingalls seemed to object to marriage in general, for some inexplicable reason, and since his own marriage was so happy, the mystery only deepens in regard to understanding his attitudes about matrimony.[82] Ingalls definitely gave his approval to his daughter's choice, and perhaps his reluctance concerning her marriage is typical of the father who feels he is more likely to lose a daughter rather than gain a son. In the meantime, however, Ingalls' political prospects seemed to flicker once more, if only for a moment. The *Times* picked up the story that Ingalls and State Senator Lucien Baker of Leavenworth were in a political death-struggle and that Baker had won. The story claimed that Ingalls was supporting the candidacy of J. Ralph Burton, a former political enemy of Ingalls'. Ingalls was alleged to be supporting Burton, with the understanding that if Burton won in his bid for the state Senate, then he in turn would support Ingalls in a bid to return to the U.S. Senate in 1897. Burton lost, however, and thus the potential political alliance perished.[83] A few months later the *Times* claimed that Ingalls had not given up and that he was openly in the field to regain his Senate seat.[84] J. C. Richardson, chairman of the Democratic State Central Committee of Kansas, claimed that Ingalls had no chance for reelection because he had no following in Kansas.[85] Richardson was essentially correct, and Ingalls' candidacy never gained serious momentum.[86]

Ingalls' speaking engagements for 1895 carried him to the campus of the University of Kansas, where he delivered the commencement address for the graduating law students that year. The sum and substance of his address was that the law profession was the most honorable of the professions and that, as such, it called for the highest principles on the part of its practitioners.[87]

Ingalls maintained a sense of humor. One incident in particular illustrates this point. While on tour in Pennsylvania, he suffered a sharp pain in his left side while lying in bed prior to falling asleep for the night. He wrote that he thought he was suffering a heart attack and that the end was at hand. "I turned over to relieve the distress," he related, "when a great burst of wind belched up and I went to sleep after saying, 'Into thy hands I commend my spirit.' "[88] It was while Ingalls was in Pennsylvania that he learned that Ethel had given birth to a son and that he was a grandfather. Ingalls wrote a humorous and proud letter to Ethel on February 8, 1896, and on February 14 he learned of the unexpected death of the newborn infant.[89] He immediately wrote Ethel, apologizing for his light-hearted letter of the eighth and expressed a desire to comfort Ethel, however, he confessed, "but I know of nothing."[90] He pointed out that his heart had never ceased to bleed for his daughter Ruth, who died at age six, and Addison, who passed away when he was four. "There may be some solution of these mysteries compatible with justice and love," he wrote, "but it has never been disclosed to me."[91]

In March of 1896 Ingalls was offered a lucrative position with the Hearst newspaper chain. Ingalls discussed the offer in a letter to his wife.[92] It appears that William Randolph Hearst wanted Ingalls to cover the Presidential campaign of 1896. In any event Ingalls wrote his wife a few days after the Hearst offer, saying that he had declined to interview the "prominent and pronounced candidates," claiming that there was really no candidate other than William McKinley. Ingalls believed that McKinley had no special talents and described him as "a very ordinary commonplace man, nothing striking, startling or original about him—not even entitled to the vogue he enjoys in connection with the principle of tariff protection, for others were much more responsible for the measure that bears his name than he: but, still he is a clean capable average American citizen and the people want him and I think they will have him and break the machine."[93] The *Times* meanwhile carried a story in which they claimed Ingalls was seeking election to the U.S. House of Representatives.[94] The story added, however, that Ingalls could not hope for election unless he endorsed the gold plank in the Republican platform.[95] Ironically, after McKinley's election, Ingalls denounced silver and the overall silver solution to economic problems as being the "silver trust," the "largest trust on earth." He made it perfectly clear that nobody hated trusts more than he did. Once more Ingalls had become a political magician with his ability to do an about-face while in full political stride.[96]

McKinley secured the Republican nomination, as Ingalls had predicted, but William Jennings Bryan's nomination by the Democrats came as a surprise to Ingalls and to many others. Ingalls referred to Bryan's nomination as "a freak of destiny" and remarked, "What a commentary on the caprices of self government, that a man scarcely thought of before, almost unknown, hardly eligible, should stampede a great convention by half an hours speech and a very commonplace one at that so far as the matter goes; merely a repetition of what he has been saying on the stump and platform for years —and what an example of the irony of fate if he should chance be elected. Stranger things have happened," concluded Ingalls. "The nomination will appeal powerfully to the pride of locality, and the platform will be the creed of the unemployed and the discontented."[97]

After the November elections Ingalls' lecture circuit took him to Greeley, Colorado. While there, he complained that Kansas was despised everywhere and was generally held in contempt. He claimed that it was regarded as a kind of political bedlam, "an aggregation of freaks, cranks, lunatics, knaves and fools." Ingalls concluded that the Republicans, by their folly, were to blame.[98]

With McKinley's election, rumors began to circulate once more that Ingalls was in line for a place in the cabinet. Ingalls declared to his wife, however, that nothing could induce him to go into the cabinet and that the idea was repulsive, so much so that he exclaimed, "I would rather break rock on the highway."[99]

In March of 1897, possibly on assignment for the Hearst newspaper chain, Ingalls covered the James J. Corbett and Robert Fitzsimmons championship fight. In his usual colorful manner, Ingalls described the rather dull affair with tongue-in-cheek comments.[100] There were those who, in response to Ingalls reportage, felt that he had sullied his dignity by taking on such an assignment. After the Carson, Nevada, assignment, Ingalls returned to Washington, D.C., and visited some old friends and familiar haunts, including the Senate chamber. He attempted to call on President McKinley, but finding a long line ahead of him, he retired without an interview. His trip to Washington and his attempt to see McKinley prompted still another rumor that he was seeking a foreign post. The rumors had it that Ingalls wanted to be made minister to Switzerland, but finding the post filled, he was willing to take a post in South America. The alleged reason for Ingalls' seeking such a post was so that he could fulfill literary contracts without "having to work meantime to keep the pot boiling."[101] It seems very doubtful, on the basis of Ingalls' personal correspondence, that there was any substance to the rumor. Concerning McKinley, Ingalls summarized his impression of him by commenting that he was "fagged and worn" and that his ailing wife was yielding to the strain.[102] The strain was to increase for McKinley with the advent of war with Spain, and the strain was also felt by Ingalls. Ingalls' son Sheffield looked upon the Spanish-American War with eager anticipation. For him it was an opportunity for adventure and heroic deeds. He apparently thought seriously of enlisting, and in response to this desire, Ingalls wrote him a rather sarcastic letter. Ingalls lauded "Sheff's" patriotism and told him to suit himself about enlisting. He then pointed out that there would be good pay in the army, $192 per annum, and the refining associations of camp and field, as all volunteers from Atchison would consist of lawyers, scholars, merchants, and professional men and that there would not be "a bum, nor a saloon loafer nor a gutter snipe in the ranks." He went on to point out that those who stayed behind would live out the rest of their lives under the imputation of cowardice, "because they were unwilling to sacrifice life and blood at the altar of their country." Ingalls claimed that war was a great thing for Napoleon, Alexander, Caesar, Grant, Sherman, and the like, who ran no risk and got all the glory, while the private soldiers do all the work, face all the danger, "and are thrown into a ditch with their bloody rags on to be covered with dirt like dead dogs and never heard of again, it is grandest and noblest of all."[103] Sheffield did not join the army.

Ingalls spoke one way about the war as a parent and quite another way as a public figure. He wrote the introduction for a hurried and shoddy book entitled *America's War for Humanity Related in Story and Picture Embracing a Complete History of Cuba's Struggle for Liberty and the Glorious Heroism of America's Soldiers and Sailors,* which was published in 1898. In his introduction Ingalls claimed the war was undertaken "with no ignoble or selfish purpose, but moved, rather, by that lofty moral impulse which has inspired the heroes of every history, and the martyrs of every religion."[104] Obviously, Ingalls did not think the stakes were high enough for his son to be either a "hero" or a "martyr." Ingalls was personally critical of the war with Spain, in general, and with Admiral Dewey, in particular. He once referred to him as "an entirely new kind of ass. He should have a guardian appointed, or be sent to an asylum. He is another popular idol with the bran and saw dust stuffing running out."[105] Also, when Dewey was talked of as a Presidential candidate, Ingalls was appalled and exclaimed, "A presidential candidate without any politics or platform. It must be that the Almighty set this world going as a continuous vaudeville performance for the amusement of fallen angels."[106] In any event, the "performance" was about to draw to a close for Ingalls, and he was approaching that inevitable and impossible race with the "man on the pale horse."

11

RACING WITH THE "GENTLEMAN ON THE PALE HORSE"

In October of 1898 Ingalls came down with pneumonia while on a speaking tour in Minnesota. He recovered sufficiently to return to Washington, D.C., where his wife and daughters were, but in January of 1899 he was stricken with what he described as the "grip." Again he recovered, but then had a second attack in which he became so ill that the doctors feared he might not recover. His eldest son, Ellsworth, who was in Texas at the time, was sent for, but by the time he arrived, Ingalls was out of danger. A month later Ingalls was stricken with a painful kidney infection, but once more he recovered. Following this latest illness, Ingalls claimed his heart beat became "irregular and intermittent." His heart trouble appeared to clear up in a short time, and then in May of 1899 he complained of an inflammation of the larynx, and he suffered a temporary loss of his voice.[1] From this latest illness Ingalls never recovered. He first sought medical attention for his hoarseness in March, 1899, probably at Battle Creek, Michigan, for he described the "multitudes at Battle Creek eagerly striving for a brief postponement of the sentence of death even at the price of prolonged suffering. I was impressed with the conviction that men have little faith in the prophecies of the future."[2]

By July, 1899, Ingalls was still waiting for the complete return of his voice, which had been made worse by the long speaking tour that he had just completed.[3] The next month he entered a hospital in Washington, D.C., for treatment and reported that he was improving and that the doctors expected him to recover completely.[4]

He was released from the hospital, but his voice trouble required further medical attention.[5] He had already been contemplating a move, possibly to Denver, Colorado, where he had been offered a position with the Denver *Post*. He hoped that the change of climate might do his health some good.[6] Ingalls decided to try the dry air of the Southwest and went to Las Cruces, New Mexico Territory, as he put it, "in my race with the gentleman on the Pale Horse."[7] By this time he wrote that he was speaking "with much difficulty."[8] Whether the change of climate was helpful to Ingalls is debatable, but he nevertheless claimed that he was better than he had been the previous winter, "I know, for I haven't wept since I left home."[9] Still he admitted that he continued to be hoarse and that there was no noticeable improvement in his throat.[10]

In December, 1899, Ingalls decided to leave Las Cruces, New Mexico, and go to Tucson, Arizona, for treatment. He conceded that Tucson might not have things to his liking, but, on the other hand, the "tedium" in Las Cruces was intolerable.[11] The few remaining days at Las Cruces found Ingalls engaged in retrospection. He recalled the pleasant evenings "at home, by a great fire with books, and talk and a good dinner coming. But I musn't think of it," he admitted, "or I shall break down."[12]

En route to Tucson, Ingalls passed through El Paso, Texas, and the trials of the trip began to take their toll of him in his weakened condition. He complained of the hardships, but nevertheless concluded that he would hold out as long as possible.[13] Upon his arrival in Tucson, he noted that it was a pleasant place, an interesting town. He even thought that he might enjoy living there.[14] He took up his residence in a one story "dobe" at 150 West Jackson Street. His quarters consisted of one large room.[15] It was here that Ingalls reflected upon the death of his lovely and talented daughter Constance, who had just passed away in the prime of young womanhood. "The world seems so changed without Constance. It is incredible that her restless, impatient spirit is at last at rest.—But perhaps it is not!"[16]

Although Ingalls hoped for a cure as a result of the dry climate of the Southwest, he decided that even if he regained the use of his voice, he would never again use it for public speaking. He did not make the claim with regret, but stated, "I do not repine—I have lived long—I have done much. I have reached the border. My years have been prolonged far beyond the average life of man. Most of my companions have already departed, and I wait also for the night which cometh when no man can work!"[17] In the same communication he revealed his continued interest in politics and claimed that if he were a candidate for Congress, Ed Howe would oppose him.

"Curtis ought to buy him, it would not cost much," he concluded. He went on to say that if his name were presented as a candidate for Congress at Topeka, his son Sheffield should declare he would not accept. "The same way about the Vice-Presidency," he wrote, "my nomination is impossible and I would not consider it if it were, but the talk does not hurt. It distracts attention from other matters that might be more annoying."[18]

A few days later Ingalls once more complained of his illness, claiming that sometimes it seemed impossible to endure the torment of it. He reflected upon his "elastic and vigorous" youth which by comparison to his present condition seemed like a "terrible dream."[19] On January 21, 1900, he underwent his most exhaustive physical examination to date. He reported that the doctors found his lungs sound and clear, but that there was an extensive inflammation in the larynx, "with infiltration of serum in the vocal chords, whatever that may be," he exclaimed. The doctors diagnosed his illness as "Odoeina." His temperature was 98.4°; the doctors did not rule out the possibility that he was suffering from tuberculosis of the larynx, but he did not have the attendant symptoms, such as fever and night sweats. His weight was down to one hundred and twenty pounds, which contributed to his general feeling of weakness. There was a small "ulceration" in his throat, but the doctors claimed it gave no indication of being malignant; nevertheless, his throat pained him severely when he swallowed, so much so that he had little desire to eat. His voice continued husky and his spirits low.[20]

On February 4, 1900, Ingalls learned that his eldest son, Ellsworth, was suffering from heart disease. In his pocket notebook Ingalls penned the words, "Dear boy, Get well!"[21] His own illness did not deprive him of his love and concern for his family, and his heart ached when they suffered misfortune. One touching incident was Ingalls' last meeting with his son Ralph. Ralph had volunteered for the Army at the outbreak of the war with Spain. He was now a captain and, as such, was headed for the Philippine Islands for a tour of duty. He visited for a day with his father at Tucson, and Ingalls described their last conversation as follows: "We talked about home, and its inmates, and at ten minutes before seven, shook hands and said good bye. I stood in the door way as he departed, and watched him till he disappeared in the darkness on his journey to the Philippines."[22]

In March, Ingalls was asked by the New York *Journal* to cover the "Bryan" convention in Kansas City, where the Democratic National Convention was scheduled to convene that summer. Ingalls gave his conditional acceptance, dependent upon the state of his

health, and wrote his daughter Ethel, who, with her husband, re-
sided in Kansas City, asking her to reserve a room for him. "Please
don't suggest my staying with you," he wrote, "you know my habits
and moods well enough to understand that I cannot work unless I
am alone."[23] A few weeks later Ingalls reported that a Mr. Farrelley
had offered him the job of covering both political conventions,
Democratic and Republican, and that he had replied that he would
do this for $1,000 plus expenses for each convention. He admitted
that this was more than he had been offered, but confided that he
didn't really want the job.[24] Two weeks later, on April 14, 1900, he
feared ill health would forbid his covering the conventions; but
when the June convention of the Republican party approached,
Ingalls planned to leave for Philadelphia and cover his assignment if
at all possible.[25] He had previously remarked that it would be odd
if the Republican Convention took "the bit in its teeth" and nominated Theodore Roosevelt. "It is not unlikely," he stated, "the combination would be strong."[26] In spite of his interest in and the
opportunities to cover the national political conventions, Ingalls'
health became worse just prior to his planned departure for Philadelphia, and he was unable to attend either the Republican or the
Democratic Convention.

Ingalls' wife had always wanted her husband to write and pub-
lish a book, and Ingalls once remarked that he might be tempted,
"if the work were not too great, and the offer liberal enough."[27]
Apparently neither condition was met, for Ingalls never wrote a
book, other than the incomplete manuscripts which burned with his
house in 1888. He often lamented the fact that he had not written
more, and he was frequently dispirited to the point of despair. In
one such mood, he commented on Atchison's future as follows,
"Whenever Atchison property comes up anything near its value, I
should like to unload [his property there] for it will never be anything but a good local trading point and county seat."[28] In his more
resolute moments he stoically faced the future, claiming, "There is
nothing to do except to endure with fortitude to the end."[29] On his
"better" days Ingalls' spirits improved, and once he commented on
Booth Tarkington, claiming that his "descriptions of western life and
landscape and the character sketches are brilliant . . . the author is
quite a youth."[30] Ingalls' own writing prowess caused a continued
demand for his work. In May, 1900, the New York *Journal* asked
Ingalls to become a regular member of its staff at a handsome annual
salary.[31] Ingalls declined their offer, and turning their letter over, he
wrote his reasons for doing so on the reverse side: "I had decided

not to proceed under the salary arrangement. I have never worked for wages, as a hired man, and it is too late to begin now. I couldn't wear the yoke, not work in harness. My feeling of independence would be gone, and my machinery will not go under compulsion. Then too I am a Republican and must maintain my personal attitude if I am to retain any influence with the public." In addition Ingalls cited his declining health for refusing their offer.[32]

By May, 1900, there were signs that the general public was beginning to believe that Ingalls would not recover. Ingalls' wife wrote him that the word was being circulated that he would not be returning to Atchison for the summer, as he had planned, and perhaps never. Ingalls replied almost violently, by declaring that the perpetrators of such stories were "dirty, and small and mean, and contemptible. . . . It makes me sick to think with what nasty reptiles we are obliged to associate in this dirty world."[33] In June, Ingalls had what he described as "a set back," and by July his condition had appreciably worsened.[34] On July 5, 1900, he received a telegram from "Lou," his wife, whom he now called "Mamma," telling him that she was leaving for his side in a few days, sooner if necessary.[35] The day before, on July 4, he had written that instead of heading home for Atchison, as he had originally planned, he had gone instead to a health resort in Las Vegas, New Mexico, in one last, desperate attempt to get well.[36] In Las Vegas he described his treatment, which included hot fomentations twice a day, electric shocks, and inhalations of iodoform and creosote, morning and evening.[37]

In spite of his painful throat and generally declining health, it is surprising the amount of writing Ingalls accomplished during the last months of his illness. His pocket notebook, beginning with March 26, 1900, indicates that he sent the following: Article to Black, "Immortality"; April 11, article "Socialism" to *Journal*; April 19, article "Office Holding" to *Journal*; May 1, "Women Article" to *World*; May 10, article "On Christianity" for *Journal*. He also mentioned writing something for the *Saturday Evening Post* on May 29; this entry is the last mention of his literary efforts contained in his notebook.[38]

By June 11 Ingalls complained of being very weak, and in the same month his sons Ellsworth and Sheffield spent some time with him. On July 13 Ingalls recorded the words "Mamma comes at 2 P.M." By July 16 Ingalls was keeping only scant and intermittent notes in his pocket memo. Ingalls made only two more entries after July 16. One was on July 18, which read, "Life insurance all paid up and papers filed." On August 11 he made his final entry: "Lay out on balcony 11–2. Flies distracting—alcohol rub and foments."[39] The gentleman on the "pale horse" was about to win the race.

12

THE FITFUL FEVER ENDED
AND
THE VERDICT OF HISTORY

On August 15, 1900, Ingalls' condition suddenly became much worse at about 9 P.M., and his wife sent for Sheffield, who was in another room, just down the hall from his father's room. Ingalls remained conscious and alert till near the end, and he repeated the Lord's Prayer with his wife. Shortly after 2 A.M. on August 16, he lapsed into a coma and died within the hour. His son Sheffield later told reporters: "His conduct all through his illness has been one of great fortitude. He loved his family and was beloved by them, and it was really in his home life that the noble qualities of his heart and mind were shown. He was devoted, kind, patient and indulgent. He was anxious for the end to come, as he had felt for the last six months that his life work and career of usefulness was over."[1]

Ingalls' remains were placed in a copper-lined cedar coffin and were transported by a special railway car to Atchison for the funeral ceremony and interment. When his remains arrived in Atchison at 7 P.M. on August 17, there were approximately a thousand persons assembled at the Atchison depot to meet his train. Ingalls was then taken to his Atchison home, Oak Ridge, where a few close friends were permitted to call. The funeral took place at 2 P.M., Sunday, August 19, 1900, in Trinity Episcopal Church in Atchison and was open to the public. The funeral service was simple, in keeping with Ingalls' request. Chopin's sonata Opus 35 was played as the bier entered the church. The ceremony itself consisted of a reading of the Episcopal burial service by the Reverend J. E. Sulger, followed by two hymns sung by the Trinity Church boys choir: "From Every Stormy Wind that Blows," the favorite hymn of Ingalls' father, who had died in 1892, and "Nearer, My God, To Thee."

Following the church ceremony, the bier was removed to Mt. Vernon Cemetery in Atchison, accompanied only by the family and pallbearers, which was in keeping with the family's request. At the graveside, the Reverend Mr. Sulger conducted a brief interment ceremony, pronounced the benediction, and committed the remains to the sexton as the family retired from the scene. Ingalls was laid to rest beside his five children who had preceded him in death, Ruth, Addison, Faith, Louisa, and Constance Ingalls Shick, the only one of those five children to reach maturity. Surviving Ingalls were his wife and six children—Ethel G. Blair, Marion, Muriel, Ellsworth, Sheffield, and Ralph Ingalls—and his mother, who was now ninety years of age. In addition there were three brothers and two sisters surviving.[2]

Ingalls' death received national attention, and news of his passing was featured in hundreds of United States newspapers and several foreign papers.[3] Owing to Ingalls' frequent public statements and eulogies which sounded agnostic, there was considerable comment in the press regarding Ingalls' religious beliefs or lack of them. The *Lutheran Evangelist* on August 25, 1900, spoke of Ingalls' religion as follows: "Senator Ingalls came of godly stock, and had a mighty conflict between his reason, as has every thinking man, and the faith with which we accept the truths of revelation, which are not contrary to reason, but which are sometimes above and beyond it, the sublime truths of God and eternity upon which the lost world's hope of freedom and salvation are builded. He was a believer in Christianity and its faith."[4] On August 23, 1900, the periodical *Christian Work* of New York City denounced Ingalls as a man who had no moral nature. The New York *Sun* on August 17, 1900, said, "Mr. Ingalls was generally looked upon as an agnostic, but a few minutes before his death he repeated with Mrs. Ingalls the Lord's Prayer." The New York *World* on August 16, 1900, alluded to Ingalls' essay on "Immortality": "I belong to no church and subscribe to no creed, but I believe in God and immortality, and that we shall reap what we sow here and hereafter."[5] This was the sum and substance of the *World* commentary.

The Indianapolis *Journal* of August 20, 1900, called Ingalls "an independent spirit." On September 1, 1900, *Harper's Weekly*, speaking of Ingalls' political defeat in 1891, said "It was the professed inactivity of his moral nature that beat him." The *Christian Advocate*, published in St. Louis, Missouri, on August 22, 1900, began an article on Ingalls with the words "Say nothing of the dead unless it be good." What they said, however, was not good. In its article that Methodist publication claimed that Ingalls "was severe on the churches . . . and in his death, who mourned?" Thus the *Christian Advocate* displayed its brand of "Christian" charity. The Presbyterian *Journal* for September, 1900, titled its Ingalls article "The Death of an Agnostic." The article stated, in contrast to its title, "We question if Senator Ingalls was ever an agnostic at heart. . . . When he came to face death his better and real [self] usurped its place."

On August 17, 1900, the St. Louis *Post-Dispatch* stated that "he would have been nobler had he been able to see more nobility in the mass of men." The Philadelphia *North American* (no date) interviewed several ministers to gain their views on Ingalls' religious convictions. The Reverend Charles M. Alford, a Presbyterian, referred to Ingalls as an agnostic, but added, "I am gratified to know that Mr. Ingalls made the change before death"—that is, the change to Christianity. Father Hugh Lane of the Roman Catholic church said, "I think Mr. Ingalls was saved. We Catholics say that at the hour of death our Lord gives intense grace, so that in a moment a person can say an act of contrition, and that act of contrition will save him." Here Father Lane must have been referring to Ingalls' last-hour recital of the Lord's Prayer. The Reverend O. J. Randall, who was not denominationally identified, said simply, "It [Ingalls' death] indicated that the agnostics' lack of faith does not deeply satisfy the human soul at the hour of its most crucial test—the moment of dissolution." And then, sounding like an agnostic himself, the Reverend Mr. Randall concluded, "God alone knows what the end is." The Reverend N. S. Thomas, an Episcopal clergyman who claimed to know Ingalls personally, said, "I positively deny the assertion that Mr. Ingalls was an agnostic. . . . He might have had his own peculiar ideas on the inspiration of the Bible and other religious subjects, but he was as firm a believer in Jesus Christ as I am, and his last words were entirely in keeping with his previous professions."[6] The St. Louis *Star* of August 27, 1900, reporting on Ingalls' death, claimed that "he was impressed with the idea that death is simply a natural transition from one life to another . . . [believing] that the Omnipotent is loving and merciful and that whatever judgement might be dealt out to his soul in the next world would be based upon justice."

It is apparent that Ingalls was as perplexing in death as he had been in life. Contemporaries, including intimate acquaintances, could not agree on just what it was that Ingalls believed, or perhaps did not believe. If an accurate appraisal of Ingalls' religious convictions is difficult, and it is, it is because Ingalls was in a constant state of flux with regard to theology. Ingalls once referred to life as "an uncivil host . . . to invite us to an entertainment which we are compelled to attend whether we like it or not, and then to unceremoniously take us by the arm and bow us out into the night, stormy and dismal, to go stumbling about without so much as a lantern to show us the way to another town."[7] On another occasion he remarked that life was becoming more and more unintelligible, referring to "its cruelties, its ferocities, its brutal injustice, its wanton and gratuitous agonies, its savage malevolence to the innocent and the helpless. It is idle to say that it is punishment for sin, for evil destiny attends the good as well as the wicked and all are alike overwhelmed in common destruction. To create beings knowing that they will suffer what falls to the lot of man, with the promise of everlasting hell-fire by way of epilogue, does not appear to my imperfect comprehension compatible either with eternal wisdom or infinite love."[8]

In his eulogies delivered in the Senate, Ingalls always referred to death as "the profoundest mystery of human destiny." He always spoke of the deity in abstract and impersonal terms.[9] After a eulogy that he delivered on Senator B. H. Hill, Ingalls wrote his wife that a Baptist paper in New York called him a heathen and an infidel. He promised to "come back" at the paper.[10] On the other hand, Ingalls received a letter from a friend who enclosed a complimentary clipping from the Boston *Post*, which claimed that Ingalls' eulogy of Hill stamped Ingalls as the most scholarly man in the Senate.[11]

After Ingalls had delivered a seemingly agnostic eulogy for Congressman J. N. Burnes, he received a critical letter from J. A. Powelson, M.D., who claimed that Ingalls' words were beautiful, but asked Ingalls why had he not referred to Holy Scripture, which afforded consolation and hope? He rejected Ingalls' thesis that death was a mystery, "an unfathomable abyss."[12] Ingalls replied to the letter a few days after receiving it, stating that the great majority of men could neither comprehend God nor did they believe the Bible. If they did, as he put it, everything would be dogmatically concluded by the recitation of texts. He summarized his response by claiming that he contented himself with reason and hope, rather than with faith and authority.[13]

In spite of Ingalls' lack of "orthodoxy," he had once recommended the very orthodox book Drummond's *Natural Law in the Spiritual World* to his father.[14] Ingalls' father had been surprised and pleased that his son had recommended this book to him and stated, "I ask myself may it not be possible that the arguments [that] have been so strongly put in the Burns [*sic*] and other eulogies have been the means of Providence of influencing your own mind?"[15] Ingalls had purchased his own copy of Drummond and made critical marginal notations in it.[16] On page 197 Drummond claimed that "the world itself is about as good a world as might be." In the margin of this page Ingalls wrote, "Earthquakes, draughts, cyclones, epidemics, inundations, etc. etc." On page 154 Drummond stated, "It becomes evident, then, that as we ascend in the scale of life we rise also in the scale of longevity." In the margin of this page Ingalls wrote, "The Galapagos tortoise, a reptile, lives several hundred years." On page 92 Drummond praised "nature's" way of doing things, claiming that moles "had taken to spending their lives beneath the surface of the ground," and as a result he claimed that nature "has taken her revenge upon them . . . she has closed up their eyes." And Ingalls made the marginal remark, "But 'Nature' placed the mole underground, and the fish [blind fish] in the cavern." And although he may have recommended the book to his orthodox father, it did not "hold water" for Ingalls himself. He was unable or unwilling to accept the unknown by faith, while reason seemed at odds with a world which, to Ingalls, was the essence of all that was unreasonable.

Once Ingalls concluded a melancholy letter to his wife as follows: "But—tra-la-la! What is the use of sniffling about it! We must go. Let us make our exit with easy grace and dignity, and not like a boor, ignorant how to leave the room without tripping on the door mat, or stumbling over the ottoman. It is not more unlikely that we shall live again than that we should have lived at all."[17]

Perhaps one of the more penetrating insights into Ingalls' religious life is revealed in a brief passage he wrote a few months before his death. Obviously responding to a query contained in a letter from his wife, Ingalls replied, "I don't remember ever to have said I did not think Christ was Divine. Truth to tell I do not know anything about it. If he called himself the Son of God, he called himself also the Son of Man. That is a matter for Ecclesiastics. The important thing is the purity of his life, and to follow, as far as we may, his perfect example. Help the poor, Reclaim the Erring, Love your enemies. Do unto others as ye would they should do unto you. We can safely leave the insoluble dogmas of theology to the illumination of the world beyond the grave, If we do our duty here."[18]

Ray Harold Sandefur, one of Ingalls' biographers, claimed that Ingalls believed in God, the divinity of Christ, and the immortality of the soul.[19] It is safe to say that Ingalls believed in all of these things, but not consistently, nor with deep conviction. Ingalls could be "orthodox" one day and agnostic the next. By and large he tended towards agnosticism; and in deference to those who insist that he was a "Christian," let it be said more accurately that he was a "Christian agnostic."

Ingalls posed as much of a problem politically as he did theologically. Throughout his eighteen years of service in the Senate, Ingalls had introduced over nine hundred bills and/or joint resolutions. He had favored pensions, high protective tariffs, Negro civil rights, free silver, and the regulation of trusts, among hundreds of other proposals of a wide variety. He had opposed prohibition, female suffrage, Democrats in general, and Cleveland in particular. In commenting on his political career, his obituaries usually referred to several speeches and incidents in his career as a politician and rarely cited specific legislative accomplishments. Among the most frequently mentioned incidents were his dispute with Vorhees, his "Fiat Justitia" speech, and his eulogies delivered from the Senate floor. Almost all the obituaries of any length referred to the "peculiar" circumstances of his election to the Senate in 1873 and to his famous *World* interview, in which he made the "iridescent dream" comment. The most prominent word used in describing Ingalls was "picturesque," and his rhetorical ability was considered to be his major political asset, while his sarcasm was said to be his worst handicap. A number of papers accused him of being politically immoral, while others praised his political integrity. In appraising Ingalls the politician, the following comments were frequently used: A master of epigrams and biting sarcasm, a man of great genius, a man of invective, a brilliant orator, merciless and severe, a conspicuous character, a fearless man, and an ultra partisan.[20] When Ingalls was either praised or criticized, the commentary was usually related to Ingalls' personal traits. He was seldom referred to as a "great legislator" or a "great statesman." He was more apt to be called a "great man." There was little notice of his political posture regarding the leading issues of his time. The obituaries leave the impression that Ingalls was a nationally known figure, possibly a great man, certainly unique if not eccentric, without stating satisfactory reasons for their claims. In the Senate, Ingalls had served on a considerable number of standing committees, namely, the committees on Indian Affairs, the District of Columbia, Pensions, Education and Labor, Privileges and Elections, from which he asked to be excused in 1879, and the Judiciary. During the second session of the Forty-fourth Congress, December 4, 1876, to January 23, 1877, he served as chairman of the Committee on Pensions. He became chairman of the Committee on the District of Columbia in 1881 and served in that capacity to the end of his Senatorial career. His greatest honor in the Senate was his election to the position of permanent President Pro Tem of that body on February 25, 1887, where he served until 1891.[21]

In approaching a solution for economic and commercial problems, Ingalls made two major speeches and proposed an amendment to the Sherman Anti-Trust Bill. The first of the two speeches was made on February 15, 1878, in support of the Bland-Allison Act in spite of President Hayes's opposition to the bill.[22] Ingalls' second speech came very late in his career, on January 14, 1891, when once more he championed the cause of free silver.[23] It is of some interest to note that Ingalls considered himself a Westerner and that in championing silver, he was representing his sectional interest. Also, it should be noted that one of these two speeches was made eleven months prior to his attempt to be reelected and the other, approximately two weeks prior to an attempt to be reelected.

His proposed amendment to the Sherman Anti-Trust Bill was made on March 21, 1890. This was a time when the nation's farmers in general, and Kansas farmers in particular, were demanding federal legislation in behalf of a "soft" or elastic currency, the curbing of trusts, and the elimination of grain speculation. It was also at a time when the Kansas Farmers' Alliance, meeting in Topeka during the latter part of March, 1890, had resolved that Ingalls had not represented the farmers in the Senate and that therefore they would not support his bid for reelection.[24] Ingalls, with his ear to the ground, "got the message." But Ingalls' amendment to the Sherman Anti-Trust Law did not please Sherman, the Senate, or the farmers of Kansas, and there was considerable speculation as to whether Ingalls' gesture in behalf of the farmers was the result of political expediency or was sincerely advocated.

In the area of civil rights, or "social justice," Ingalls gained attention as the enemy of the woman-suffrage movement. The tone of his opposition is revealed in a speech written in his own hand, which reads in part as follows: "Its [female suffrage's] advocates, outside this chamber, so far as I know them, are the unsexed of both sexes. Men (long hair) without manhood: women (S.H.) [short hair] without womanhood: males without virility, and females without fecundity. . . . I am sure I voice the sentiments of a vast majority of the women of America in protesting agt [against] this movement to abolish the distinction between the sexes as a loathsome unnatural heresy—an obscure dogma at war alike with the ordinances of nature and the laws of God."[25]

In support of the Grand Army of the Republic, Ingalls became highly emotional and at times almost irrational in his reasoning. On one occasion, in speaking of "the soldiers of the Republic," he claimed that they went to battle for a moral cause, "for the precepts of the New Testament, for the Golden Rule as the fundamental law of our national existence."[26] Conversely, all Confederates (Democrats) were enemies of the cherished and hallowed values of the Union (Republicans). Ingalls would not go so far as to say that all Democrats were traitors and horsethieves, but all such were Democrats in his thinking; at least he claimed as much for public consumption. On one occasion he had argued that whoever opposed increasing G.A.R. pension benefits must be in sympathy with the South and that such sympathies sprang from loyalty to the Confederacy.[27]

In regard to prohibition, the sum and substance of all Ingalls said on this topic finds him planted squarely "on the fence." In an article published in the *Forum* in August, 1889, Ingalls had said in substance that prohibition was pleasing to everybody: the prohibitionists had their law, and the antiprohibitionists had their liquor.[28]

Ingalls seemed to find it difficult to find a "solution" for any of man's problems, whatever their nature. He was conscious of the increasing rapidity of changes that were taking place in the world around him, but was seemingly perplexed by it all. In a Memorial Day speech delivered in 1895, he had claimed that "the U.S. now, today, at this moment, is in the midst of a vast social, industrial, economic and political revolution, the course of which is obscure, but the consequences of which are certain to be infinitely momentous . . . involving the personal liberty of the citizen, the right of majority rule, and the federal union of independent states. . . . The battles of the past have been to secure the political equality of all men before the law. The battles of the present and the future will be to secure to all men an equal opportunity in the race of life." He described the present enemies of these opportunities as "monopolies, trusts and combinations" and spoke of "the tyranny of labor organizations" as a new enemy. Ingalls did not propose a course of action for the dilemma he had outlined.[29]

Ingalls was customarily inconsistent in his approach to the issues of his day. William Jackson Armstrong, a leading columnist of the day, denounced Ingalls' inconsistency in an article published in the *Arena*, entitled "Mr. Ingalls and Political Economy."[30] He claimed that at one time Ingalls was the most pronounced orator in the land against the rapid concentration of capital, but now he had reversed himself. He went on to state that at heart Ingalls was probably a Socialist, "but by history he has been what he has judged he could afford to be." Armstrong claimed that if Ingalls were allowed to be his own historian, he would doubtless be able to give a considerably modified version of his public and personal inconsistencies. Ingalls, according to Armstrong, always built his verbal arguments on "premises" which "are a haphazard mixture of falsehoods and half-truths." Armstrong quoted Ingalls' comments concerning wealth, poverty, and social justice, which had appeared in a syndicated column, and then meticulously began to pick Ingalls' logic to pieces. In summary, Armstrong claimed that Ingalls had no solutions and that his argument could be reduced to "rich and poor have always existed, . . . man is a discontented animal, at best, . . . human legislation is impotent for remedy."[31] This probably comes very close to conveying Ingalls' basic fatalistic view of human problems. Ingalls leaves the impression over and over again that life is a series of uncontrollable or accidental catastrophes and that mankind has very little influence in altering the course of "fate."

Understandably, the press had difficulty in assessing Ingalls, either as a person or as a politician. D. R. Anthony in the Leavenworth *Daily Times* claimed that Ingalls was "one of the great men that Kansas produced, perhaps the greatest," but he gave no reason for this judgment.[32] On August 19, 1900, the Atchison *Champion* headlined the article about Ingalls' death with the words "A Mighty Voice is Stilled." The article claimed that Ingalls "was the most conspicuous figure that has yet come out of the political life of the West. Gauged by any standard he measured up to greatness." The article backed up these claims by referring to Ingalls' literary talent and his rhetoric. There was no mention of legislative accomplishments.

An undated clipping from the Chicago *Record* claimed that "Ingalls was a critic, rather than a creator of political proceedings. Considerable as was the work he did, both for the state of Kansas and for the nation at large, and conspicuous as was his position, his name is not exclusively identified with any single act of constructive legislation. The regret which will be felt at his death is that which must follow the loss of any man of signal ability who seems not to have developed his talents to the best purpose." The Topeka *Journal* claimed that "he [Ingalls] was in no sense a politician and the petty intrigues that go with politics disgusted him."

On August 23, 1900, the Atchison *Weekly Globe* printed tributes to Ingalls, one of which was from William Allen White, who said, "Ingalls was a great man who missed being a useful man in politics by a narrow margin, and showed his real worth in his letters." The Chicago *Tribune* said that "the death of John James Ingalls takes from public life one of the most picturesque and striking figures the country has ever known. . . . Not since the days when Randolph of Roanoke and Burgess of Rhode Island lashed each other with cutting phrases has the Senate of the United States known a wit so caustic or a tongue so ready." The Kansas City *Times* of August 16, 1900, claimed that Ingalls had a "singular aptitude for politics and marked ability made him a leader of his party." On the same date the Kansas City *Star* wrote that Ingalls followed his theory "to get through life with as little discomfort as possible . . . duty was a restraint to him and he approached it as the galley slave to his toil. Even the obligations of public life were detestful to him. He despised the demands made upon him by his constitutents."

The Washington *Post,* in its obituary on August 16, 1900, noted four things about Ingalls, namely, his mastery of "splendid English," his ability as a eulogist, his satirical power, and his literary talent. The Paris edition of the New York *Herald* claimed that Ingalls "was for many years a striking and characteristic figure in American politics." The Denver *Republican* of August 16, 1900, claimed that "as matters stand today, there are two men in the Middle West who are capable of writing the great American political novel. One is William Allen White, and the other is John J. Ingalls." The New York *Sun* of August 17, 1900, stated that Ingalls was "a brilliant and interesting character. . . . He had lost his political grip in Kansas principally because of his sharp tongue." The Atlanta (Georgia) *Journal* headlined its Ingalls obituary "Ingalls had a proneness for Logical Gymnastics," and then went on to quote "some of the epigrams and figures of speech that made him famous." In summary, the press invariably conceded greatness to Ingalls, but not as a statesman. He was called great because of his oratory and/or literary contributions. It is doubtful if Ingalls would have cared what the final press appraisal of him was. He had not worried very much about the press in life, and certainly in death there would be no quarrel.

A number of the obituaries raised suggestions, such as, had Ingalls devoted himself exclusively to writing, his fame would have been secure for years to come. One paper, however, paid tribute to the more specific legislative accomplishments of Ingalls. The Tucson (Arizona) *Star* of August 19, 1900, claimed that Ingalls was the champion of the territories: "He led the fight which gave to six other territories statehood." The *Star* went on to claim that Ingalls took pleasure in his work in behalf of the territories and referred to his efforts in this endeavor as "triumphs of justice to the state builders of the West."[33]

Contemporary opinion about Ingalls often fell into stereotyped patterns, although there were occasionally sharp differences in the appraisals rendered on him. Even the task of raising a monument over Ingalls' grave was debated for a time, as no suitable stone could be found. In December of 1890 Ingalls had made a specific request concerning a "monument." He wrote to his wife that "our ground in the cemetery should have a 'monument.' I hate these obelisks, urns, and stone cottages, and should prefer a great natural rock—one of the red boulders—known as the 'lost rocks' of the prairie—porphyry from the north—brought down in glacier times—with a small surface smoothed down—just large enough to make a tablet in which should be inserted the bronze letters of our name—'Ingalls'—and nothing else."[34] On December 20, 1903, the St. Joseph *Gazette* carried an article stating that "after the lapse of a long time, the grave of John James Ingalls . . . has been marked by a monument." The article went on to describe the monument as "a great, rough, unhewn stone, a boulder brought down from the north in primeval floods, untouched by the hand of all save God and Nature." A bronze tablet was imbedded in the stone, bearing the word "Ingalls," but in addition there were the lines taken from Ingalls' immortal essay "Blue Grass": "When the fitful fever is ended, and the foolish wrangle of the market and forum is closed, grass heals over the scar which our descent into the bosom of the earth has made, and the carpet of the infant becomes the blanket of the dead."

Efforts were undertaken concurrently to erect a fitting monument to his memory as a public servant. Perhaps M. M. Murdock of the Wichita *Daily Eagle* was the first to suggest the idea of a statue of Ingalls. He headlined one of his editorials "Why Not a Statue of Ingalls," and then proceeded to extol Ingalls' unique talents and personal traits. A short time later Balie P. Waggener, a Democrat of Atchison, introduced a resolution in the Kansas legislature, providing for a bust of Ingalls to be placed in Statuary Hall in Washington, D.C. After some delay the resolution was adopted, and Charles Niehaus of New York was selected as the sculptor. On December 13, 1904, the Senate passed a resolution naming Saturday, January 21, 1905, as the day "appropriate to the reception and acceptance from the State of Kansas of the statue of John James Ingalls."[35] Ingalls had been given the highest honor a state can bestow on its departed. Ingalls had for some time now been in the "abyss of the unknown," which brings to mind a plea once penned to his wife: "You must never forsake me, here or hereafter. If you go before me to the undiscovered country, guard me. If I precede you, search for me till you find me, with entreaties and importunities that will permit no denial, but will rescue me, though ages intervene, from the profoundest abyss."[36] Lou, Ingalls' wife, died at eighty-three years of age on April 15, 1926. Ingalls' place in subsequent histories has not been large. Generally brief and uncomplimentary notice has been given to him by such historians as Matthew Josephson, Richard Hofstadter, Walter Nugent, Gene Clanton, and James C. Malin.[37] From time to time his name still appears, but generally only in reference to his literary talents. The most recent and notable mention came on February 14, 1970, when Hugh Downs, of NBC Television, concluded a special one-hour show devoted to the Great Plains with a quote from Ingalls' "Blue Grass."

Ingalls once expressed regret that "my history has been written by my enemies."[38] This biography is not the product of an "enemy," nor of an advocate. In standing by the graves of Ingalls, his wife, nine of their eleven children, and three of their grandchildren, the lines of "Blue Grass" haunt the stillness. Ingalls, like men of all ages, was troubled by the adversities of life, though the brevity of his life, like that of all men, was as grass before the storms of winter. The green grass that covers the earthly remains of Ingalls is symbolic of the epitaph he once wrote, perhaps in anticipation of his own death: "Grass is the forgiveness of Nature—her constant benediction . . . unobtrusive and patient, it has immortal vigor and aggression." In like manner, the enigmatic figure of Ingalls, the man given to iridescent dreams, has found its place in history, though the riddle of his life may forever escape solution.

NOTES

ABBREVIATIONS USED IN NOTES:

ALI —Anna Louisa Ingalls
EIms.—Manuscript by Ethel Ingalls
ETI —Elias T. Ingalls
IP —Ingalls papers in collections of the Kansas State Historical Society

JJI —John James Ingalls
KSHS—Kansas State Historical Society
KUIP—Ingalls papers in Kansas Collection of the University of Kansas Library

Chapter 1

1. JJI, *Edmund Ingalls and Some of His Descendants,* p. 4. This is a nineteen-page booklet published privately in Atchison, Kans., in 1881.

2. JJI to ETI, Dec. 16, 1958, in the "John J. Ingalls Collection" in the ms. division of the KSHS, Topeka, hereafter cited as IP.

3. *Ibid.*

4. Copy of a letter from Margaret Ingalls to Ellsworth Ingalls, May 25, 1930. IP. A portion of this letter states that "The whole Chase family always detested Grandfather Ingalls."

5. Several other Ingalls compositions reveal these inner conflicts. Especially noteworthy are "Essay on Creation," "Greylock," and "The Sea." IP.

6. "The Sun Lover, or The Autobiography of a Monomaniac." IP. Also *New York Times* of Aug. 17, 1900, reported that he was able to read before he was three years of age.

7. The visions alluded to come from an Ingalls composition entitled "Pictures From Memory." IP. In this composition he recorded incidents in his life that he was able to recall from memory. In all, twenty-five remembrances are recorded, numbered one through twenty-five. They seem to be in chronological order. Assuming this to be so, Ingalls began having his nightmares at the age of thirteen, as the nightmare incidents are numbered

thirteen. In later years Ingalls' father openly expressed concern over his son's eccentricities. One specific example is to be found in a letter he wrote to him on Sept. 28, 1865. IP.

8. ETI to JJI, Feb. 4, 1871. IP.

9. JJI to his daughter Marion Ingalls, Jan. 19, 1900. IP.

10. From a memoir written by Mrs. John J. Ingalls, the former Anna Louisa Chesebrough. It was entitled "My Husband John James Ingalls." IP.

11. ETI to JJI, Dec. 26, 1869. IP.

12. "Pictures From Memory." IP. This is remembrance number three on the list, and again if this is the correct chronological order, Ingalls first remembered being in a Baptist church with his father at age three.

13. ETI to JJI, Dec. 26, 1869. IP.

14. ETI to JJI, Nov. 27, 1870. IP.

15. The age at which he was baptized is inscribed in his baptismal booklet which was comparable to a baptismal certificate. IP.

16. "Pictures From Memory." IP. Also *New York Times,* Aug. 17, 1900.

17. Copy of a letter written by Margaret Ingalls to Ellsworth Ingalls, May 25, 1930. IP. This letter described Elias T. Ingalls as a resourceful, inventive man who invented the machine mentioned here. In all, the let-

ter claims he invented seventeen different kinds of machines for the manufacture of shoes. Also he invented a steam-radiator system for heating homes.

18. *Catalogue of the Officers and Students of Williams College for the Academic Year 1851-52*, pp. 5 and 15.

19. *Ibid.*

20. In a letter to the author from William J. Cartwright, researcher at Williams College Library, he stated, "While we do not have class records, we do have preserved 'Minutes of the Faculty' covering those early days . . . . During his college course, Ingalls was fined three times for absence from church . . . . He was not the only one, but I mention it to give a glimpse of the college life then, not to be critical of Ingalls." May 12, 1964.

21. William J. Cartwright to Burton J. Williams, May 12, 1964. Also a program in the James A. Garfield papers in the ms. division of the Library of Congress, Washington, D.C., states that John J. Ingalls was president of the "Adelphic Union Debate." Garfield, also a student at Williams College, graduated in 1856, a year later than Ingalls.

22. Ingalls himself had boasted of his academic prowess. Others conceded that he was brilliant although eccentric.

23. JJI to "Dear Friend," June 10, 1852. Ms. division of the Williams College Library, Williamstown, Mass.

24. *Ibid.*

25. *Ibid.*

26. This was an independent publication of the Williams College student body. Vol. 1, no. 1, of the 1853-1854 *Williams Quarterly* contained six poems by Ingalls entitled "The Sculptor to His Statue," "May Dreams," "Life's Autumn," "Vespers," "Storm at Midnight," and "The Erlking." These poems are the least pessimistic

of Ingalls' extant college compositions; in fact some are idealistic.

27. JJI to Morris Ingalls, his brother, June 26, 1855. IP.

28. *Ibid.*

29. IP. The recurrent theme of hopelessness and frustration is typical of most of Ingalls' extant college compositions.

30. IP.

31. "Essay on Creation." IP.

32. "The Sun Lover, or The Autobiography of a Monomaniac." IP.

33. *Ibid.*

34. *Ibid.*

35. "The Admirable Crichton." IP.

36. From an untitled essay in IP.

37. "Two Sabbaths." IP.

38. JJI to his daughter Muriel Ingalls, May 31, 1900. IP.

39. The 1882 Sketch of Ingalls contained in the *Williams College Reports* reminded everyone that the subject of his commencement oration was "Mummy Life." William J. Cartwright, in a letter to the author, stated that the college did not have a copy of the "Mummy Life" address. Aug. 19, 1964.

40. This appeared under the title "A Brace of College Characters," *The Williams Quarterly*, vol. 3, no. 1, Sept., 1855.

41. JJI to John Graham, Oct. 14, 1855. This letter was in the papers of President James A. Garfield in the ms. division of the Library of Congress, Washington, D.C. An examination of the Williams College catalogues for the four years Ingalls was a student there did not reveal John Graham to be a student.

42. *Ibid.*

43. *The Williams College Class Report*, 1857.

44. *Ibid.* For the "log" story see Frederick Rudolph, *Mark Hopkins*

and the Log: *Williams College, 1836–1872* (New Haven, Conn.: Yale Univ. Press, 1956), pp. vii, 227.

45. *A Collection of the Writings of* *John James Ingalls: Essays, Addresses, and Orations* (Kansas City, Mo.: Hudson-Kimberly Publishing Co., 1902), p. 36.

Chapter 2

1. JJI to ETI, Sumner, K.T., Oct. 5, 1858. IP.

2. *Ibid.*

3. This quotation is taken from a typed ms. written by Ethel Ingalls. It is a biographical account of both her father and mother and was written in collaboration with her mother, Anna Louisa Chesebrough Ingalls, probably about 1905, or five years after Ingalls' death. Hereafter this ms., a part of the Ingalls Papers in the KSHS will be referred to as EIms.

4. *Ibid.*

5. A reference to a moral commitment as a reason for his Kansas migration is to be found in a letter quoted in *The Writings of John J. Ingalls,* p. 36: "A few days later, my studies completed, I joined the uninterrupted and resistless column of volunteers that marched to the lands of the free."

6. There is no question regarding Ingalls' politics, however; he was a Republican who was strongly opposed to slavery. His opposition to slavery was more than political; it was personal. In his lifetime he championed the cause of Negro civil rights, publicly and privately, and although he did not favor "miscegenation" in any sense of the word, he did show deep affection for the Negro domestic servants employed in his Atchison home. Ingalls was not like many of the "Free State" advocates who were simultaneously anti-Negro.

7. This quotation from an Ingalls letter is contained in EIms. Another reference to this "lithographic fiction" is to be found in a letter Ingalls wrote to his father, dated at Sumner, K.T., Oct. 5, 1858. IP.

8. *National Intelligencer,* Oct. 13, 1857. In 1860 these letters were incorporated in a book by Gilpin entitled *The Central Gold Region: the Grain, Pastoral, and Gold Regions of North America.* For an interesting account of Gilpin's experiences on the Santa Fe Trail see the article by Thomas L. Karnes entitled "Gilpin's Volunteers on the Santa Fe Trail," *Kansas Historical Quarterly,* vol. 30, no. 1 (Spring, 1964), pp. 1–14. For a penetrating analysis of Gilpin's contribution to Great Plains regionalism see James C. Malin, *The Grassland of North America* (Lawrence, Kans., 1961), pp. 173–258.

9. Sumner *Kanzas Gazette,* Sept. 12, 1857. In the article entitled "Sumner, Its Rise and Progress," it was pointed out that Sumner had "a New York *Weekly Tribune* Club of forty one subscribers, besides many other important improvements that we have not time to enumerate."

10. JJI to ETI, Sumner, K.T., Oct. 6, 1858. IP.

11. Mrs. John J. Ingalls, "My Husband John James Ingalls." This statement is especially significant in view of the "panic" of 1857 which was followed by news of a Kansas gold strike in 1858. Ingalls also had an opportunity to learn of the "West" through a member of his graduating class, Dwight Hubbard, who was a resident of St. Louis, Mo. *Catalogue of the Officers and Students of Williams College, 1854–1855.*

12. This quote is from an article Ingalls wrote in 1896, which he entitled "Kansas." It appeared in a booklet entitled *A Kansas Souvenir: A Book of Information Relative to the Moral,*

Educational, Agricultural, Commercial, Manufacturing and Mining Interests of the State. It was issued by the Kansas Immigration and Information Association in 1896. In this article Ingalls briefly reviewed his migration to Kansas in 1858.

13. JJI to ETI, Sumner, K.T., Oct. 6, 1858. IP.

14. Edmund Burke, *The Works of the Right Honorable Edmund Burke* (10 vols.; Boston: Little, Brown and Company, 1866), VII, 150.

15. JJI to ETI, Boston, Mass., Sept. 23, 1858. IP.

16. Elms. JJI to ETI, Elmira, N.Y., Sept. 24, 1858.

17. JJI to ETI, Cleveland, Ohio, Sept. 25, 1858. IP.

18. JJI to ETI, St. Louis, Mo., Sept. 29, 1858. IP.

19. JJI to ETI, Sumner, K.T., Oct. 5, 1858. IP. Ingalls mentioned in this letter that it was in St. Louis that he experienced his first real feelings of downheartedness and melancholy and that he was relieved to board the Pacific Railroad train for the West. In following his commentary en route to Sumner, it appears that his depression and despondency increased in proportion to the distance traveled west. At Buffalo he was elated with Niagara Falls; from Cleveland he related that he was thrilled by the Great Lakes; in Indiana he reported the effects of the scenery were "depressing in the extreme"; and while in St. Louis he was so depressed that he could hardly wait to leave that place. In Kansas City, however, he viewed the scene more favorably. This suggests that there was, at least in Ingalls' mind, something romantic or uplifting about the "Far West" and that the sparsely settled regions in between were just scoured enough by human habitation to be despoiled, having as yet been unable to produce a culture worthy of the name. The "frontier," however, to which Ingalls

was headed, he regarded as "dramatic," "fascinating," "tempting," "mysterious," and as a place that provided an opportunity to "conquer."

20. JJI to ETI, St. Louis, Mo., Sept. 29, 1858. IP.

21. JJI to ETI, Sumner, K.T., Oct. 5, 1858. IP.

22. *Ibid.*

23. JJI to ETI, Sumner, K.T., Oct. 5, 1858. IP. There were two letters written on this date, one in the morning and one in the afternoon; this quote comes from the latter.

24. *Ibid.*

25. The original contract for the grading of Washington Avenue is among the IP. The cost and the name of the contractor are clearly delineated in the provisions of the contract. E. W. Howe is in error when he states that the cost was $20,000, and it is doubtful if the laborers and teams were imported from St. Louis as stated. See *Kansas Historical Collections*, XII, 438.

26. JJI to ETI, Sumner, K.T., Oct. 5, 1858. IP.

27. *Ibid.*

28. JJI to ETI, Sumner, K.T., Oct. 6, 1858. IP.

29. JJI to ETI, Sumner, K.T., Oct. 24, 1858. IP.

30. *Ibid.*

31. JJI to ETI, Sumner, K.T., Nov. 5, 1858. IP.

32. JJI to ETI, Sumner, K.T., Oct. 24, 1858. IP.

33. The original constitution is a part of the IP. The constitution of the Sumner Company is composed of several sheets of lined paper pasted together to form a continuous piece of paper approximately two feet long. It is written in script and there are occasional misspellings.

34. JJI to ETI, Sumner, K.T., Nov. 5, 1858. IP.

35. JJI to ETI, Sumner, K.T., Oct.

11, 1858. IP. In this letter Ingalls had nothing but the highest praise for Richardson, describing him as a "very honest, reliable, sagacious man, of long experience in Western life, though not yet quite thirty years old, and talks more fairly than any man whom I had previously met."

36. JJI to ETI, Sumner, K.T., Dec. 12, 1858. IP.

37. It is interesting to note Ingalls' uncertainty with regard to the question as to just where he might most profitably locate. His Free State sentiments did not seem to figure very strongly as a determinant in making the final decision. In a letter to his father dated at Sumner on Nov. 14, 1858, he stated his position on the whole matter very precisely: "I do not consider myself permanently located here. If any other place should seem to me to offer greater scope for any kind of labor which I can perform I shall enter upon it readily: but at present I regard the City of Sumner as my home." IP.

38. JJI to ETI, Sumner, K.T., Dec. 2, 1858. IP.

39. JJI to ETI, Sumner, K.T., Oct. 11 and Nov. 14, 1858. IP. The books he felt to be "absolutely indispensable" were: *Bouvier's Law Dictionary,* 2 vols.; *Chitty On Contracts; Greenleaf on Evidence,* 3 vols.; *Davis' Massachusetts Justice; Davis' Criminal Justice; Story's Bills and Promissory Notes,* 2 vols.; *Walker on American Law,* 2 vols.; *Oliver's Conveyances; Interest Tables; Greenleaf's Cruise* (Real Estate), 3 vols.; and *Parson's Mercantile Law.*

40. JJI to ETI, Sumner, K.T., Nov. 21, 1858. IP.

41. *Ibid.* The difficulty of getting paid in cash was a major problem for Ingalls, who related that he was usually paid in goods or services. "Out of one client I get a desk made for my office; out of another, a tailor, I get my old cloak manufactured into an excellent sack coat, which is the most extraordinary of garments for comfort, if nothing more." JJI to ETI, Sumner, K.T., Nov. 5, 1858. IP.

42. ETI to JJI, Haverhill, Mass., Oct. 28, 1858. IP.

Chapter 3

1. JJI to ETI, Sumner, K.T., Nov. 6, 1858. IP.

2. JJI to ETI, Sumner, K.T., Nov. 17, 1858. IP.

3. JJI to ETI, Sumner, K.T., Nov. 14, 1858. IP.

4. JJI to ETI, Sumner, K.T., Dec. 12, 1858. IP.

5. JJI to ETI, Sumner, K.T., Dec. 22, 1858. IP.

6. JJI to ETI, Sumner, K.T., Dec. 8, 1858. IP.

7. JJI to ETI, Sumner, K.T., Dec. 2, 1858. IP.

8. JJI to ETI, Lawrence, K.T., Jan. 2, 1859. IP.

9. JJI to ETI, Sumner, K.T., Dec. 22, 1858, and Jan. 2, 1859. IP.

10. JJI to ETI, Sumner, K.T., Feb. 16, 1859. IP.

11. JJI to ETI, Sumner, K.T., Mar. 1, 1859. IP.

12. JJI to ETI, Lawrence, K.T., Jan. 12, 1859. IP. The Walsh referred to was Hugh Sleight Walsh.

13. ETI to JJI, Haverhill, Mass., Jan. 22, 1859. IP.

14. JJI to ETI, Lawrence, K.T., Jan. 12, 1859. IP.

15. JJI to ETI, Lawrence, K.T., Feb. 11, 1859. IP. For an appraisal of the role of Governor Medary in this period of Kansas history see James C. Malin, *On The Nature of History* (Lawrence, Kans., 1954), "The Nature of the American Civil War: The

Verdict of Three Kansas Democrats," pp. 197–236.

16. JJI to ETI, Lawrence, K.T., Jan. 2, 1859. IP.

17. JJI to ETI, Sumner, K.T., Feb. 16, 1859. IP.

18. JJI to ETI, Sumner, K.T., Mar. 15, 1859. IP. Ingalls was obviously in error in his account of the founding of Topeka and Manhattan, as these towns predated the Pike's Peak gold rush.

19. *Ibid.*

20. JJI to ETI, Sumner, K.T., Mar. 29, 1859. IP.

21. JJI to ETI, Sumner, K.T., May 13, 1859. IP.

22. JJI to ETI, Sumner, K.T., June 10, 1859. IP. The vote tally given in Atchison *Freedom's Champion,* June 11, 1859, showed that Robert Graham led Ingalls by eighteen votes.

23. JJI to ETI, Wyandotte, K.T., July 5, 1859. IP. Atchison *Freedom's Champion,* July 16, 1859, reported that the delegates included thirty-four Republicans, seventeen Democrats, and one Independent. All of the convention officers were Republicans. There were eighteen farmers, twenty attorneys, nine merchants, three "manufacturers," three physicians, one land agent, one mechanic, one lawyer, one editor, one surveyor, one clergyman, and one journalist. Fourteen delegates were originally from Ohio, nine from Pennsylvania, six from Indiana, four from Kentucky, four from Vermont, four from New York, three from Maryland, three from New Hampshire, one from Georgia, and one from Virginia. Two delegates were originally from England, while Ireland, Germany, and Scotland had one each. This issue of the *Champion* also listed all committee appointments. Ingalls was a member of the Schedule Committee, the Amendment and Miscellaneous Committee, and the Phraseology and Arrangement Committee. Ironically, Ingalls' home state, Massachusetts, was not listed, although he was a member of the delegation.

24. This essay is written in Ingalls' own hand and is in the IP in the KSHS.

25. *Ibid.*

26. JJI to ETI, Sumner, K.T., Aug. 14, 1859. IP. In regard to Ingalls' claim that he designed the state seal and motto see *The Writings of John James Ingalls,* pp. 481–482.

27. "Wyandot Constitution." Ingalls and several others were scheduled to speak at a number of Republican rallies in support of the constitution. Atchison *Freedom's Champion,* Aug. 13, 1859, listed Ingalls as the speaker scheduled for rallies that were to be held at Sumner on Aug. 17, Port William on Aug. 18, Pardee on Aug. 20, and Kapioma on Aug. 27. The speech that Ingalls claimed to have made in Atchison was not reported in the *Champion.*

28. JJI to ETI, Sumner, K.T., Sept. 4, 1859. IP.

29. JJI to ETI, Sumner, K.T., Oct. 18, 1859. IP.

30. JJI to ETI, Sumner, K.T., Oct. 29, 1859. IP.

31. Atchison *Freedom's Champion,* Dec. 10, 1859. The headlines for this issue read as follows: "Atchison County Redeemed, Her Freemen Wake Up, Glorious Victory Rejoice! Freemen Rejoice!" Also the Dec. 17, 1859, edition of the *Champion* spoke of the election under the titles "The Victory" and "Let The Eagle Scream."

32. The problems of providing himself with even a subsistence living are seen in letters to his father dated from Sumner, K.T., on Mar. 29, Aug. 14, and Oct. 18, 1859. IP.

33. On Dec. 17, 1859, the Atchison *Freedom's Champion* reported that the Pike's Peak Express had just returned from Denver bearing a total

of $32,000 in gold dust. On Feb. 25, 1860, the *Champion* reported the completion of the Atchison and St. Joseph Railroad, and the paper boasted that this put Atchison within seventeen hours of Chicago.

34. JJI to ETI, Sumner, K.T., Jan. 25, 1860. IP.

35. JJI to ETI, Sumner, K.T., Apr. 3, 1860. IP. In *Kansas Historical Collections*, XII, 471, Ingalls is listed as one of the incorporators of the towns of Arazo and Detroit, Arapahoe County, in what was to become Colorado Territory. His interest in these towns no doubt was a contributing factor in his desire to journey to the Pike's Peak country.

36. JJI to ETI, Sumner, K.T., Jan. 25, 1860. IP.

37. Atchison *Freedom's Champion*, Apr. 21, 1860.

38. *Kansas Historical Collections*, XII, 438. In all the extant correspondence of Ingalls there is no mention of the tornado that was supposed to have been so completely devastating to Sumner.

39. Atchison *Freedom's Champion*, June 9, 1860.

40. Mrs. John J. Ingalls also believed that the alleged tornado was the reason for her husband's move from Sumner to Atchison. See her ms. entitled "My Husband John J. Ingalls." IP. Ingalls discussed his legal partnership and his commuting between Sumner and Atchison in a letter to his father dated at Sumner, K.T., Oct. 7, 1860. IP. The date of the letter indicates that Ingalls was still a resident of Sumner some four months after the town was allegedly destroyed by the tornado.

41. JJI to ETI, Sumner, K.T., Oct. 7, 1860. IP. The first professional notice of Ingalls as a law partner with Adams and Leland appeared in the Atchison *Freedom's Champion* on July 28, 1860.

42. Atchison *Freedom's Champion*, Oct. 20 and 27, 1860.

Chapter 4

1. JJI to ETI, Lawrence, K.T., Jan. 19, 1861. IP.

2. *Ibid.*

3. *Ibid.*

4. Atchison *Freedom's Champion*, Feb. 26, 1861.

5. *Ibid.*

6. *Ibid.*

7. *Ibid.*

8. JJI to ETI, Atchison, Kans., Mar. 21, 1861. IP.

9. *Ibid.*

10. *Ibid.*

11. *Ibid.* Atchison *Freedom's Champion*, Dec. 31, 1859, and subsequent issues, hailed Samuel C. Pomeroy as the best possible choice as a U.S. Senator to represent Kansas.

12. JJI to ETI, Atchison, Kans., Mar. 21, 1861. IP. Ethel Ingalls in her ms. described Lane and Pomeroy. The descriptions are apparently based on some of her father's letters and read as follows: "James Henry Lane had an extraordinary assemblage of mental, moral and physical traits. A lean, haggard and sinewy figure with a Mephistophelian leer upon his shaven image, his movements were alert and restless. Professing religion, he was never accused of hypocrisy for his followers knew that he partook of the sacrament as a political device to secure the support of the church and that with the same nonchalant alacrity, had he been running for office in Hindustan, he would have thrown his offspring to the crocodiles of the Ganges or bowed [with] Parsees at the shrine of the Sun."

In another place Ethel described the Lane and anti-Lane political factions. The language of the manuscript is in the first person and the speaker is obviously Ethel's mother, Anna Louisa Chesebrough Ingalls: "There were two factions—Lane and anti-Lane. My father [Ellsworth Chesebrough] was anti-Lane—a Pomeroy man, as was all of Atchison. But, strange to say, I always admired Jim Lane, and I never missed an opportunity to hear him when he spoke in Atchison. He was a natural orator, although not a scholar. He had a high rasping voice, his utterance was clear and easily heard, and he never failed to arouse enthusiasm; few could resist his appeal. Always, he convinced his listeners of his sincerity, and he was largely responsible for raising the Thirteenth Kansas Regiment. When dashing Jim Lane came to town, great bonfires blazed on Commercial street. A dry-goods box draped in red calico was his platform. The band would play and a crowd would gather. The *Champion*, Atchison's daily [weekly] newspaper, was against him, so he was not well advertised. Word of his coming, however, brought men and women from all directions.

"He would begin his speech quietly, confidentially. Soon he warmed up, took off his coat and vest, loosened his tie and was ready for the fray.

"Once he took breakfast in my father's house, after the hatchet was buried. I considered him very good looking. He was tall and slender, a typical westerner. His death was a great shock to me and to all his friends. He was unhappy in his family life—a contrast to Pomeroy who posed as a religious statesman and Sunday school man.

"Mrs. Pomeroy, his second wife, was a superior woman, a temperance worker and abolitionist. She died during the war and he married a rich widow who never was appreciated in Kansas, but was popular in Washington." EIms., IP.

13. JJI to ETI, Atchison, Kans., Mar. 21, 1861. IP.

14. JJI to "Dear Bro.," Topeka, Kans., Apr. 12, 1861. IP.

15. *Ibid.* Obviously Ingalls was referring to Pomeroy's administration of relief funds destined for destitute Kansas settlers.

16. *Ibid.*

17. JJI to ETI, Topeka, Kans., May 15, 1861. IP.

18. JJI to ETI, Atchison, Kans., July 1, 1861. IP. This sale of Sumner shares is interesting in light of the fact that Sumner had suffered from a severe tornado and a general exodus of the population was taking place, which eventually included Ingalls himself. Perhaps Ingalls was looking forward to the future union of the towns of Atchison and Sumner, an idea he had suggested earlier. If this were to occur, then the Sumner stock would be expected to rise in the not-too-distant future. In any event there is no mention of the payment of $15,000 for the shares, and in all likelihood his father and brother merely advanced him sufficient funds to supply him with his immediate needs. Shortly after the sale of his Sumner shares, Ingalls left for Denver City, Colo. Terr.

19. Atchison *Freedom's Champion*, July 6, 1861.

20. JJI to ETI, Atchison, Kans., July 12, 1861. IP. Obviously Ingalls did not intend to remain in Colorado. In all probability he was more interested in "scouting out" the prospects of the Territory and looking into the possibilities of the several Colorado corporations to which he had previously referred.

21. JJI to ETI, Rocky Mountains, Aug. 23, 1861. IP.

22. JJI to ETI, Central City, Colo. Terr., Sept. 5, 1861. IP.

23. JJI to ETI, Atchison, Kans., Sept. 27, 1861. IP. In letters to his wife

and daughter Ethel, written many years later, Ingalls vividly recalled his trip to Colorado and gave expression to his thoughts as follows: "The first time I saw Denver was in 1861, after a journey of 600 miles on a bay bronco, with my belongings on a yellow mule, across a treeless and unpeopled desert. But the romance of the lonely, and mysterious Plains has vanished with the subjugation of the desert and the abolition of the frontier. It was a desolate and shabby hamlet in those early days, and I remember the eagerness with which I retired with my mail, the accumulation of six weeks, to the shady side of a slab saloon, and read about the distant world which I had left so long before—It is a marvel among cities, but for some unexplicable reason, it has always seemed to me a desolate cheerless lonesome place, to be shunned and avoided." JJI to Ethel Ingalls, Atchison, May 19, —. IP.

In another letter written to his wife he again gave expression to reflections on his 1861 Denver trip: "The snowy Sierra above was rosy, and Pike's Peak glowed as if luminous with an internal flame. The long, long years since that youthful morning when I beheld the splendid spectacle for the first time seemed to vanish for an instant, but the shadows of fate soon closed down again and I walked in dust and ashes to the Oxford Hotel." JJI to ALI, Denver, Colo., Nov. 15, 1896. IP.

24. JJI to ETI, Atchison, Kans., Sept. 27, 1861. IP.

25. JJI to ETI, Atchison, Kans., Oct. 16, 1861. IP.

26. Atchison *Freedom's Champion,* Oct. 19, 1861, referred to the county "Union Convention," listing the candidates for the office of state senator. One of Ingalls' opponents, ironically, was Ellsworth Chesebrough, his future wife's father, whom he easily defeated.

27. JJI to ETI, Atchison, Kans., Oct. 16, 1861. IP.

28. *Ibid.* With reference to Ingalls' Pike's Peak journey see the article by the author entitled "The Platte, The Plains and the Peak: Grand Theory and Local History," *Great Plains Journal,* Fall, 1968, pp. 1–15.

29. Atchison *Freedom's Champion,* Nov. 9, 1861. A short time later Ingalls was elected to fill a vacancy in the state senate which resulted when John A. Martin was commissioned in the Kansas Militia.

30. *Ibid.* Also JJI to ETI, Atchison, Kans., Nov. 19, 1861. IP.

31. JJI to ETI, Atchison, Kans., Nov. 19, 1861. IP.

32. JJI to ETI, Topeka, Kans., Feb. 23, 1862. IP.

33. Atchison *Freedom's Champion,* Apr. 26, 1862.

34. Ellsworth Chesebrough to Samuel C. Pomeroy, Atchison, Kans., Apr. 20, 1862. IP.

35. *Ibid.*

36. JJI to F. G. Adams, Atchison, Kans., May 3, 1862. IP.

37. ETI to JJI, Haverhill, Mass., Sept. 30, 1862. IP.

38. JJI to ETI, Atchison, Kans., Sept. 30, 1862. IP. Also, Atchison *Freedom's Champion* carried an account of the convention in its Oct. 4, 1862, issue.

39. JJI to ETI, Wyandot, Kans., Oct. 24, 1862. IP.

40. *Ibid.*

41. JJI to ETI, Atchison, Kans., Nov. 19, 1862. IP.

42. *Ibid.*

43. ETI to JJI, Haverhill, Mass., Sept. 30, 1862. IP.

44. JJI to ETI, Atchison, Kans., Sept. 30, 1862. IP. Ingalls and his father had considerably different opinions towards Lincoln's wartime policy regarding the Negro. Though both In-

galls and his father opposed slavery, they had not been able to agree on the best policy for obtaining freedom for the Negro slaves.

45. John A. Martin to JJI, Nashville, Tenn., Nov. 12, 1862. IP.

46. *Ibid.*

47. The information contained in the preceding paragraph was taken from a letter from JJI to ETI, Atchison, Kans., Dec. 25, 1862. IP.

48. JJI to ETI, Atchison, Kans., Jan. 8, 1863. IP.

49. *Ibid.*

50. JJI to ETI, Atchison, Kans., Jan. 17, 1863. IP.

51. *Ibid.*

52. JJI to ETI, Atchison, Kans., Sept. 5, 1863. IP.

53. *Ibid.* This letter is the most graphic account of the raid that has been seen by the author. Also see the author's article entitled "Quantrill's Raid on Lawrence: A Question of Complicity," *Kansas Historical Quarterly,* vol. 34, no. 2 (Sumner, 1968); pp. 143–149.

54. *Ibid.* Obviously Ingalls must have reported that Stebbins was mismanaging the paper.

55. *Ibid.*

56. John A. Martin to JJI, Chattanooga, Tenn., Oct. 18, 1863. IP.

57. *Ibid.*

58. *Ibid.* Again on Jan. 1, 1864, Martin wrote to Ingalls from Strawberry Plains, Tenn., urging the return of the regiment. IP.

59. A. D. Horton to JJI, Washington, D.C., May 1, 1864. IP.

60. *Ibid.*

61. John F. Martin, Adj., to JJI, Topeka, Kans., May 13, 1864. IP. There is no clear explanation as to why Ingalls was commissioned a major in the Kansas State Militia in 1864 when he had previously been commissioned a colonel in 1861.

62. John A. Martin to JJI, Lookout Mountain, Tenn., Sept. 6, 1864. IP.

63. *Ibid.* Apparently Ingalls never shared the enthusiasm Martin showed for Lincoln or for the draft.

64. JJI to ETI, Camp Near Big Blue Ridge, Mo., Oct. 21, 1864. IP. An interesting account of Ingalls' part in repulsing Price's invasion is contained in *Lippincott's Monthly Magazine,* XLVI (July, 1890), 141–149.

65. *Ibid.*

66. Atchison *Freedom's Champion,* Sept. 22, 1864, announced that Ingalls had been nominated as Lieutenant-Governor on the "Republican Union Ticket." By this time the motto of the *Champion* had been changed from "It is better to be right than President" to "Union and Liberty."

67. Pardee Butler to JJI, n.p., Nov. 3, 1864. IP.

68. JJI to ETI, Atchison, Kans., Dec. 17, 1864. IP.

69. *Ibid.*

70. Atchison *Freedom's Champion,* Sept. 1, 1864.

71. JJI to ETI, Atchison, Kans., Dec. 17, 1864. IP.

72. Atchison *Freedom's Champion,* Dec. 29, 1864.

Chapter 5

1. JJI to ETI, Atchison, Kans., Jan. 16, 1865. IP.

2. This is the date reported in EIms. Actually the date was 1859; the erroneous date is either an error of type or memory. IP.

3. Mrs. John J. Ingalls, who collaborated with Ethel Ingalls in writing this ms., spoke in the first person and stated, "My mother was born and died in New York City and is buried in Greenwood cemetery, Brooklyn." Also

a copy of a letter from "Aunt" Mary Addison DeGoll to Fanny Chesebrough stated that the cause of death was tuberculosis. She claimed that Mrs. Chesebrough was seized with a coughing spell after which she noticed blood on her handkerchief. The letter concluded with the statement that "the scarlet stain on her handkerchief was in that period a virtual sentence of death."

Anna Louisa Chesebrough spoke of her birth and that of her sister as follows: "I was born in New York City April 9, 1843, at 122 Pearl Street, corner Whitehall St. My sister Fanny was born on Spring St., June 28, 1844." No doubt the sudden death of Ellsworth Chesebrough's young wife influenced him to move to a climate that he hoped would be better when it appeared that Fanny was developing the same ailment that killed her mother. All of the above information appears in EIms., IP.

4. As a result of this application of the Kearney name, Anna Louisa signed her name Anna Louisa K. Chesebrough.

5. Anna Louisa's sister, Fanny, was present for the commencement and wrote a long descriptive letter to her Grandmother Chesebrough, telling of the honors her sister, Lou, had received.

When Ellsworth Chesebrough arrived in Atchison, he immediately leased a store building and, taking Lou with him, went to St. Louis to purchase a supply of goods. While in St. Louis he probably made contact with the school that Lou graduated from. EIms., IP.

6. Ethel Ingalls claimed that he was forty-eight years old when he died "and much talked of for governor when he died in the autumn of 1864." She described the fatal illness as erysipelas. EIms., IP.

7. Atchison *Freedom's Champion*, Oct. 20, 1864, listed Ellsworth Chese-brough along with Marcus Parrott and Robert McBratney as candidates for electors. Chesebrough died on Oct. 24, and on Oct. 27, 1864, the *Champion* listed W. F. Cloud as his replacement. Also on Oct. 27, 1864, the *Champion* carried a one-third-column eulogy of Chesebrough. John J. Ingalls, who was editing the *Champion* at this time, probably wrote this tribute to the father of his future wife.

8. Leavenworth *Daily Conservative*, Dec. 14, 1864. The ad read, "For those desiring to enter into business where the business is already established. The entire stock of E. Chesebrough, deceased, late of Atchison, Kansas, is offered for sale at a bargain. The situation of this stand is unsurpassed. The sales during the last year have exceeded $200,000.00 Terms reasonable. Mrs. E. Chesebrough, Administratrix."

9. The gown worn by Lou was later worn by her daughter Ethel at the inaugural ball of Benjamin Harrison. EIms., IP.

10. A note from ALI to JJI dated May 9, 1865, refers to this practice. The note was signed "Ever your Friend Louisa Chesebrough." IP.

11. Ethel Ingalls commented that it was likely that in the spring the northward migration of the animals was conducted along more sheltered and remote routes. EIms., IP.

12. A copy of the letter reads as follows: "My love for you has become the one absorbing and controlling impulse of my life. If it is hopeless, return this note to me unanswered. If there may be any future for us, tell me when I can see you alone and say to you what I wished but dared not say an hour ago.

"Do not in any event deny me the privilege of remaining always
    Your friend
    J. J. Ingalls"
The letter was not dated. EIms., IP.

---

13. JJI to ETI, Atchison, Kans., Sept. 24, 1865. IP.

14. Ethel Ingalls in her ms. stated that Mrs. Ellsworth Chesebrough asked this because Mr. Chesebrough was so recently deceased and because she was hardly able to bear the loss of her daughter at this time. Ethel suggested, however, that Mrs. Chesebrough may have suffered a disappointment in love, thinking that Ingalls' visits to her home had been directed towards her rather than Lou. Ethel stated that Mrs. Chesebrough more or less dominated Ingalls' visits with her brilliant conversation and probably construed Ingalls' attention to her conversation as personal rather than intellectual. Mrs. Chesebrough at this time was forty and Ingalls was thirty-one. EIms., IP.

15. JJI to ETI, Atchison, Kans., Aug. 2, 1865. There are no extant letters written en route; however, he did make the trip that he referred to in a letter to his father dated at Atchison, Kans., Sept. 24, 1865. IP.

16. A copy of Lou's letter relating her mother's change of heart was dated Aug. 4, 1865. IP. It reads as follows:

"My Darling,

"I have good news for us both. Mamma has undergone a metamorphosis. She has consented to our marriage in September. Will that suit you Dearest? I can hardly realize it, but it is really true. Fortune seems to favor us now and I am too happy. Love, come over this evening right early to see

Your own loving
Lou"

17. The marriage is recorded in the marriage records of the Atchison County courthouse in book no. 1, p. 274, and simply reads: "I hereby certify that on this day at 7 P.M. at the house of Mrs. Ellsworth Chesebrough in this city, John James Ingalls Esq. and Miss Anna Louisa Chesebrough, both of Atchison, were joined together in Holy Matrimony by me" (signed Thomas H. Vail, Bishop of the [Episcopal] Diocese of Kansas). The certificate was filed Sept. 30, 1865. Simultaneously Lou's sister, Fanny, was married to Andrew Hughes of the well-known Bella Hughes family.

In her ms., Ethel Ingalls provides a detailed description of the costumes and the general ceremony. John A. Martin, editor of the Atchison *Freedom's Champion* was one of the groomsmen. After the ceremony the principals in the wedding party went to St. Louis on their honeymoon. EIms., IP.

18. ETI to JJI, Haverhill, Mass., Sept. 28, 1865. IP.

19. *Ibid.*

20. JJI to ETI, Atchison, Kans., Oct. 28, 1865. IP.

21. "My Husband John James Ingalls" by Mrs. Ingalls. IP.

22. *Ibid.*

23. *Ibid.*

24. Mrs. Ingalls related the interesting details of their move to the river-bluff property as follows: "Your father purchased the property on the River Bluff—we moved in June just before Ellsworth was born—It was a very small house—1 story & a half—2 rooms above and 2 below—no hall —a small kitchen on the west—later Papa built a servants bedroom—We had a nice cistern but our drinking water came from Dickens' spring.

"We were attracted by the river— We owned only the two lots—north to south—but later purchased all the rest of the block (no streets) it seemed quite in the country—We made no change in the house until after Ethel's birth—then we built a wing to the south—2 stories—but only finished two down stairs rooms— which we used for bedrooms—the house had many changes and it expanded in many directions. . . . In the large bedroom was Papa's Desk, which Ethel now has—& on this Papa wrote Blue Grass, Regis Loisell, etc. all the articles that appeared in the famous Kansas Magazine—So he had great power of concentration—Ralph & Addison & Constance & Marion were born in this room." "My Husband John James Ingalls" by Mrs. Ingalls. IP.

25. "My Husband John James Ingalls" by Mrs. Ingalls. IP.

26. JJI to ETI, Atchison, Kans., July 20, 1865. IP.

27. *Ibid.*

28. *Ibid.*

29. JJI to ETI, Atchison, Kans., July 29, 1865. IP.

30. JJI to ETI, Atchison, Kans., Aug. 2, 1865. IP.

31. JJI to ETI, Atchison, Kans., July 20, 1865. IP.

32. *Ibid.*

33. ETI to JJI, Haverhill, Mass., Aug. 31, 1866. IP.

34. JJI to ETI, Atchison, Kans., Feb. 21, 1867. IP.

35. *Ibid.*

36. JJI to ETI, Atchison, Kans., Mar. 13, 1867. IP.

37. *Ibid.*

38. JJI to ETI, Atchison, Kans., July 30, 1867. IP.

39. JJI to ETI, Atchison, Kans., May 24, 1867. IP.

40. JJI to ETI, Atchison, Kans., Aug. 25, 1868. IP.

41. Only one year's diary is known to be extant, that being for the year 1869. The surviving grandchildren remember that there were a number of diaries at one time, but where they are now, or what has become of them, is a mystery. Ethel Ingalls claimed that her mother began keeping a diary on Jan. 1, 1866. EIms., IP.

42. The diary is part of IP.

43. Anna Louisa Chesebrough is listed as a member of Trinity Church in the "Parish Families Book" No. 1, p. 9. Entries of family names begin as early as Nov. 15, 1863. The records of the church are at the Trinity Episcopal Church in Atchison and were made available to the author through the courtesy of Mrs. Robert Behrend, church secretary.

44. In the "Parish Families Book" no. 2, p. 19, Ingalls is listed as having been baptized. He was not listed, however, as having been confirmed nor was he considered a communicant.

45. Basic information in this chapter, thus far, came from EIms., IP., except where otherwise noted.

46. ETI to JJI, Haverhill, Mass., Oct. 15, 1869. Copy of a letter in IP.

47. "Uncle" Pendleton was actually Tarleton Pendleton. He was born in the Shenandoah Valley of Virginia in 1822. Early in the war he escaped from his owners, who had moved from Kentucky to St. Joseph, Mo. He fled to Atchison and took a job as waiter in a restaurant where Ingalls first met him. Ingalls grew fond of him, and when he married Lou, he took Pendleton into the service of the Ingalls family. All the children referred to him as "Uncle," and to distinguish him from Uncle Frank, Ingalls' brother, who was minister of the Congregational church in Atchison, the children referred to him as "black uncle." Ingalls himself delivered the following graveside eulogy for his faithful friend and servant: "For more than twenty years he has been in the service of my family. During this long period he has always manifested the same interest in my affairs as if they had been his own. I never knew him to do a dishonest action or to speak an untruthful word. He was faithful, upright and loyal in all the relations of life.

"At the open grave all men are equal. In the democracy of death the rich man is as poor as the poorest and the poor as rich as the richest. Here the wealthy man leaves his possessions, the proud man surrenders his honors and dignities — the worldly man relinquishes his pleasures and nothing remains but those moral qualities which define our relations to our fellow creatures and to God. Pendleton could neither read nor write. His long life of humble toil is ended—his name will be heard no more among men. But he leaves the memory of virtues which the highest may imitate with advantage and an example which all may follow with profit and safety. It was such as he that were in the mind of the Divine Teacher on the mountain of Judea when he declared that the lowly of spirit should possess the Kingdom of Heaven; that the meek should inherit the earth and that the pure in heart should see God. Here we leave him. He is at rest. May his soul abide in peace and felicity until the great day when the Lord shall come to judge the quick and the dead."

All of the information of this note comes from a copy of the history of and eulogy for Pendleton which is in IP.

48. JJI to ETI, Atchison, Kans., Mar. 27, 1870. IP.

49. The docket book for the U.S. Circuit Court at Topeka shows that the trial did not reach the courts until May 26, 1870. The trial lasted three days, with P. H. Sheridan and J. H. Paige as defendants in the first case and P. H. Sheridan in the second. The cattleman claimed that he was beaten, bruised, wounded, and imprisoned on Feb. 1, 1869, at the hands of the defendants near Camp Supply, Indian Territory, and that steers, cows, yearlings, and calves to the number of 250 head were taken from him. He asked $25,000 for his injuries and $7,900 for the cattle and personal property taken.

50. Topeka *Commonwealth* reported the proceedings on May 27, 29, and 31. A. H. Horton and a Mr. Wheaton were named as counsels for the defendants, and Ingalls was not mentioned at all. The docket book named four attorneys for the defendants, Messrs. Horton, Clove, and Wheaton, with Ingalls' name being added to the list later. The jury decided the case in favor of the defendants. Ingalls, however, did not get the publicity he had hoped for. The docket book for the U.S. Circuit Court at Topeka, Kans., is in the clerk's office of the District Court at Topeka, Kans.

51. JJI to ETI, Atchison, Kans., May 6, 1871. IP.

52. *Ibid.*

53. *Ibid.* Atchison *Daily Champion* was replete with such predictions of Atchison becoming the railroad center of Kansas. John A. Martin, the editor, was a great promoter and played up every aspect of the towns potential, often with a careless regard for the facts.

54. JJI to ETI, Atchison, Kans., Oct. 1, 1871. IP. Also, in Topeka *Commonwealth*, Apr. 19, 1870, there is a two-column description of Atchison. Under the subtitle "Other Lions," the *Commonwealth* speaks of JJI as one in the front rank of the bar of Atchison and "one of the most accomplished orators in the state," remarking that "all the appointments of his establishment give evidence of a prosperous business."

55. ALI to JJI, Atchison, Kans., Dec. 3, 187–. IP.

56. JJI to ETI, Atchison, Kans., Nov. 28, 1872. IP.

57. *Kansas Magazine* (Topeka: Kan-

sas Magazine Publishing Company, 1872), Feb. and Sept. issues.

58. See H. Clay Park, "The Rise and Fall of Sumner," *Collections of the Kansas State Historical Society, 1911–1912* (Topeka: State Printing Office, 1912), XII, 434–438.

59. Elms., IP.

60. *Ibid.*

61. *Kansas Collections*, II, 438.

62. *Kansas Magazine*, II (Sept., 1872), 272.

63. *Ibid.*

64. For a brief analysis of "Blue Grass" and "Catfish Aristocracy" see an article by the author entitled "John James Ingalls: Geographic Determinism and Kansas," in *Midwest Quarterly*, vol. 6, no. 3 (Spring, 1965), pp. 285–291.

Chapter 6

1. Samuel L. Clemens and Charles Dudley Warner, *The Gilded Age* (Hartford: 1873).

2. Henry Adams, *The Education of Henry Adams* (Boston and New York: 1927), p. 294.

3. Matthew Josephson, *The Robber Barons: The Great American Capitalists, 1861–1901* (New York: 1934).

4. *Nation*, XVI (May 22, 1873), 349.

5. JJI to ETI, Atchison, Kans., June 30, 1872. IP.

6. A holograph ms. speech of Ingalls', p. 26. The ms. is not dated and bears no title. Some of the statements found in the ms. are similar to statements Ingalls was to make in later years when he opposed civil-service reform under the Cleveland administration. IP.

7. JJI to ETI, Atchison, Kans., Sept. 14, 1872. IP.

8. *Ibid.*

9. *Ibid.*

10. Samuel C. Pomeroy to Samuel N. Wood, Washington, D.C., Dec. 3, 1872. Ms. division of KSHS.

11. Samuel C. Pomeroy to JJI, Topeka, Kans., Jan. 17, 1873. IP.

12. Kansas *House Journal*, 1873, p. 47.

13. Original telegram from JJI to his wife, Topeka, Kans., Jan. 28, 1873. IP.

14. Kansas *Daily Commonwealth*, Jan. 30, 1873.

15. *Ibid.* It must be remembered that York's statements, which are alleged to be quotations, were written from memory. No officer of the House or Senate took down York's statements as he spoke. In fact the *House Journal* and the *Senate Journal* of 1873 do not even mention York's speech. The only reference to York's part in the entire exposé is contained in a resolution passed by the House as follows: "Resolved, that the thanks of the Convention be and the same is hereby tendered to Hon. A. M. York for the services he has rendered this Convention and the people in exposing the corruption of S. C. Pomeroy" (*House Journal*, 1873, p. 244). The Kansas City *Journal* of June 6, 1906, carried a story of this election written by "Capt." Henry King, who stated that Col. W. H. Rossington later went to his desk and wrote the so-called York speech, "as in his opinion [it] ought to have been delivered and that was the speech that was printed everywhere."

16. Kansas *Daily Commonwealth*, Jan. 30, 1873.

17. A copy of the "Joint Roll—Senate and House—1873." The total vote tallied here agrees with that reported in *House Journal*, 1873, p. 242. An unidentified clipping in Marion Ingalls' scrapbook, entitled "Ingalls of Kansas," claimed that after York's speech everyone was afraid to vote for Pomeroy. "Ingalls was the next

leading candidate and he was elected. The legislators felt that in casting their votes for him they would be free from suspicion, and in this way, in a measure accidental, he received his first election." IP. *Harper's Weekly,* XVII (Mar. 1, 1873), 174, gives an account of the legislative activity on the day of Ingalls' election, including a lithograph picture of the scene of pandemonium. Tacoma, Washington, *Ledger,* Aug. 17, 1900, claimed that "Chance Sent Him to the Senate." The article claimed that Pomeroy's opponents were in such confusion when York made his speech exposing the incumbent Senator that in that moment "they were willing to unite on anyone." For a detailed, though undocumented, account of Ingalls' dramatic election, see Wichita *Eagle,* Aug. 19, 1900. For the most recent and provocative treatment of the election see the article by James C. Malin entitled "Some Reconsiderations of the Defeat of Senator Pomeroy of Kansas, 1873," *Mid-America,* vol. 48, no. 1 (Jan., 1966), pp. 47–57.

18. For a dramatic account of this election and its aftermath see "Gotterdammerung in Topeka: The Downfall of Senator Pomeroy," by Albert R. Kitzhaber, in *Kansas Historical Quarterly,* XVIII (Aug., 1950), 243–278.

19. A copy of the plea *State of Kansas* v. *Samuel C. Pomeroy,* Apr. 5, 1875. Ms. division of KSHS.

20. Atchison *Daily Champion* on Jan. 30, 1873, and for weeks afterward, persisted in defending Pomeroy throughout the entire proceedings, claiming that Pomeroy would explain all to the satisfaction of everyone when he had time to make an adequate reply.

21. JJI to James A. Garfield, Atchison, Kans., Feb. 7, 1873. Garfield papers, ms. division of Library of Congress. It is interesting to note that Garfield and Ingalls were distant relatives. Ingalls' father, Elias, was a first cousin of Mehitabel Ingalls, who was Garfield's grandmother.

22. Copy of the original Senate resolution concerning Ingalls' election in 1873. Dated at Topeka, Kans., Feb. 26, 1873, and signed by W. H. Smallwood, Secretary of State. IP.

23. *Nation,* XVI (Feb. 6, 1873), 87.

24. *Harper's Weekly,* XVII (Mar. 1, 1873), 170.

25. *New York Times,* Feb. 14, 1873, p. 1–1.

26. P. W. Hitchcock to JJI, Washington, D.C., Jan. 29, 1873. IP.

27. This diary entry was incorporated in EIms., IP.

28. *The Writings of John James Ingalls,* p. 9.

29. The original invitation is in IP.

30. *New York Times,* April 26, 1873, p. 7–1.

31. JJI to ALI, Washington, D.C., Sept. 30, 1873. IP.

32. JJI to ALI, Washington, D.C., Dec. 1, 1873. IP.

33. JJI to ALI, Washington, D.C., Nov. 29, 1873. IP.

34. *Ibid.*

35. The preceding information is taken from a letter that Ingalls wrote to his wife dated at Washington, D.C., Mar. 16, 1874. IP.

36. EIms., IP.

37. Much of this information comes from EIms.; however, Ingalls refers to it in letters dated Feb. 18, Mar. 6, May 18, and Dec. 22, 1874; Feb. 2, 1875; June 19, 1888; and thereafter. This is a selective, not an inclusive, list of letters that Ingalls wrote to his wife in which he referred to Ruth's death. IP.

38. ETI to JJI, Louisville, Ky., Feb. 18, 1874. IP.

39. JJI to ALI, Washington, D.C., Mar. 6, 1874. IP.

40. JJI to ALI, Washington, D.C.,

May 18, 1874. IP. Subsequent letters to his wife are replete with similar thoughts.

41. JJI to ALI, Washington, D.C., Mar. 17, 1874. IP.

42. JJI to ALI, Washington, D.C., Mar. 13, 1874. IP.

43. JJI to ALI, Washington, D.C., Mar. 3, 1874. IP.

44. JJI to ALI, Washington, D.C., Mar. 16, 1874. IP.

45. *Ibid.*

46. JJI to ALI, Washington, D.C., May 23, 1874. IP.

47. See *Congressional Record*, 43rd Cong., 1st sess. (Dec. 1, 1873–June 23, 1874), 2, pts. 1–6; also 43rd Cong., 2nd sess. (Dec. 7, 1874–Mar. 3, 1875), 3, pts. 1–3.

48. This account of the scandalous newspaper story is contained in a letter that Ingalls wrote to his father, dated at Atchison, Kans., Aug. 21, 1874. IP. *New York Times* also carried a brief article in which the charges were discussed. Aug. 18, 1874, p. 1–3.

49. JJI to ETI, Atchison, Kans., Oct. 18, 1874. IP.

50. JJI to ALI, Washington, D.C., Dec. 7, 1874. IP.

Chapter 7

1. JJI to ETI, n.p., Jan. 9, 1875. IP.

2. *Ibid.*

3. JJI to ALI, Washington, D.C., Dec. 7, 1874. IP.

4. JJI to ALI, Washington, D.C., Jan. —, 1875. IP.

5. JJI to ALI, Washington, D.C., Jan. 3, 1875. IP.

6. JJI to ALI, Washington, D.C., Jan. 31, 1875. IP. Surprising, because he was usually critical of church; however, he was never critical of Jesus.

7. JJI to ALI, Washington, D.C., Feb. 2, 1875. IP.

8. JJI to ALI, Washington, D.C., Feb. 9, 1875. IP.

9. *Ibid.*

10. JJI to ALI, Washington, D.C., Feb. 19, 1875. IP.

11. JJI to ALI, Washington, D.C., Mar. 5, 1875. IP.

12. JJI to ALI, Washington, D.C., Mar. 17, 1875. IP. Ingalls had been appointed to the committees on Indian Affairs, Pensions, and Education and Labor. He had introduced fifty-nine bills dealing with a variety of subjects, including exploitation of mineral lands, relief of settlers on homestead and preemption lands, rights of single women, incorporation of the Colorado Irrigation and Land Company, a military road from Kansas to Texas, relief of certain Indians, and increasing pension benefits. He was meticulous in all his Senatorial duties, raising detailed questions and making penetrating analyses of proposed bills which frequently exposed flaws or a waste of funds. It was not too much, therefore, for Ingalls to claim that he had been "generally successful."

13. JJI to ETI, Atchison, Kans., Nov. 5, 1875. IP.

14. *Ibid.*

15. JJI to ETI, Washington, D.C., Feb. 12, 1876. IP.

16. *Ibid.*

17. JJI to ETI, Atchison, Kans., Sept. 22, 1876. IP.

18. *Ibid.*

19. *Ibid.* On Dec. 24, 1883, in the Atchison *Daily Globe*, Ed Howe spoke of Ingalls in the following manner: "The tall form of Senator Ingalls, which resembles a strand of barbed wire on end, was bobbing around the city today."

20. *Ibid.*

21. JJI to ALI, Washington, D.C., Jan. 28, —. IP.

22. JJI to ETI, Atchison, Kans., Oct. 25, 1876. IP.

23. JJI to ETI, Atchison, Kans., May 26, 1877. IP.

24. See *The Writings of John J. Ingalls,* pp. 366 ff.

25. JJI to James A. Garfield, Atchison, Kans., Nov. 17, 1878. Garfield papers in ms. division, Library of Congress. Garfield replied favorably to Ingalls' letter at Washington, D.C., Dec. 15, 1878. IP.

26. JJI to ETI, Washington, D.C., Dec. 16, 187–. IP.

27. See *Congressional Record,* 45th Cong., 2nd sess. (Feb. 15, 1878), 7, pt. 2, 1052.

28. *Ibid.* The foregoing summary of Ingalls' activities in his first term as a United States Senator was compiled from the *Congressional Record,* 43rd 44th, and 45th Congs. (Jan., 1873–Jan., 1879), vols. 2–8.

29. JJI to ETI, Healing Springs, Va., July 1, 1878. IP.

30. JJI to ETI, Atchison, Kans., Nov. 5, 1878. IP.

31. ALI to JJI, Atchison, Kans., Jan. 25, 1879. IP.

32. Kansas *Senate Journal,* 1879, p. 129.

33. EIms., IP.

34. Undated letter, with no heading and simply signed, "Your Son." IP.

35. *Ibid.* On Feb. 6, 1879, the Kansas House adopted a resolution calling for an investigation of Ingalls' election. See *Kansas Special Committee, Report for 1879.*

36. *Special Committee, Report for 1879.*

37. The official title of the pamphlet, which was filed Feb. 9, 1880, is *Election of John J. Ingalls, Brief of Counsel for the Memorialists.*

38. JJI to ETI, Washington, D.C., Mar. 22, 1879. IP.

39. JJI to ETI, Washington, D.C., June 23, 1879. IP.

40. Samuel C. Pomeroy to P. H. Coney, n.p., June 25, 1879. Ms. division of KSHS.

41. JJI to ETI, Topeka, Kans., Oct. 18, 1879. IP.

42. JJI to ETI, Washington, D.C., Jan. 14, 1880. IP.

43. The information relative to the Senate investigation of Ingalls was gleaned from the *Congressional Record,* 46th Cong., 1st sess., 9, pt. 1, 15, 75; pt. 2, 2196, 2255–2257; also 2nd sess., 10, pt. 1, 153, 937–938.

44. Atchison *Daily Champion,* Mar. 7, 1880. Also, unidentified clippings in ALI's scrapbook. IP.

Chapter 8

1. John A. Martin to JJI, Atchison, Kans., Apr. 29, 1880. IP.

2. JJI to ETI, Washington, D.C., June 6, 1880. IP.

3. JJI to ETI, Atchison, Kans., Aug. 1, 1880. IP.

4. *Ibid.*

5. JJI to ETI, Washington, D.C., Dec. 17, 1881. IP.

6. *Ibid.*

7. EIms., IP.

8. *Ibid.*

9. JJI to ALI, n.p., Jan. 9, —. IP.

10. D. W. Wilder to JJI, Hiawatha, Kans., Apr. 20, 1882. IP. "Blue Grass" had originally appeared in an 1872 edition of *Kansas Magazine,* and Wilder was reprinting it in honor of its tenth anniversary.

11. *Nation,* XXXIV (May 4, 1882), 369.

12. JJI to ALI, Atchison, Kans., Sept. 13, 1882. IP.

13. JJI to ALI, Ottawa, Kans., Nov. 1, 1882. IP.

14. JJI to ALI, Washington, D.C., July 2, 1882. IP.

15. See *Congressional Record,* 44th Cong., 2nd sess. (Feb. 27, 1877), pt. 3, 1967.

16. Matthew Josephson, *The Politicos, 1865–1896* (New York: Harcourt, Brace and Co., 1938), p. 322.

17. *New York Times,* July 6, 1881, p. 4–4.

18. *New York Times,* July 2, 1881, p. 2–6.

19. JJI to ALI, Washington, D.C., Feb. 4, 1883. IP.

20. *Ibid.*

21. EIms., IP. Mrs. Dahlgren's husband published a book in 1856 entitled *Shells and Shell Guns.* Also, a biography was done of Admiral Dahlgren by Lieutenant C. Stewart Peterson, entitled *Admiral John A. Dahlgren, Father of U.S. Naval Ordnance* (New York: Hobson Book Press, 1945).

22. *Nation,* XXXVIII (June 19, 1884), 516–517.

23. *New York Times,* June 18, 1884, p. 1–3.

24. An Ingalls holograph ms. entitled "The Future Relation of the Republican Party to Prohibition in Kansas." IP.

25. *Ibid.*

Chapter 9

1. JJI to ALI, Washington, D.C., Jan. 27, 1885. IP.

2. JJI to ALI, Washington, D.C., Feb. 2, 1885. IP.

3. An Ingalls holograph ms. with no title. The content reveals that the address was delivered in 1885. IP.

4. JJI to ALI, Washington, D.C., Mar. 5, 1885. IP.

5. *New York Times,* May 26, 1886, p. 5–3.

6. *Ibid.,* July 20, 1886, p. 1–3. The *Times* referred to this dispute as "A Comedy in the Senate."

7. EIms., IP. Apparently Ethel copied a portion of her father's Cleveland ms. and included it in her own.

8. An untitled holograph ms. written by ALI. IP.

9. EIms., IP.

10. *Ibid.* Also an unidentified clipping in Marion Ingalls' scrapbook. IP.

11. Grover Cleveland to Mrs. John J. Ingalls, Washington, D.C., Feb. 11, 1886. IP.

12. See *Congressional Record* (Mar. 20, 1886), 17, pt. 3, 2785 ff.

13. A portion of Ingalls' holograph ms. in which he made an attack on Cleveland and civil-service reform. No date or title. IP.

14. *Congressional Record* (Mar. 26, 1886), 17, pt. 3, 2786.

15. *Ibid.,* pp. 2785–2790.

16. *Harper's Weekly,* XXX (Apr. 10, 1886), 226–227 and 240.

17. JJI to ALI, Washington, D.C., June 16, 1886. IP.

18. *New York Times,* Feb. 24, 1887, p. 1–6.

19. *Ibid.,* Feb. 25, 1887, pp. 2–1 and 4–1.

20. JJI to ALI, Washington, D.C., Feb. 24, 1887. IP.

21. *Congressional Record* (Mar. 26, 1886), 19, pt. 2, 1775.

22. Frances F. Cleveland to Mrs. John J. Ingalls, Washington, D.C., Jan. 3, 1888. IP.

23. JJI to ALI, Washington, D.C., Feb. 23, 1887. IP.

24. Chase County *Leader,* Mar. 10, 1887. For a thorough treatment of the Irish question in Kansas see James C. Malin, *Confounded Rot About*

Napoleon (Lawrence, Kans., 1961), pp. 78 ff.

25. *Congressional Record,* 49th Cong., 2nd sess. (Jan. 25, 1887), 18, pt. 2, 1808–1809.

26. *Kansas House Journal,* Feb. 2, 1887, p. 337; *Kansas Senate Journal,* Feb. 2, 3, 4, 1887, pp. 261, 291, 302, 303.

27. JJI to ALI, Washington, D.C., Jan. 26, 1887. IP.

28. JJI, "The Sixteenth Amendment," *Forum,* IV (Sept., 1887), 1 ff.

29. An Ingalls holograph ms., no title or date. IP.

30. *North American Review,* CXLVI (June, 1888), 651–656.

31. EIms., IP.

32. Luther Stearnes Cushing, *Manual of Parliamentary Practice,* rev. by John J. Ingalls (New York: A. L. Burt, 1895).

33. Copy of a brief essay entitled "How Senator Ingalls Bears It" and bearing the name of W. A. Croffut. IP.

34. Carrie Mize to ALI, Atchison, Kans., Jan. 11, 1888. IP. The desk that was saved was recently given to the KSHS by Mrs. Warren Price, Jr., granddaughter of the late Senator Ingalls.

35. JJI to ALI, Atchison, Kans., Nov. 6, 1888. IP.

36. ETI to JJI, Haverhill, Mass., Oct. 13, 1889. Also JJI to Ethel Ingalls, Washington, D.C., Sept. 23, 1890. IP.

37. The dispute is to be found in full in the *Congressional Record* (Mar. 6, 1888), 19, pt. 2, 1777; (Apr. 26, 1888) 19, pt. 4, 3383; (May 1, 1888), 3556, 3566 ff., and 3572. Also an interesting account is contained in the New York *Tribune,* May 2, 1888. Also see Ray H. Sandefur, "The Ingalls-Vorhees Debate of 1888," *Kansas Historical Quarterly,* Aug. 1949,

pp. 243–253. The *New York Times,* Mar. 7, 8, 9, 1888, attacked Ingalls as a "Malignity in the Senate," etc. The *Times* claimed that Ingalls was not willing to stop until every Union soldier was placed on the pension rolls. On March 8, 1888, the *Times* claimed that Ingalls was now out of the Presidential race. The article claimed that Ingalls' bitter attack on the South was evidence of his indifference to a Presidential nomination. The article also cited the fact that Ingalls had offended Union Army veterans by his attacks on Generals McClellan and Hancock. The *Times* summarized its complaints about Ingalls on March 9, 1888 (p. 1–7), by claiming that "of all the 76 members of the Senate he is the one Senator the most difficult to be misunderstood." Ironically, Ingalls praised McClellan and Hancock in a speech he made at Kit Carson Post in which he praised "'those gallant generals,' Grant, Sheridan, Sherman, Hancock, McClellan, and Logan" (*New York Times,* Mar. 30, 1888, p. 5–2). The *Times* gave still more coverage to the Ingalls-Vorhees feud on April 27, May 2, 3, 1888.

38. EIms., IP.

39. *Ibid.*

40. JJI to P. I. Bonebrake, Washington, D.C., Mar. 6, 1888. IP. The *New York Times* claimed that Ingalls desperately wanted to be on the national ticket because he knew his own party was planning for his defeat in 1890. It was also claimed that he could capture the Irish vote (*New York Times,* June 12, 1888, p. 1–3). The *Times* denounced Ingalls and the Western Union Telegraph Co., because Ingalls had free use of the wires (*ibid.,* p. 2–7).

41. Washington *Post,* Feb. 28, 1888; New York *Sun,* Feb. 28, 1887; and Topeka *Commonwealth,* June 14, 1888.

42. Telegram from Eugene F. Ware

to JJI, Fort Scott, Kans., Feb. 25, 1888. IP.

43. JJI to ALI, Washington, D.C., June 19, 1888. IP.

44. JJI to ALI, Washington, D.C., June 25, 1888. IP.

45. ALI to JJI, Stonington, Conn., June 25, 1888. IP.

46. ALI to JJI, Stonington, Conn., June 26, 1888. IP.

47. JJI to ALI, Washington, D.C., Oct. 6, 1888. IP.

48. JJI to ALI, Atchison, Kans., Nov. 6, 1888. IP. The "Guthrie gang" refers to Ingalls' old enemies within the Republican party. In another contradiction, Ingalls wrote a letter to an unknown recipient. According to the *Times*, he is alleged to have written: "But if he [Cleveland] keeps on as he has begun, his Administration will grow in popular favor" (*New York Times*, Sept. 30, 1888, p. 16–4).

49. JJI to E. A. Augier, Atchison, Kans., Nov. 17, 1888. In the Benjamin Harrison papers in the ms. division, Library of Congress.

50. Mrs. John J. Ingalls to President-elect Benjamin Harrison, n.p., Jan. 20, 1889. Benjamin Harrison papers in the ms. division, Library of Congress.

51. *Harper's Weekly*, XXXIII (Sept. 14, 1889), 734.

52. *Harper's Weekly*, XXXIII (Oct. 26, 1889), 850.

53. *Congressional Record* (Jan. 23, 1890), 21, pt. 1, 802 ff. Also see a brief article published by the author in the Atchison *Daily Globe*, Mar. 19, 1965. The *Times* interviewed Ingalls on the race question and quoted him as saying that "the voluntary separation of the races is among the possibilities of the near future." Ingalls claimed that the time would come when the Negroes "will insist upon their equality under the law, and then

there will be a crisis which may become a catastrophe" (*New York Times*, Dec. 3, 1888, p. 1–7). Apparently Ingalls did have some insights into future political developments. After Ingalls' "Fiat Justitia" speech, the *Times* took the time and space to roundly denounce his discourse (*ibid.*, Jan. 24, 1890, p. 5–1).

54. Topeka *Daily Capital*, Mar. 26, Sept. 3, 4, and 5, 1890.

55. JJI to Ethel Ingalls, Washington, D.C., Mar. 12, 1890. IP. In July of 1888 *Harper's Weekly* gave a penetrating analysis of Ingalls as a politician. Much of what was said was uncomplimentary, but there were some compliments paid to Ingalls. *Harper's* conceded that he was "the most admirable presiding officer of his side of the Chamber. His clear quick mind has made him an excellent Parliamentarian." See *Harper's Weekly*, XXXII (July 7, 1888), 498.

56. *Congressional Record*, 51st Cong., 1st sess., 21, pt. 3, 2648–2649. Ingalls offered his amendment on Mar. 21, 1890. For a detailed study of the controversial amendment see David F. McFarland, Jr., "The Ingalls Amendment to the Sherman Anti-Trust Bill," *Kansas Historical Quarterly*, May, 1942, pp. 173–198.

57. New York *World*, Apr. 13, 1890. Earlier the *Times* had claimed that Ingalls was in danger of being defeated in his bid for reelection. The *Times* pointed out that J. Ralph Burton, of central Kansas, and George R. Peck, general solicitor of the Santa Fe Railroad, were both out after Ingalls' seat (*New York Times*, Nov. 13, 1889, p. 1–5).

58. For another account of Ingalls and plagiarism see James C. Malin, *Confounded Rot About Napoleon* (Lawrence, Kans., 1961), pp. 99–100.

59. Kansas Democratic Platform, 1890.

60. *Nation,* XV (June 19, 1890), 480.

61. JJI to ALI, Washington, D.C., July 14, 1890. IP.

62. JJI to P. I. Bonebrake, Washington, D.C., Aug. 18, 1890. IP.

63. The House at this time consisted of twenty-six Republicans, seven Democrats, and ninety-two Alliance men. In the Senate there were thirty-eight Republicans, one Democrat, and one Alliance man. This made a total of sixty-four Republicans, eight Democrats, and ninety-three Alliance men.

64. *New York Times,* Feb. 19, 1890, p. 2–2. The *Times* story may be referring to the letter written by William A. Peffer to Ingalls in which these questions and others were posed. See Malin, *Confounded Rot About Napoleon,* pp. 91 and 92.

65. *New York Times,* July 6, 1890, p. 16–7.

66. *New York Times,* Sept. 18 and 19, 1890, p. 1–2.

67. *Ibid.,* Sept. 20, 1890, p. 1–4.

68. *Nation,* LI (Nov. 30, 1890), 371.

69. *New York Times,* Nov. 8, 1890, p. 4–1.

70. *Ibid.,* Nov. 25, 1890, p. 1–4.

71. *Ibid.,* Dec. 11, 1890, p. 5–1.

72. JJI to J. W. Steele, Atchison, Kans., Jan. 3, 1891. IP.

73. For the complete text see *Congressional Record* (Jan. 14, 1891), 22, pt. 2, 1278–1283. The text of the speech was also printed in its entirety in the Atchison *Daily Globe,* Jan. 17, 1891.

74. *Ibid.*

75. Atchison *Daily Globe,* Jan. 27–29, 1891. Ethel Ingalls claimed in her ms. that D. D. and C. C. Burnes met with a committee in Topeka and agreed with some of Ingalls' friends that money spent "advisedly" would stem the tide of Populism and save Ingalls' seat in the Senate. Ethel claimed that her father refused to listen to such a proposition and that the Burnes brothers were the sons of Col. John N. Burnes who had been a Confederate and was a Democrat. He was, however, a close personal friend of Ingalls'. Col. Burnes had business interests in Atchison. For another and somewhat different commentary on Ingalls' defeat see the article by the author entitled "The Kansas Alliance vs. 'Mr. Republican': The Case for The Accused," *Kansas Quarterly,* Fall, 1969, pp. 40–48. Also for an interesting account of the circumstances surrounding Ingalls' bid for reelection see William Allen White, *Autobiography* (New York: The Macmillan Co., 1946), pp. 190–191.

76. *New York Times,* Dec. 22, 1890, p. 5–3.

77. *Ibid.,* Jan. 28, 1891, p. 4–2.

78. Atchison *Daily Globe,* Jan. 27, 1891.

79. *Ibid.*

80. *Literary Digest,* vol. 2, no. 14 (Jan. 31, 1891), p. 23.

81. *Nation,* LII (Feb. 5, 1891), 104.

82. JJI to ALI, Washington, D.C., Feb. 8, 1891. IP. For an account of how Ingalls took his defeat see James C. Malin, *Confounded Rot About Napoleon,* pp. 103–112.

83. Atchison *Daily Globe,* Feb. 10, 1891.

84. Atchison *Daily Globe,* Feb. 13, 1891.

85. Atchison *Daily Globe,* Feb. 21, 1891.

86. JJI to ALI, Washington, D.C., Mar. 10, 1891. IP.

87. St. Louis *Globe-Democrat,* quoted in Topeka *Advocate,* Feb. 18, 1891.

Chapter 10

1. *New York Times,* Feb. 26, 1891, p. 1–5.

2. *Ibid.*

3. *New York Times,* Mar. 14, 1891, p. 2–2.

4. JJI to Ethel Ingalls, Atchison, Kans., Apr. 20, 1891. IP. In this letter Ingalls referred to himself as a "farmer." Also in a letter to his son Sheffield, dated Tucson, Ariz. Terr., Feb. 17, 1900, Ingalls claimed that his plan upon leaving the Senate was "to make a stockfarm: an estate on which I could live the life of a 'country gentleman' amid blue grass pastures and groves of oak in my declining years."

5. JJI to ALI, Washington, D.C., Aug. 19, 1890. IP. In this letter Ingalls gave extensive instructions concerning the management and leasing of the Walnut Township farm.

6. JJI to Sheffield Ingalls, Tucson, Ariz. Terr., Feb. 17, 1900. IP.

7. JJI to ALI, Washington, D.C., Feb. 8, 1891. IP. All the information concerning these lucrative positions is contained in the letter cited here.

8. JJI to ALI, Washington, D.C., Feb. 25, 1891. IP.

9. For a critical analysis of Ingalls as a legislator see James C. Malin's book entitled *Confounded Rot About Napoleon,* pp. 173 ff.

10. The first installment appeared on Mar. 7, 1891.

11. Atchison *Daily Globe,* Mar. 19, 1891.

12. Blakely Hall to JJI, New York, N.Y., Apr. 8, 1891. IP.

13. It is interesting to note that upon Ingalls' death, one of the most frequently mentioned items of all his literary efforts was the poem, or sonnet, entitled "Opportunity."

14. The complete sonnet "Opportunity" follows:

Master of human destinies am I!
    Fame, love and fortune on my footsteps wait.
    Cities and fields I walk; I penetrate
Deserts and seas remote, and passing by
    Hovel and mart and palace, soon or late
    I knock unbidden once at every gate!
If sleeping, wake; if feasting, rise before
    I turn away. It is the hour of fate,
    And they who follow me reach every state
    Mortals desire, and conquer every foe
Save death; but those who doubt or hesitate,
    Condemned to failure, penury and woe,
Seek me in vain and uselessly implore.
I answer not, and I return no more!

15. JJI to ETI, Atchison, Kans., July 30, 1871. IP.

16. ETI to JJI, Haverhill, Mass., Apr. 26, 1864. IP.

17. JJI to ALI, Tucson, Ariz. Terr., Jan. 3, 1900. IP.

18. *New York Times,* July 1, 1891, p. 4–7.

19. *Ibid.*

20. *New York Times,* Aug. 2, 1891, p. 5–3.

21. *Ibid.*

22. *Ibid.*

23. JJI to ALI, Washington, D.C., Aug. 4, 1891. IP.

24. JJI to ALI, Lookout Mountain, Tenn., Aug. 9, 1891. IP.

25. JJI to Ethel Ingalls, Detroit, Mich., Oct. 30, 1891. IP.

26. Datelined Atchison, Kans., June 4: *New York Times,* June 5, 1891, p. 1–4.

27. *New York Times,* Nov. 22, 1891, p. 12–7.

28. Atchison *Daily Globe,* Jan. 5, 1892. The cost of the building was estimated to be $100,000.

29. *Ibid.,* Feb. 27, 1892.

30. *Ibid.,* Mar. 3, 1892.

31. *Ibid.,* May 2, 1892.

32. *Ibid.,* May 6, 1892.

33. *Ibid.,* May 6, 1892.

34. *Ibid.,* May 14, 1892.

35. *Ibid.,* June 7, 1892.

36. *Ibid.*

37. For a discussion of Ingalls' chances for reelection to the United States Senate see James C. Malin's *Confounded Rot About Napoleon,* pp. 173 ff.

38. JJI to ALI, the *S.S. Ems* at sea, June 25, 1892. IP.

39. JJI to ALI, the *S.S. Ems* at sea, June 28, 1892. IP.

40. *Ibid.* Ingalls' letter was twenty-two pages long and covered a wide range of subjects, which included this account of his personal finances.

41. JJI to ALI, *S.S. Ems* at sea, June 29, 1892. IP.

42. JJI to ALI, *S.S. Ems* at sea, July 3, 1892. IP. Ingalls' letters to his wife written on board the *S.S. Ems* actually composed a chronological journal which he kept throughout the voyage from New York to Southampton, England.

43. JJI to ALI, Berlin, Germany, July 7, 1892. IP.

44. Ingalls' personal pocket notebook, July 13, 1892. The Kansas Collection of the University of Kansas Library. Hereafter this will be referred to as KUIP.

45. JJI to ALI, Dresden, Germany, July 15, 1892. IP.

46. Ingalls' personal pocket notebook, July 17, 1892. KUIP.

47. *Ibid.,* July 19, 1892.

48. *Ibid.,* July 31, 1892.

49. *Ibid.*

50. *Ibid.,* Aug. 4, 1892.

51. *Ibid.*

52. *Ibid.,* Aug. 5, 1892.

53. JJI to ALI, Rome, Italy, Aug. 5, 1892. IP.

54. *Ibid.*

55. JJI to ALI, Milan, Italy, Aug. 5, 1892. IP. Lorenzo D. Lewelling, a Populist, was elected Governor of Kansas in Nov., 1892.

56. JJI to ALI, Lucerne, Switzerland, Aug. 8, 1892. IP.

57. Ingalls' personal pocket notebook, Aug. 9, 1892. KUIP. The *Herald* he referred to was the New York *Herald.*

58. JJI to ALI, Lucerne, Switzerland, Aug. 10, 1892. IP.

59. JJI to ALI, Paris, France, Aug. 14, 1892. IP.

60. Ingalls' personal pocket notebook, Aug. 14, 1892. KUIP.

61. *Ibid.*

62. *Ibid.,* Aug. 19, 1892.

63. The original note is included in IP.

64. JJI to ALI, London, England, Aug. 21, 1892. IP.

65. *Ibid.*

66. JJI to ALI, London, England, Aug. 27, 1892. IP.

67. The original essay is in IP.

68. JJI to ALI, Brghmptn [*sic*], New York, Dec. 9, —. IP.

69. *Ibid.*

70. JJI to Ethel Ingalls, Burlington, Iowa, Jan. 26, 1893. IP.

71. *Ibid.*

72. JJI to ALI, Chicago, Ill., Oct. 8, 1893. IP.

73. JJI to ALI, Chicago, Ill., Oct. 12, 1893. IP.

74. *Harper's New Monthly Magazine,* LI (Apr., 1893), 698 ff.

75. H. M. Alden to JJI, New York, N.Y., Jan. 12, 1888. IP.

76. *Ibid.*

77. Ingalls' personal pocket notebook, June 26, 1894. KUIP.

78. The photograph is in IP.

79. Ingalls' personal pocket notebook, June 26, 1894. KUIP.

80. Ingalls' personal pocket notebook, no date. KUIP. The *Times* carried a story almost precisely like that which appears in his notebook. He was interviewed in Kansas City, Mo., by a reporter from the Topeka *Capital*, and the story was picked up by the *Times*. *New York Times*, Nov. 16, 1894, p. 15–6.

81. Atchison *Daily Globe*, Oct. 25, 1894.

82. JJI to Ethel Ingalls, S.S. *Fairfax*, June 30, 1894. IP.

83. *New York Times*, Jan. 27, 1895, p. 14–6.

84. *Ibid.*, June 13, 1895, p. 1–5.

85. *Ibid.*, July 6, 1895, p. 4–6.

86. On this attempt at gaining re-election see James C. Malin, *Confounded Rot About Napoleon*, pp. 129 ff.

87. Ingalls' original draft of the address is in IP.

88. JJI to ALI, Bradford, Pa., Feb. 7, 1896. IP.

89. JJI to Ethel Ingalls, on a train bound for Boston, Mass., Feb. 8, 1896. IP.

90. JJI to Ethel Ingalls, Boston, Mass., Feb. 14, 1896. IP.

91. *Ibid.*

92. JJI to ALI, Marquette, Mich., Mar. 23, 1896. IP. Neither Hearst's letter to Ingalls nor Ingalls' reply is extant. One can only speculate con-cerning the offer, salary, and assignment.

93. JJI to ALI, Ishpeming, Mich., Mar. 27, 1896. IP. No doubt Ingalls was referring, in part, to his own efforts to secure a high protective tariff. Ingalls had consistently supported a high-tariff policy as a Senator. Although he spoke out in behalf of free silver, which the Populists proposed, he was never able to compromise his views regarding the tariff question, regardless of pressure from his constituency in Kansas. It was only after he left public office that he began to revise his views on the tariff.

94. *New York Times*, Mar. 8, 1896, p. 4–2.

95. *Ibid.*, Mar. 6, 1896, p. 1–6.

96. *Ibid.*, Nov. 17, 1896, p. 5–5.

97. JJI to ALI, near Indianapolis, Ind., on the train, July 10, 1896. IP.

98. JJI to ALI, Greeley, Colo., Nov. 21, 1896. IP.

99. *Ibid.*

100. San Francisco *Examiner*, Mar. 18, 1897.

101. *New York Times*, July 3, 1897, p. 1–5.

102. JJI to ALI, Washington, D.C., May 26, 1897. IP.

103. JJI to Sheffield Ingalls, Washington, D.C., Apr. 28, 1898. IP.

104. There is no one named as the author of the book, which was published in New York and St. Louis by the N. D. Thomas Publishing Co. in 1898.

105. JJI to ALI, Tucson, Ariz. Terr., Apr. 9, 1900. IP.

106. JJI to ALI, Tucson, Ariz. Terr., Apr. 4, 1900. IP.

Chapter 11

1. JJI to "Dear Sheridan," Tucson, Ariz. Terr., Apr. 24, 1900. IP. This was Barney Sheridan of the Paola, Kansas, *Western Spirit*.

2. JJI to ALI, Plymouth, Ind., Mar. 5, 1898. IP.

3. JJI to ALI, n.p., Oct. 29, 1898. IP.

4. JJI to Ethel Ingalls, Washington, D.C., Nov. 30, 1898. IP.

5. JJI to Ethel Ingalls, Atchison, Kans., July 6, 1899. IP.

6. JJI to ALI, Atlantic City, N.J., May 22, 1899. IP.

7. JJI to ALI, Las Cruces, N. Mex. Terr., Oct. 7, 1899. IP.

8. JJI to ALI, Las Cruces, N. Mex. Terr., Oct. 8, 1899. IP.

9. JJI to ALI, Las Cruces, N. Mex. Terr., Nov. 4, 1899. IP.

10. JJI to ALI, Nov. 8, 1899. IP.

11. JJI to ALI, Las Cruces, N. Mex. Terr., Dec. 1, 1899. IP.

12. JJI to ALI, Las Cruces, N. Mex. Terr., Dec. 7, 1899. IP.

13. JJI to ALI, El Paso, Tex., Dec. 26, 1899. IP.

14. JJI to ALI, Tucson, Ariz. Terr., Dec. 28, 1899. IP.

15. JJI to Marion Ingalls, Tucson, Ariz. Terr., Dec. 31, 1899. IP.

16. *Ibid.*

17. JJI to ALI, Tucson, Ariz. Terr., Jan. 3, 1900. IP.

18. *Ibid.* It is interesting to note Ingalls' comment about Howe, as Howe had long been an admirer of Ingalls' and his staunch supporter. See Calder M. Pickett, *Ed Howe: Country Town Philosopher* (Lawrence and London: University Press of Kansas, 1968), pp. 144 ff.

19. JJI to ALI, Jan. 17, 1900. IP.

20. JJI to ALI, Tucson, Ariz. Terr., Jan. 21, 1900. IP.

21. Ingalls' personal pocket notebook, Feb. 4, 1900. KUIP.

22. JJI to Muriel Ingalls, Tucson, Ariz. Terr., Feb. 21, 1900. IP.

23. JJI to Ethel Ingalls, Tucson, Ariz. Terr., Mar. 26, 1900. IP.

24. JJI to ALI, Tucson, Ariz. Terr., Apr. 14, 1900. IP.

25. JJI to ALI, Tucson, Ariz. Terr., Apr. 28 and June 21, 1900. IP.

26. JJI to ALI, Tucson, Ariz. Terr., June 20, 1900. IP.

27. JJI to ALI, Tucson, Ariz. Terr., Apr. 5, 1900. IP.

28. JJI to ALI, Tucson, Ariz. Terr., Apr. 9, 1900. IP.

29. JJI to ALI, Tucson, Ariz. Terr., Apr. 22, 1900. IP.

30. JJI to Marion Ingalls, Tucson, Ariz. Terr., May 11, 1900. IP. Ingalls had just read Booth Tarkington's book *Gentleman from Indiana.*

31. Rudolph Black to JJI, New York, N.Y., May 19, 1900. IP.

32. *Ibid.*

33. JJI to ALI, Tucson, Ariz. Terr., May 20, 1900. IP.

34. JJI to Ethel Ingalls, Tucson, Ariz. Terr., June 17, 1900. IP.

35. ALI to JJI, Atchison, Kans., July 5, 1900. IP.

36. JJI to ALI, Las Vegas, N. Mex. Terr., July 4, 1900. IP.

37. JJI to ALI, Las Vegas, N. Mex. Terr., July 6, 1900. IP.

38. The information concerning Ingalls' literary productions just noted was taken from his personal pocket notebook. KUIP. The *Journal* and the *World* were New York City newspapers.

39. Ingalls' personal pocket notebook. KUIP.

Chapter 12

1. Kansas City *Times,* Aug. 16, 1900.

2. The information concerning Ingalls' death and funeral service was compiled from several sources, including Trinity Episcopal Church *Parish Record* at Atchison, Kansas; Atchison *Daily Globe;* Washington *Post;* Kansas City *Times;* Chicago *Tribune;* Las Vegas (N. Mex.) *Republic;* Las Vegas (N. Mex.) *Daily Optic,* dating from

Aug. 16 to Aug. 21, 1900. These clippings are included in the scrapbook of ALI in IP.

3. Several hundred newspaper clippings dealing with Ingalls' death and a summary of his career are contained in five large scrapbooks which formerly belonged to Mrs. Ingalls and her daughters Ethel, Marion, and Muriel. The scrapbooks are now a part of IP.

4. *Lutheran Evangelist,* Aug. 25, 1900, published weekly in Dayton, Ohio, and Washington, D.C., "on the basis of the General Synod of the Evangelical Lutheran Church in the United States."

5. See Ingalls' essay "The Immortality of the Soul," in his *Writings,* p. 199.

6. Undated clipping in the scrapbook of ALI. IP.

7. JJI to ALI, Washington, D.C., Dec. 10, 1890. IP.

8. JJI to Ethel Ingalls, Washington, D.C., Apr. 19, 1898. IP.

9. See Ingalls' eulogies of James N. Burnes, *Congressional Record* (Feb. 25, 1889), 20, pt. 3, 2291, and Benjamin Hill (Jan. 25, 1883), 14, pt. 2, 1573, as representative examples.

10. JJI to ALI, Washington, D.C., Feb. 10, 1883. IP.

11. E. J. Edwards to JJI, Washington, D.C., Feb. 6, 1883. IP. Ingalls' eulogy of Senator Hill is included in *The Writings of John James Ingalls,* pp. 268–271.

12. J. A. Powelson to JJI, New York, N.Y., Feb. 26, 1889. IP. Ingalls' eulogy of Congressman Burnes is included in *The Writings of John James Ingalls,* pp. 272–276.

13. JJI to J. A. Powelson, Washington, D.C., Mar. 7, 1889. IP.

14. ETI to JJI, Haverhill, Mass., Apr. 10, 1889. IP. The book is by Henry Drummond, *Natural Law in the Spiritual World* (New York: John B. Alden, Publisher, 1887).

15. ETI to JJI, Haverhill, Mass., Apr. 10, 1889. IP.

16. Ingalls' personal copy is in the possession of his granddaughter Mrs. Sally Ingalls Keith.

17. JJI to ALI, Atchison, Kans., Sept. 13, 1882. IP.

18. JJI to Muriel Ingalls, Tucson, Ariz. Terr., Jan. 1, 1900. IP. See Ingalls' ms. entitled "The Jesus Business," ms. division, KSHS. Also see his essays "The Immortality of the Soul" and "Why Christianity Has Triumphed" in *The Writings of John James Ingalls,* pp. 199–203 and 208–212 respectively.

19. See Ray Harold Sandefur, "Analysis of Selected Public Speeches of John James Ingalls" (Ph.D. diss., State University of Iowa, 1950), p. 366.

20. These are some of the phrases and words that are frequently used in describing Ingalls as based on the examination of several hundred obituary notices contained in the scrapbook of Ingalls' wife, Anna Louisa Ingalls. IP.

21. See the *Congressional Record* (Feb. 25, 1887), 18, pt. 3, 2233.

22. See the *Congressional Record* (Feb. 15, 1878), 7, pt. 2, 1051.

23. See the *Congressional Record* (Jan. 14, 1891), 22, pt. 2, 1278 ff.

24. Wichita *Daily Eagle,* Mar. 28, 1890.

25. An Ingalls holograph ms. bearing no date or title. IP.

26. An Ingalls holograph ms., no date or title. IP.

27. *Congressional Record* (Dec. 12, 1887), 19, pt. 1, 22.

28. See Ingalls' article entitled "Prohibition and License," *Forum,* VII (Aug., 1889), 673–682.

29. An Ingalls holograph Memorial Day speech for 1895. No title or date. IP.

30. *Arena,* VIII (Oct., 1893), 592 ff.

31. *Ibid.*

32. An undated clipping in ALI scrapbook, IP. Hereafter all newspapers cited in the text are from this scrapbook collection of clippings unless otherwise noted.

33. Ingalls had persistently sympathized with the problems of the territories and always urged their speedy admission into the Union. For example, he introduced bills to organize the Territory of Oklahoma in 1873 and to enable New Mexico to become a state in 1874. See *Congressional Record*, 43rd Cong., 1st sess., 2, pts. 1–6, 12.

34. JJI to ALI, Dec. 10, 1890. IP.

35. See *Statue of Hon. John James Ingalls* (Washington: Government Printing Office, 1905).

36. JJI to ALI, Washington, D.C., Mar. 3, 1874. IP.

37. See Matthew Josephson, *The Politicos* (New York: Harcourt, Brace and Co., 1938), p. 322; Richard Hofstadter, *The American Political Tradition* (New York: Vintage Books, 1957), p. 177; Walter T. K. Nugent, *The Tolerant Populists* (Chicago: University of Chicago Press, 1963), p. 51; O. Gene Clanton, *Kansas Populism: Ideas and Men* (Lawrence and London: University Press of Kansas, 1969), pp. 43–45, 54–57, 90, 104, 110, 153; and James C. Malin, *Confounded Rot About Napoleon*, pp. 78 ff.

38. JJI to ALI, Rockwood, Pa., Dec. 20, 1893. IP.

BIBLIOGRAPHY

Manuscript Collections

Horton, Albert H. Letters and papers in the ms. division, Kansas State Historical Society, Topeka, Kans.

Ingalls, John J. Letters and papers in the ms. division, Kansas State Historical Society, Topeka, Kans.

Ingalls, John J. Letters and papers in the ms. division, Williams College Library, Williamstown, Mass.

Ingalls, John J. Letters and papers in the Senate Committee Papers of which he was a member, 1873–1891. National Archives, Washington, D.C.

Ingalls, John J. Letters, papers, and personal notebooks in the Kansas Collection of the University of Kansas Library, Lawrence, Kans.

Ingalls, John J. Letters to and from, in the ms. collections of the following persons: Chester A. Arthur, Grover Cleveland, James A. Garfield, Benjamin Harrison, Rutherford B. Hayes, Carl Schurz. The papers of all the foregoing-named persons are in the ms. division, Library of Congress, Washington, D.C.

Pomeroy, Samuel C. Letters and papers in the ms. division, Kansas State Historical Society, Topeka, Kans.

Trinity Episcopal Church. Parish Families, Books 1, 2, and 3, 1863–1900. Atchison, Kans.

Government Documents and Public Records

Atchison County Clerk Records. Atchison, Kans., 1865.

Biennial Report of the State Board of Agriculture, 1877–1878.

Congressional Directory. Washington, D.C.: Government Printing Office, 1873–1891.

Congressional Record. Washington, D.C.: Government Printing Office, 1873–1891.

Election of John J. Ingalls. Brief of Counsel for the Memorialists, 1880.

Holmes, J. T., vs. *Sheridan, P. H., and Paige, J. H.* Docket Book of the United States Circuit Court, no. 1810, Topeka, Kans.

Kansas *House Journal.* Topeka, Kans.: 1873 and 1887.

Kansas *Senate Journal.* Topeka, Kans.: 1873, 1879, and 1887.

Senatorial Election, 1879. Report of the Special Committee of the Kansas House of Representatives. Topeka, Kans.: Kansas Publishing House, 1879.

Statue of John James Ingalls. Washington, D.C.: Government Printing Office, 1905.

Statutes of Kansas Territory, 1855.

Articles and Pamphlets

Armstrong, William Jackson. "Mr. Ingalls and Political Economy," *Arena*, Oct., 1893.

"By the Way," *University Review,* Mar., 1893.

Chase, George B. *A Genealogical Memoir of the Chase Family of Chesham, Bucks, in England, and of Hampton and Newbury in New England, With Notices of Some of Their Descendants.* Boston: H. W. Dutton and Son, 1869.

Diggs, Annie L. "The Farmers' Alli-

ance and Some of Its Leaders," *Arena*, V (Apr., 1892).
——. "The Women in the Alliance Movement," *Arena*, VI (July, 1892).
Gates, Paul W. "The Homestead Law in an Incongruous Land System," *American Historical Review*, XLI (July, 1936).
Hicks, John D. "Birth of the Populist Party," *Minnesota History*, IX (Sept., 1928).
Ingalls, John J. "Fetichism in the Campaign," *North American Review*, June, 1888.
——. "Kansas 1541–1891," *Harper's New Monthly Magazine*, Apr., 1893.
——. "Prohibition and License," *Forum*, Aug., 1889.
Ingalls, Mrs. John J. *Our Yesterdays.* Topeka, Kans., 1915.
"Kansas History and Kansas Newspapers," *Graduate Magazine of the University of Kansas*, June, 1906.
Kitzhaber, Albert T. "Gotterdammerung in Topeka: The Downfall of Senator Pomeroy," *Kansas Historical Quarterly*, Aug., 1950.
Lease, Mary E. "Do Kansas Women Want the Right to Vote?" *Agora*, II (Jan., 1893).
Levinson, Harry. "Petticoat Politician," *Kansas Magazine*, 1949.
McFarland, David F. "The Ingalls Amendment to the Sherman Anti-Trust Bill," *Kansas Historical Quarterly*, May, 1942.
Malin, James C. "At What Age Did Men Become Reformers?" *Kansas Historical Quarterly*, XXIX (Autumn, 1963).
——. "Notes on the Literature of Populism," *Kansas Historical Quarterly*, I (Feb., 1932).
——. "Some Reconsiderations of the Defeat of Senator Pomeroy of Kansas, 1873," *Mid-America*, Jan., 1966.
Miller, Raymond C. "Background of Populism in Kansas," *Mississippi*

Valley Historical Review, XI (Mar., 1925).
Nugent, Walter T. K. "Some Parameters of Populism," *Agricultural History*, XL (Oct., 1966).
Osnes, Larry G. "The Birth of a Party: The Cincinnati Populist Convention of 1891," *Great Plains Journal*, Fall, 1970.
Park, H. Clay. "The Rise and Fall of Sumner," *Collections of the Kansas State Historical Society*, 1911–1912.
Peffer, William A. "The Farmers' Alliance," *Cosmopolitan*, X (Apr., 1891).
——. "The Farmers' Defensive Movement," *Forum*, VIII (Dec., 1889).
——. "Government Control of Money," *Farmers' Alliance History and Agricultural Digest*, 1891.
Pollack, Norman. "Hofstadter on Populism: A Critique of *The Age of Reform*," *Journal of Southern History*, XXVI (Nov., 1960).
Saloutos, Theodore. "The Professors and the Populists," *Agricultural History*, XL (Oct., 1966).
Sandefur, Ray H. "The Ingalls-Vorhees Debate of 1888," *Kansas Historical Quarterly* (Aug., 1949).
Ware, E. F. *The Kansas Bandit; or, the Fall of Ingalls.* 2nd ed., Fort Scott, Kans.: James A. Aoulton, n.d.
Webb, William C. *The Ingalls Case, A Review of the Investigations of John J. Ingalls.* Topeka, Kans., 1879.
Weinstein, Allan. "Was There a 'Crime of 1873'?" *Journal of American History*, LIV (Sept., 1967).
Williams, Burton J. "John James Ingalls, Geographic Determinism and Kansas," *Midwest Quarterly*, Spring, 1965.
——. "John James Ingalls: The

Sumner Years," *Kansas Historical Quarterly*, Winter, 1967.

———. "The Kansas Alliance v. 'Mr. Republican': The Case for the Accused," *Kansas Quarterly*, Fall, 1969.

———. "Mormons, Mining and the Golden Trumpet of Moroni," *Midwest Quarterly*, Autumn, 1966.

———. "Quantrills Raid on Lawrence: A Question of Complic-

ity," *Kansas Historical Quarterly*, Summer, 1968.

Williams College *Catalogue of the Officers and Students, 1851–1855.*

Williams College *Class Reports,* 1857, 1882, 1895.

Woodward, C. Vann. "The Populist Heritage and the Intellectual," *American Scholar,* XXIX (Winter, 1959–1960).

Unpublished Dissertations and Manuscripts

Case, Nelson. "Personal Recollections and Impressions Concerning Some of My Acquaintances of More or Less Prominence." Vol. 4, 1906–1912.

Sandefur, Ray Harold. "Analysis of Selected Public Speeches of John

James Ingalls." State Univ. of Iowa, 1950.

Svenson, Karl A. "The Effect of Popular Discontent on Political Parties in Kansas." State Univ. of Iowa, 1948.

Interviews and Correspondence

Barnes, Constance Ingalls. Interview with the author, June 25, 1964, Atchison, Kans.

Cartwright, William J. Letters to the author, Williamstown, Mass., June 10 and Aug. 19, 1964.

Davis, Major General Ellsworth Ingalls. Interview with the author,

Mar. 23, 1964, Bethesda, Md.

Keith, Mrs. Sally Ingalls. Interviews with the author, on Mar. 8, 1964, and on numerous occasions subsequently.

Price, Mrs. Frances Davis. Interview with the author, Mar. 23, 1964, Bethesda, Md.

Books

Adams, Henry. *The Education of Henry Adams.* Boston, Mass., and New York: Houghton Mifflin, 1927.

America's War for Humanity Related in Story and Picture, Embracing a Complete History of Cuba's Struggle for Liberty, and the Glorious Heroism of America's Soldiers and Sailors. New York and St. Louis, Mo.: N. D. Thompson Publishing Co., 1898.

Bryce, James. *The American Commonwealth.* 3rd ed., 2 vols. New York: Macmillan and Co., 1895.

Buck, Solon J. *The Agrarian Cru-*

sade: *A Chronicle of the Farmer in Politics.* New Haven, Conn.: Yale Univ. Press, 1921.

———. *The Granger Movement: A Study of Agricultural Organization and Its Political, Economic, and Social Manifestations, 1870–1880.* Cambridge, Mass.: Harvard Univ. Press, 1913.

Clemens, Samuel L., and Warner, Charles Dudley. *The Gilded Age.* Hartford, Conn.: American Publishing Co., 1873.

Connelley, William E. *Ingalls of Kansas.* Topeka, Kans., 1909.

———. *The Life of Preston B.*

Plumb, 1837–1891. Chicago: Browne and Howell Co., 1913.

Cushing, Luther Stearns. *Manual of Parliamentary Practice*. Rev. by John J. Ingalls, New York: A. L. Burt, 1895.

Drummond, Henry. *Natural Law in the Spiritual World*. New York: John B. Alden, Publisher, 1887.

Durden, Robert F. *The Climax of Populism: The Election of 1896*. Lexington, Ky.: Univ. of Kentucky Press, 1965.

Fite, Gilbert C. *The Farmers' Frontier, 1865–1900*. New York: Holt, Rinehart and Winston, 1966.

Gates, Paul W. *The Farmer's Age: Agriculture 1815–1860*. New York: Holt, Rinehart and Winston, 1960.

——. *Fifty Million Acres: Conflicts Over Kansas Land Policy, 1854–1890*. Ithaca, N.Y.: Cornell Univ. Press, 1954).

Ginger, Ray. *Age of Excess: The United States From 1877 to 1914*. New York: Macmillan, 1965.

Glad, Paul W. *McKinley, Bryan, and the People*. Philadelphia and New York: J. B. Lippincott Co., 1964.

——. *The Trumpet Soundeth: William Jennings Bryan and His Democracy, 1896–1912*. Lincoln, Nebr.: Univ. of Nebraska Press, 1960.

Goldman, Eric F. *Rendezvous with Destiny: A History of Modern American Reform*. Rev. ed., New York: Vintage Books, 1956.

Harvey, William Hope. *Coin's Financial School*. Chicago: Coin Publishing Co., 1894.

Hicks, John D. *The Populist Revolt: A History of the Farmers' Alliance and the People's Party*. Minneapolis, Minn.: Univ. of Minnesota Press, 1931.

Hofstadter, Richard. *The Age of Reform: From Bryan to F.D.R.*

New York: Alfred A. Knopf, 1956.

——. *The American Political Tradition*. New York: Vintage Books, 1957.

Howes, Charles C. *This Place Called Kansas*. Norman, Okla.: Univ. of Oklahoma Press, 1952.

Ingalls, John J. *A Collection of the Writings of John James Ingalls: Essays, Addresses, and Orations*. Kansas City, Mo.: Hudson-Kimberly Publishing Co., 1902.

Ingalls, Sheffield. *History of Atchison County*. Lawrence, Kans.: Standard Publishing Co, 1916.

Johnson, Walter. *William Allen White's America*. New York: H. Holt, 1947.

Josephson, Matthew. *The Politicos, 1865–1896*. New York: Harcourt, Brace & Co., 1938.

Kansas: A Guide to the Sunflower State. New York: Federal Writers Project, The Viking Press, 1939.

Kansas State Historical Society. Collections of the Kansas State Historical Society. 17 vols.

Kirkland, Edward C. *Dream and Thought in the Business Community, 1860–1900*. Ithaca, N.Y.: Cornell Univ. Press, 1956.

McNeal, Thomas A. *When Kansas Was Young*. Topeka, Kans.: Capper Publications, 1934.

Malin, James C. *A Concern About Humanity: Notes on Reform, 1872–1912, at the National and Kansas Levels of Thought*. Lawrence, Kans., 1964.

——. *Confounded Rot About Napoleon*. Lawrence, Kans., 1961.

——. *The Grassland of North America*. Lawrence, Kans., 1961.

——. *On the Nature of History*. Lawrence, Kans., 1954.

——. *Winter Wheat in the Golden Belt of Kansas: A Study in Adaptation to Subhumid Geographical Environment*. Lawrence,

Kans.: Univ. of Kansas Press, 1944.

Meixell, Granville H. *John J. Ingalls, His Life, His Public Services, and His Personal Characteristics.* Atchison, Kans.: Home Printing Co., 1896.

Morgan, H. Wayne, ed. *The Gilded Age: A Reappraisal.* Syracuse, N.Y.: Syracuse Univ. Press, 1963.

Nevins, Allan. *Grover Cleveland: A Study in Courage.* New York: Dodd, Mead and Co., 1933.

———. *Letters of Grover Cleveland, 1850–1908.* Boston and New York: Houghton Mifflin Co., 1933.

Nichols, Roy Franklin. *The Disruption of American Democracy.* New York: Macmillan Co., 1948.

Nugent, Walter T. K. *The Tolerant Populists: Kansas, Populism and Nativism.* Chicago: Univ. of Chicago Press, 1963.

Peterson, C. Stewart. *Admiral John A. Dahlgren, Father of U.S. Naval Ordnance.* New York: Hobson Book Press, 1945.

Pollack, Norman, ed. *The Populist Mind.* Indianapolis, Ind., and New York: Bobbs-Merrill Co., Inc., 1967.

———. *The Populist Response to Industrial America: Midwestern Populist Thought.* Cambridge, Mass.: Harvard Univ. Press, 1962.

Richardson, Albert Deane. *Beyond the Mississippi.* Hartford, Conn.: American Publishing Co., 1873.

Rudolph, Frederick, *Mark Hopkins and the Log: Williams College, 1836–1872.* New Haven, Conn.: Yale Univ. Press, 1956.

Saloutos, Theodore, and Hicks, John D. *Agricultural Discontent in the Middle West, 1900–1939.* Madison, Wis.: Univ. of Wisconsin Press, 1951.

Shannon, Fred A. *The Farmer's Last Frontier: Agriculture, 1860–*

1897. Vol. V: *The Economic History of the United States.* New York: Farrar and Rinehart, 1945.

Sharkey, Robert P. *Money, Class, and Party: An Economic Study of Civil War and Reconstruction.* Baltimore, Md.: Johns Hopkins Press, 1959.

Sievers, Harry J., S.J. *Benjamin Harrison: Hoosier Statesman.* New York: University Publishers, Inc., 1959.

Smith, Henry Nash. *Virgin Land: The American West as Symbol and Myth.* Cambridge, Mass.: Harvard Univ. Press, 1950.

Smith, Theodore Clark. *The Life and Letters of James Abram Garfield.* 2 vols. Hamden, Conn.: Archon Books, 1968.

Socolofsky, Homer E. *Arthur Capper: Publisher, Politician, and Philanthropist.* Lawrence, Kans.: Univ. of Kansas Press, 1962.

Spring, L. W. *A History of Williams College.* Boston: Houghton Mifflin Co., 1917.

———. *Kansas, the Prelude to the War for the Union.* Boston and New York: Houghton, Mifflin and Co., 1885.

Stoddard, Henry L. *As I Knew Them: Presidents and Politics from Grant to Coolidge.* New York and London: Harper and Brothers, 1927.

Strong, Josiah. *Our Country.* New York: Baker and Taylor Co., 1885.

Webb, Walter P. *The Great Plains.* Boston: Ginn and Co., 1931.

White, William Allen. *The Autobiography of William Allen White.* New York: Macmillan Co., 1946.

Wilder, D. W. *The Annals of Kansas.* Topeka, Kans.: T. Dwight Thacher Publishing Co., 1886.

Woodward, C. Vann. *Reunion and Reaction: The Compromise of 1877 and the End of Reconstruc-*

tion. Boston: Little, Brown and Company, 1951.

————. *Tom Watson, Agrarian Rebel.* New York: Macmillan Co., 1938.

Zornow, William Frank. *Kansas, A History of the Jayhawk State.* Norman, Okla.: Univ. of Oklahoma Press, 1957.

INDEX

Abell, P. A., 55

abolitionism. *See* civil rights, Negro; Free State movement; slavery

Adams, F. G., 36, 42, 45

Adams, Henry, 71

Addison, Anna Louisa. *See* Chesebrough, Anna Louisa Addison

Addison, Thomas, 55

Admire, J. V., 93

American party, 39

America's War for Humanity . . . , 140

Anthony, D. R., 56, 157

Anthony, George T., 93, 131

Anthony, Susan B., 56, 111–112

Armstrong, William Jackson, 156–157

Arthur, Chester A., 99, 102, 108

Atchison, Kans.: described, 25–26, 43, 53–54, 55; railroad connection, 29, 34–35; Ingalls moves to, 36; hopes for prosperity of, 37, 48, 66–67, 146; politics in, 45; growth of, 60–61; celebrates Ingalls' election, 76–77; Ingalls ignores, 97; Ingalls' residence in, challenged, 117; post-office building for, 130; Ingalls' property in, 131; Ingalls buried at, 149–150

Atchison *Daily Globe:* on Ingalls, 123, 130–131; Ingalls' essay in, 126–127

Atchison *Freedom's Champion:* on Ingalls, 40, 42–43, 157; leased by Stebbins, 46; under Horton and Ingalls, 49; Martin resumes publishing of, 51, 53; mentioned, 34, 36

Bailey, James E., 94

Baker, Lucien, 137

Bayard, Thomas, 113

Benton, M. R., 45

Black, General John C., 107

Blaine, James G.: 1876 candidacy of, 88, 89; admired by Ingalls, 99; nominated in 1884, 102–103; Lou Ingalls on, 116

Blaine, Mrs. James G., 88

Blair, Dr. Edward Giles, 137

Blair, Mrs. Edward G. *See* Ingalls, Ethel

Bland-Allison Act, 155

"Blue Grass": publication of, 67, 68–69; factor in Senatorial election, 76; revived, 127; and Ingalls' monument, 159; mentioned, 99, 160

Bonebrake, P. I., 115, 120

bribery: in 1872 election, 74–75, 76; attempted, 81–82; Ingalls accused of, 92–93, 94–95, 97

Brown, John, 39

Brown, Joseph E., 102

Bryan, William Jennings, 120, 139

Buell, General D. C., 47

Burchard, Reverend Samuel D., 103

Burke, Edmund, 14

Burnes, J. N., 152

Burton, J. Ralph, 137

Butler, Benjamin F., 80, 102, 103

Butler, M. C., 118

Butler, Reverend Pardee, 51

Butterworth, Benjamin, 119

Cameron, Angus, 95

Cameron, Donald, 93, 101, 115

Carney, Thomas, 48

"Catfish Aristocracy," 67–68, 76

Chase, Salmon P., 50

Chautauqua lecture circuit, 128

Chesebrough, Amos (uncle of Lou Ingalls), 55

Chesebrough, Anna Louisa (Lou): on Atchison, 53–54; journeys to Kansas, 54–55; childhood of, 55–56; at Lincoln inauguration, 56, 57; courted by Ingalls, 56–57, 58; marriage of, 58–59. *See also* Ingalls, Anna Louisa

Chesebrough, Anna Louisa Addison (mother of Lou Ingalls), 55, 170–171n3

Chesebrough, Annie Euphemia Kearney (stepmother of Lou Ingalls), 54, 58, 59, 82, 172n14, 172n16

Chesebrough, Ellsworth (father of Lou Ingalls), 45, 53, 54, 55, 56

Hareston, George S., 94
Harper's Weekly: on Ingalls, 75–76, 109, 150; attacks Republican party, 117–118
Harrison, Benjamin, 116–117, 129
Hayes, Rutherford B.: Ingalls on, 87, 90; mentioned, 89, 98, 155
Hearst, William Randolph: newspapers of, 138, 139
Hill, Benjamin H., 94, 152
Hitchcock, Phineas W., 76
Hoar, George F., 95, 109
Hobbes, Thomas, 111, 112
homesteaders, bill for relief of, 81
Hopkins, Mark: President of Williams College, 5; and Ingalls' commencement address, 8; admired by Ingalls, 10; mentioned, 6, 7
Horton, Albert H.: and Atchison *Freedom's Champion*, 49, 50, 51; competes for federal judgeship, 80–81; defeated by Ingalls, 92; and Ingalls investigation, 94; attacked by Ingalls, 95; in London, 134; mentioned 111
Hossack, James A., 92, 93
Hughes, Andrew, 58, 134

immigration, restricted, 130
Indiana, 15
Indian Affairs, Senate committee on, 81, 90, 154
Indians: treaties, 49; Creek, 81; Ingalls' bill on, 90
Ingalls, Addison (son of John J.), 59, 89, 138
Ingalls, Anna Louisa (wife of John J.): on John J.'s migration, 13–14; diary of, 62–64, 76; considerateness of, 65; shares husband's hopes, 67; on "Shang," 68; and death of Ruth, 78–79; illness of, 89; campaigns for John J., 91–92, 105–106; and attack on Cleveland, 107–108, 110; on loss of home, 114; on nominations of 1888, 116; writes to Harrison, 117; during John J.'s illness, 146–147; death of, 159–160; mentioned passim. *See also* Chesebrough, Anna Louisa

Ingalls, Constance (daughter of John J.), 60, 144
Ingalls, Elias Theodore (father of John J.): married, 2; and John J.'s childhood, 3, 4, 5; as inventor, 5, 161–162n17; advises John J., 22, 27, 44, 45, 66; buys Sumner stock, 42; on the Mississippi Valley, 46; invited to Atchison, 51, 65; on John J.'s marriage, 58–59; on national issues, 61; death of, 129; on Drummond's book, 152–153; mentioned passim
Ingalls, Eliza Chase (mother of John J.), 2, 3–4, 150
Ingalls, Ellsworth (son of John J.), 59, 62, 63, 64, 65, 143, 145, 147, 150
Ingalls, Ethel (daughter of John J.): on migration to Kansas, 11–12; on Arthur administration hospitality, 99; marriage of, 137; loss of infant, 138; on Lane and Pomeroy, 167–168n12; mentioned, 59, 62, 63, 129, 146, 150
Ingalls, Francis T. (brother of John J.), 133–134
Ingalls, John J.: melancholy of, 3, 4–5, 7, 8, 100; religious attitudes of, 4, 7, 8, 63, 86, 150–154; concern for appearance, 5, 78, 88–89; and Williams College, 5–10; "Admirable Crichton" theory of, 8, 62; settles in Sumner, 11–12, 13–14, 20, 21, 164n19, 164n37; his journey to Kansas, 14–15, 16; finances of, 26–27, 42, 43–44, 67, 78, 121, 131–132, 165n41; his sarcasm, 27, 99–100, 114, 115, 154, 158; moves to Atchison, 36; in Kansas militia, 40, 43, 50, 51; travels to Colorado, 43; as farmer, 49, 125–126; courtship and marriage of, 56–57, 58–60; domestic life of, 61–65, 86–87, 89; political philosophy of, 72, 100–101, 119, 120, 122, 130, 154, 156–157; his debate skill, 99–100; "Mugwump" speech of, 107–109; Atchison home burns, 113–114; "Fiat Justitia" speech, 118, 120, 154; lecturing of, 128–129, 135–136, 137, 138, 139; tours Europe, 131–

escorts Lou Chesebrough, 57; mentioned, 47, 49, 50, 99

Lang, Jonathan Gardner ("Shang"), 67–68

Lawrence, Kans.: charter of, 25; territorial legislature at, 26; Ingalls on, 28; and Quantrill's raid, 48–49; rail connection for, 67

Lease, Mrs. Mary Elizabeth, 110–111, 125

Leavenworth, Kans., 26, 67

Lebold, C. H., 121

Leland, C. M., 36, 42, 45

Lincoln, Abraham: Ingalls on, 36, 46, 48; visits Atchison, 39; elected President, 40; inauguration of, 56, 57; war policy on Negroes, 169–170n44; mentioned, 41, 42, 43, 50, 106

Logan, John, 85, 95

McClellan, General George B., 50, 114

McCloud, W. F., 56

McCullough, William, 31

McDowell, William C., 30–31

McKinley, William: as Republican Convention chairman, 131; Ingalls on, 138, 140; election of, 139–140

Marsh, John J., 10

Martin, John A.: nominates Ingalls, 37; leases *Freedom's Champion*, 46, 49, 51; in Union forces, 46–47, 50, 51; supports Ingalls, 47, 91; on the war, 49, 50; defends Atchison, 97, 174n53. *See also* Atchison *Freedom's Champion*

Meade, Captain Richard W., 127

Medary, Samuel, 28, 29

Middleton, Mass., 1, 2–3, 136–137

Milan, Italy: Ingalls visits, 133

Miller, Warner, 107

mineral land and mining, bills on, 81, 90

Missouri River, 16, 90

Morse, Samuel F. B., 55

Mount Saint Scholastica Academy, 54

"Mugwump" speech, 107–109

"Mulligan letters," 103

Murdock, M. M., 159

Nation: on Ingalls' election, 75; on Ingalls' debating skill, 99–100;

denounces Ingalls, 109, 120, 121, 123–124

naval policy, 127

Negroes, 47–48. *See also* civil rights, Negro; slavery

New Mexico statehood movement, 81

New York *Evening Post:* Ingalls writes for, 27–28, 29

New York *Journal*, 145–147

New York Times: accuses Ingalls of corruption, 76; denounces Ingalls, 101, 121, 122, 123; endorses Ingalls, 109

New York *World:* "iridescent dream" in, 119, 122–123, 154; Ingalls' obituary in, 150

Niehaus, Charles (sculptor), 159

North American Review, 113

Oklahoma, Territory of, 81

"Opportunity" (poem), 127–128, 183n14

Osborn, Thomas A., 47, 73

Pacific Railroad Act, 40, 81

Panic of 1873, 87

Paris, France: Ingalls in, 134

Parrott, Marcus J., 41

patronage: Ingalls' use of, 85, 107; mentioned, 90, 121

Peffer, William A., 123, 124

Pendleton, "Uncle" Tarleton (servant), 65–66, 68, 173–174n47

Pensions, Senate committee on, 81, 90, 154

"The People's Party," 119–120

Pierce, Franklin, 6

Pike's Peak, 18, 29, 35, 169n23

"Pike's Peak Express Company," 26

Pisa, Italy: Ingalls visits, 133

Playter, Franklin, 92, 94

Plumb, Preston B., 129

Pomeroy, Samuel C.: elected U.S. Senator, 41; motives questioned, 44–45; Ingalls on, 45, 60; Horton talks with, 49–50; attacked for corruption, 71; defeat of, 73–75, 175–176n17; and campaign of 1878, 91–92, 93–94; Ethel Ingalls on, 167–168n12; mentioned, 47, 55, 65, 69, 80, 82, 95

populism, 119–120

Privileges and Elections, Senate committee on, 90, 93, 154

prohibition: Ingalls on, 65, 102, 128, 130, 154, 156
Purcell, E. B., 93

Quantrill, William C., 48–49

railroads: and town development, 13, 18, 24, 26, 28–29; Hannibal and St. Joseph, 28–29; and development of Kansas, 33; connection to Atchison, 34–35; Union Pacific, 48, 81; and Pomeroy, 60; Central Branch, 67; Atchison and Nebraska, 67; European, 135; mentioned, 37, 49
Republican party: and Kansas statehood movement, 29, 33; of Kansas, 34, 35–36, 37; platform of 1860, 39; during Grant presidency, 62; and Ingalls, 69, 155–156; of late nineteenth century, 71–72; "Stalwart" and "Half-Breed" feud in, 99; charged with corruption, 117–118; Ingalls' advice to, 125; of New York, 129; platform of 1896, 139
Richardson, Albert Dean, 14, 20, 165n35
Richardson, J. C., 137–138
Riggs, Samuel A., 92
Roosevelt, Theodore, 146
Rosecrans, General William S., 47
Rush, J. W., 121

St. John, John P., 102, 103, 130
St. Louis, Mo., 15
St. Peter's: Ingalls visits, 132, 133
"Salary Grab" Act of 1873, 87
Sandefur, Ray Harold, 153
Saturday Evening Post, 147
Saulsbury, Eli, 93, 94
Seymour, Horatio, 62
Sheridan, General Philip: trial of, 66, 174n49; mentioned, 106
Sherman, John, 85, 110, 116
Sherman, General William T., 50
Sherman Anti-Trust Bill: Ingalls' amendment to, 118–119, 155
silver: discovery of, 13; free, 87, 91, 123, 139, 154, 155
Simpson, Jerry, 123
"Sixteenth Amendment," 111–112, 119
slavery: in Kansas, 23, 28, 30, 48; Republican platform on, 39; and

Kansas politics, 45; Ingalls sentiments on, 47–48, 169n44. *See also* civil rights, Negro; Free State movement
Slough, "Colonel" John P., 31
Smith, Leonard T., 93
Spanish-American War, 140–141
Stanford, Leland, 133
Stanton, Edwin M., 60
Stanton, Frederick P., 41
Statuary Hall (Washington, D.C.), 159
Stebbins, G. I., 46, 51
Stotler, J., 36
Stowe, Harriet Beecher: *Uncle Tom's Cabin*, 6
Stumbaugh, F. S., 92, 93
suffrage, Negro, 112, 113, 118
suffrage, woman: Ingalls on, 111–112, 128, 130, 154; mentioned, 81, 155
Sumner, Charles: influences Ingalls, 12; town named for, 19; Ingalls on, 77; death and funeral of, 79–80, 81
Sumner, Kans. Terr.: Ingalls' arrival at, 11, 13, 16–18; descriptions of, 12, 13, 16–18; constitution of, 19–20; administrative and financial difficulties of, 23–24; charter for, 23–25, 26; compared to Atchison, 25–26; by-passed by railroads, 28–29; struck by tornado, 36, 167n40; demise of, 61, 67–68
Sumner Company: promotion tactics of, 12, 13, 17, 20; reorganization of, 24
Sumner *Kansas Gazette*, 13, 17, 20

Tabor, Horace A. W. (Haw), 101
tariffs, 113, 125, 130, 154, 185n93
Tarkington, Booth, 146
telegraph, 33, 37
Tennessee: Ingalls on, 129
Texas, 40, 67
Topeka, Kans., 29, 41, 166n18
town-site booming, 12, 20–21
Treaty of Washington, 1870, 111
Truth, 126–127, 131
Tucson, Ariz.: Ingalls in, 144
Twain, Mark: *The Gilded Age*, 71

Union party. *See* Constitutional Union party

Vance, Zebulon B., 94
Vatican: Ingalls visits, 132
Vienna, Austria: Ingalls visits, 132
Vorhees, Daniel W., 107, 114–115, 154

Waggener, Bailie P., 159
Ware, Eugene F., 116, 133
Warner, Charles Dudley: *The Gilded Age*, 71
Washington, D.C.: described by Ingalls, 77, 85–86, 124; revisited, 139
Webb, W. C., 92
Wellman, Walter, 124

Wheeler, John P., 19, 24
Wheeler, William A., 92–93
Whig party, 10, 39
"Whisky Ring" conspiracy, 87
White, William Allen, 157–158
Wilder, D. W., 49, 99
Williams College: Ingalls at, 5–10; mentioned, 76, 101
Williams Quarterly, 6
Wilson, Henry, 85, 87, 106
Wilson, Levi, 93
Wyandotte Constitutional Convention, 29, 30, 31, 32–33

York, Alexander M.: and defeat of Pomeroy, 73–75, 82, 175*n15*; mentioned, 71